A Guide to
War Publications of the
First and Second World War

Dedication

To my good friends Nick Scott and Ed Riseman.
Where have all the years gone?
And to my oldest friend Nigel Gray, our friendship dates back
to school days in Epsom in the early 1970s.
Lastly, and my no means least to Dave Grey, a more recent pal
from the north-east of England with whom I share so many interests.

A Guide to War Publications of the First and Second World War

From Training Guides to Propaganda Posters

ARTHUR WARD

Pen & Sword
MILITARY

First published in Great Britain in 2014 by
PEN AND SWORD MILITARY
an imprint of
Pen and Sword Books Ltd
47 Church Street
Barnsley
South Yorkshire S70 2AS

Copyright © Arthur Ward 2014

ISBN 978 1 78383 154 8

The right of Arthur Ward to be identified
as the author of this work has been asserted by him in accordance
with the Copyright, Designs and Patents Act 1988.

A CIP record for this book is available from the British Library
All rights reserved. No part of this book may be reproduced or
transmitted in any form or by any means, electronic or
mechanical including photocopying, recording or
by any information storage and retrieval system, without
permission from the Publisher in writing.

Printed and bound in India
by Replika Press Pvt. Ltd.

Typeset in Times New Roman by
CHIC GRAPHICS

Pen & Sword Books Ltd incorporates the imprints of Pen & Sword Archaeology,
Atlas, Aviation, Battleground, Discovery, Family History, History,
Maritime, Military, Naval, Politics, Railways, Select, Social History, Transport,
True Crime, Claymore Press, Frontline Books, Leo Cooper, Praetorian Press,
Remember When, Seaforth Publishing and Wharncliffe.

For a complete list of Pen and Sword titles please contact
Pen and Sword Books Limited
47 Church Street, Barnsley, South Yorkshire, S70 2AS, England
E-mail: enquiries@pen-and-sword.co.uk
Website: www.pen-and-sword.co.uk

Contents

Introduction 6

Chapter 1   Influencing Attitudes – Propaganda and Official Policy 15

Chapter 2   The Home Front 51

Chapter 3   Entertainment 90

Chapter 4   Children 101

Chapter 5   Civilian Militias – Home Guard and *Volkssturm* 123

Chapter 6   Military Training Guides and Manuals and ARP
            Instructions 139

Chapter 7   Looking After Your Collectables..169

Appendix 1   Inside the Third Reich...181

Appendix 2   Auxiliary Units...190

Appendix 3   Penguin Specials 195

Bibliography 200

Index 201

Introduction

This Edwardian Welsh Guards poster simply stipulated that eligibility for membership of the regiment depended on recruits either having a Welsh parent 'on one side' at least, being domiciled in Wales or Monmouth or having a Welsh surname!

Collectors of historic printed documents are prospecting along the final remaining frontier of available, authentic wartime items. Traditionally less-expensive than other more familiar items like badges and uniforms, both vigorously traded for years, lots of authentic printed ephemera remains undiscovered. Furthermore, although high-end militaria has long been subject to fakery, printed items are more difficult to forge convincingly. But, be warned, with individual wartime posters now commanding as much as £1,000, the stakes have been raised. This undiscovered country isn't going to remain fruitful for long.

Although long overlooked in favour of more substantial pieces of military clothing and equipment – including that perennial favourite, Nazi regalia – ephemeral printed items are now being collected with fervour. Not before time in my opinion, because these printed pieces often provide the enthusiast with a much better picture of the

Turn of the century postcard showing the Devonshire Regiment still resplendent in scarlet tunics.

reality of life during wartime, be that from the point of view of the front-line soldier or the civilian on the home front. Vintage paperwork adds context to individual items like badges and helmets and helps to explain what people had to endure when embroiled in the reality of *total war*.

One reason for the new-found popularity of previously disregarded items is simply because their availability provides a pleasant surprise – they were never expected to have a long life. On the contrary, they were designed to have only temporary, ephemeral, appeal. Consequently most of these items were not saved; they were simply disposed of instead. Therefore they have, by default, become quite rare.

Furthermore, given that the big ticket items that have been the traditional province of serious collectors for generations: military dress, regalia and certain medals and unit badges, are now regularly counterfeit, collectors are better off casting their net wider. Printed ephemera, though of less intrinsic value, is far more difficult to fake convincingly. Surprisingly, it's far easier to make a copy of a badge, a 're-strike', adding the odd blemish here and some tarnish there, than it is to copy a piece of 1940s heat-set lithographic printed material and achieve not only accurate colour reproduction but the texture and distinctively musty smell of vintage paper.

The dictionary definition of ephemera is 'things of only short-lived relevance', meaning that most printed items were never imbued with much value when they first appeared. Although mass-produced, often in the hundreds of thousands, relatively few original items survive today. And, as we all know, rarity is as attractive to collectors as shiny objects are to magpies. So, after long taken for granted, the myriad documents each belligerent government produced in support of their nation's war effort, are at last achieving high prices on the collectors' market.

Trench warfare didn't only spell the end of military pomp and regalia it saw the introduction of mechanised warfare as depicted on this naive French postcard.

This book aims to explore the realm of twentieth-century printed ephemera and provide details for the collector about what to look out for, who produced what and why they did so and, most importantly, where to find such collectables and what to pay for them.

At the outbreak of the Great War, Britain's authorities first began to put their own slant on why the nation had become embroiled in the conflict and what role the government was adopting, which it expected its electorate to follow. When the new War Propaganda Bureau began work on 2 September 1914, its work was so secret that it was not until 1935 that its activities were revealed to the public. Several prominent writers agreed to write pamphlets and books that would promote the government's point of view and these were printed and published by such well-known publishers as Hodder & Stoughton, Methuen, Oxford University Press, John Murray, Macmillan and Thomas Nelson. In total, the War Propaganda Bureau went on to publish over 1,160 pamphlets during the war.

In Britain, the build-up to the Second World War was characterised by the official appeasement of Hitler's expansionist behaviour. The Führer reoccupied the Rhineland, entered Austria, proclaiming union (*Anschluss*) with that sovereign country, and even dismembered Czechoslovakia following his acquisition of the Sudetenland, without the British government doing much more than expressing its displeasure. At the time government propaganda at home concentrated on informing Britain's civilian population of the dangers of modern war, which despite their confident expressions of peace in our time, they knew was a foregone conclusion.

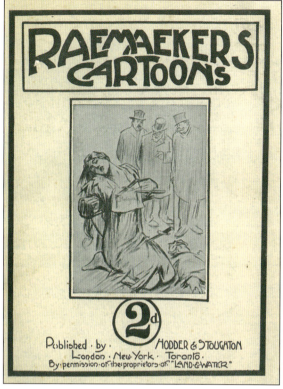

The German government placed a reward of 12,000 guilders, dead or alive, on Dutch artist Louis Raemaekers' head. Raemaekers' graphic cartoons depicted the German military in Belgium as barbarians and Kaiser Wilhelm II as an ally of Satan. The Germans also accused Raemaekers of 'endangering Dutch neutrality'.

The fear of chemical attack from enemy air fleets – 'the bomber will always get through' – and the vulnerability of modern cities to high explosives and incendiaries encouraged the development of volunteer Air Raid Precaution (ARP) services and the production of numerous leaflets informing householders about how to survive such an eventuality. Fear of aerial attack, and in particular of gas being sown by enemy bombers, presented a terrifying prospect which films like Korda's 1936 epic *Things to Come*, based on H.G. Wells' prophetic vision, did little to allay. After the war, Harold Macmillan, a Cabinet minister during the Second World War who became Prime Minister in 1957, wrote: 'We thought of air warfare in 1938 rather as people think of nuclear warfare today.'

Amazingly, as an item in this book proves, there were many quite liberally minded people who thought that Hitler's decision to incorporate the largely German-speaking Sudeten region of Czechoslovakia into the Third Reich, which triggered the Munich Crisis in 1938, was not an unreasonable ambition. But other than the occasional vociferous outburst from politicians like Winston Churchill or the gradually shifting views of previously pro-Hitler press barons like Lord Beaverbrook and Lord Rothermere, there was little official pro-war information in circulation. Despite this, in 1935 the *Daily Mail*'s Rothermere presented the prototype Bristol Blenheim aircraft, *Britain First*, as a gift to the nation and a vital addition to the RAF's bomber fleet.

Notwithstanding Britain's desire to stay out of another European war, at least until enough Spitfires had been built, the 1938 Czechoslovakian crisis saw a dramatic increase in the amount of leaflets distributed among its citizens which encouraged them to learn about and prepare for the reality of enemy aerial bombardment.

Hitler's invasion of Poland on 1 September 1939 was the spark which ignited the long-feared conflict. Britain's declaration of war on 3 September saw a distinct change in the tone and manner of official government pronouncements. Now the gloves were off and printing presses worked overtime extolling citizens to do their bit, stay firm and go about their daily life with the traditional stoicism of John Bull.

Today, I guess the most famous piece of government propaganda from this period is the iconic 'Keep Calm and Carry On' poster created by the new Ministry of Information (MOI). Ironically, although it was printed and ready for distribution when the war started, this poster was only to be employed in the event of an invasion of Britain by Germany. As this never happened, the poster was never widely seen by the public.

Collectors of wartime ephemera have a wealth of material to look out for. This naval signal from the First World War is particularly interesting. Sent from the Vice Admiral, it congratulates the efforts of the ship's company of HMS Racoon *for their part in saving the liner HMT* Southland *after it was torpedoed in the Aegean Sea by a German submarine in 1915.*

INSTRUCTIONS for the Civil Population
in the event of a Landing by the Enemy in this Country, an event less probable now than earlier in the War.

It has come to the notice of the Military Authorities that there is some doubt on the part of the Civil population, particularly in the Eastern and South-Eastern Counties, as to the preparations which have been made for the conduct and movement of the Civil population in case of invasion or other emergency.

In order to allay any apprehension on this point it is notified that complete schemes for regulating the action of the inhabitants have been framed by the Central Organising Committee under the Lord Lieutenant of the County, but that it is not proposed to publish these in detail until an emergency actually exists.

Meanwhile, however, it is considered that the following instructions may be of service in giving the Civil population a general outline of the course of action on their part which will be most helpful in enabling the authorities, both Civil and Military to put their plans into execution.

People. (1.) As it is of primary importance that the free movement of His Majesty's Troops should not be hampered by the presence of civilians on the roads, it is necessary to control the use of roads by non-combatants, and to close certain roads. The Civil population will therefore do wisely to remain in their homes (except in case of actual bombardment). Owing to Military requirements, Refugees will not be able to use the railways; nor can furniture or baggage be conveyed in any public vehicle.

Transport. (2) All motors, bicycles, carriages, carts and other vehicles, harness-horses, mules, donkeys, petrol launches and lighters, will be taken at once to pre-arranged places of assembly, where further Military directions will be given. Those not required for the service of the Troops may be detailed for the use of Civilians, or be ordered to be removed. Any which cannot be removed will, **under Military Order** (conveyed by the Police), be rendered unserviceable or destroyed.

Tools, etc. (3). Tools, such as spades, shovels, picks, axes, saws, barbed wire, etc , will be immediately collected at **The Esplanade, Cleethorpes,** and the **School House, Tetney,** for Military disposal. All available able-bodied men will assemble in gangs at the places mentioned, with the tools, etc., prepared for work.

N.B. No property is to be destroyed except under direct Military Order.

W. D. FIELD,

Grimsby,
May, 1918.

Chairman of the Grimsby District
Local Emergency Committee.

A. WATERHOUSE, LINCOLN.

At one point the German spring offensive of 1918 swept all before it, causing panic not just in France but further afield. Towns along the northeast coast of England had been subject to German naval attack early in the war and some feared an all-out maritime invasion. Taking no chances, the good fathers of Grimsby prepared this poster advising their citizens about what to do if the worst came to the worst.

It was long believed that most of the 'Keep Calm' posters were destroyed and reduced to a pulp at the end of the war in 1945. However, nearly sixty years later, a bookseller from Barter Books stumbled across a copy hidden among a pile of dusty old books bought from an auction. A small number also remain in The National Archives and the Imperial War Museum in London, and a further fifteen were discovered through the BBC's *Antiques Roadshow* programme, having been given to Moragh Turnbull, from Cupar, Fife, by her father William, who served as a member of the Royal Observer Corps.

The seemingly ubiquitous 'Keep Calm and Carry On' poster has probably become one of the most famous publications associated with the British home front in the Second World War. However, as readers of this book will discover, it was seen by hardly anyone during the war and only became famous after it was rediscovered in 2000 by Stuart Manley of Barter Books in Alnwick, Northumberland!

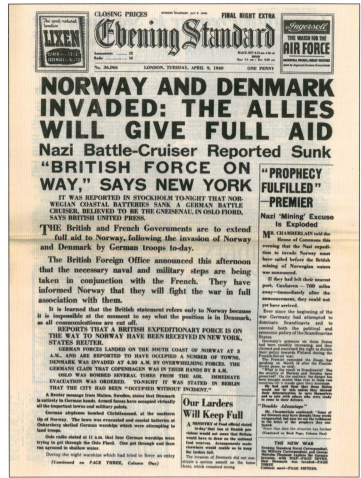

Vintage newspapers can be secured for relatively small sums but need careful conservation (see Chapter 7). This 9 April 1940 edition of the London Evening Standard *deals with the ill-fated Norwegian campaign. Ironically, like Gallipoli in the First World War, an idea of Churchill's but one which saw the First Lord of the Admiralty accede to the premiership while Neville Chamberlain paid the price for failure and lost his job.*

And this is why 'Keep Calm and Carry On' has become possibly the most famous government instruction originating from the Second World War!

The MOI was dissolved in March 1946, with its residual functions passed to the newly established Central Office of Information (COI), a centralised organisation supporting officialdom with a range of specialist information services. Fortunately today, much of what the MOI and HMSO (His Majesty's Stationery Office – responsible for printing, marketing and the public distribution of numerous illustrated publications describing the progress of particular campaigns and the activities of the civilian workers at home) produced survives and much of it is shown in this book. It is more collectable than ever before.

This book includes far more than official British government publications. To paint an accurate picture of twentieth-century wartime, we need to consider the myriad other

Postcards were a useful way fighting men of all nations could keep in touch with loved ones at home. This very collectable German example stresses the importance of a pause in the shooting so troops could catch up on their correspondence from home.

The *Daily Mirror* reported Hitler's death on 2 May 1945 and stated that Admiral Karl Dönitz would succeed him as Führer.

Safe-conduct pass signed by Dwight D. Eisenhower, then Supreme Commander Allied Expeditionary Force during Operation Torch in North Africa. When presented by a surrendering Axis soldier, the supplicant was guaranteed a welcome and lenient reception.

items that supported the war efforts at the front and at home. Therefore, examples of the kind of things that entertained and informed both the young and the old during the dark days of war are also included. Items such as postcards, song sheets, periodicals, official and unofficial publications, such as the famous *Wipers Times* from the 1914–18 conflict, feature throughout the pages of this book. I hope the combination of illustrations and narrative fact will appeal not only to the collector but also to those interested in the social history of twentieth-century warfare and the effect it had on ordinary men, women, boys and girls who had the misfortune to live throughout it.

I am grateful to the following for the assistance in preparing this book: Mirella Aslar, Zaki Jamal, Jayne Joyce and Stuart Manley and Jim Walsh at Barter Books.

Arthur Ward
Pulborough, West Sussex
September 2014

CHAPTER 1

Influencing Attitudes – Propaganda and Official Policy

Towards the end of the English Civil War, the London-based petitioner movement known as the Levellers, comprising soldier 'Agitators' of the parliamentarian New Model Army and a number of prominent politicians, produced a draft written constitution under the title of 'Agreements of the People'. Their efforts were the catalyst for a series of famous debates in the autumn of 1647 held in St Mary's Church, Putney, to decide the prospective settlement of the nation, the right of all men to have the vote and, especially, about whether Charles I had any future as the nation's king. Charles was tried at Westminster Hall in January 1649, and after it was decided that he had 'traitorously and maliciously levied war against the present Parliament and the people therein represented' he was executed. So the monarch's fate had been decided.

However, despite their best efforts the Levellers did little better and with the king out of the picture absolute power now resided with the army and in particular Oliver Cromwell, the man who was soon to become 'The Lord Protector'. By 1650 they were no longer a serious threat to the established order and the powerful remained in power.

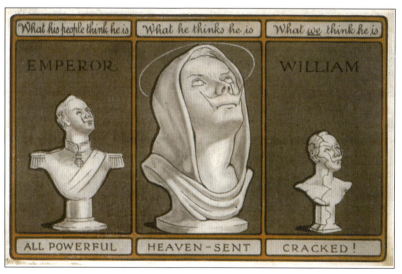

Satirical postcard showing the difference between the Kaiser's apparent self-image and how others really saw him.

But, despite this state of affairs, part of the legacy of this tumultuous period is that from the late seventeenth century Britain's authorities could no longer assume the tacit approval of the body politic for forthcoming military adventures or expeditions. From now on the people had to be persuaded that going to war was an expedient option and that the cost and inevitable suffering incurred was a price worth paying.

A tangible method used to communicate the early official propaganda used to persuade the people of the government's wisdom were handbills, sketches and cartoons. At first these were distributed within news-pamphlets and after the Restoration of the monarchy appeared in publications such as the *London Gazette* (first published on 16 November 1665 as the *Oxford Gazette*), and from 1702 of the *Daily Courant*, London's first daily newspaper (there were twelve London newspapers and twenty-four provincial papers by the 1720s).

A curious side-effect of this dissemination was the emergence of the cult of personality. As readers were provided with information about the battles their armies were fighting, they were also given details about the commanders who led the troops. Consequently, Marlborough, victor at the Battles of Blenheim in 1704 and Ramillies in 1706, which drove the French forces from Germany and the Netherlands during the War of the Spanish Succession, and later Wolfe, who stormed the heights below the

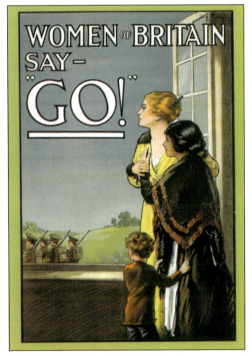

'Women of Britain Say – Go!' by E.V. Kealey. A mother and her children watch from the window of their home as some soldiers march off to war. It was originally published by the Parliamentary Recruiting Committee, London.

Patriotic German postcard from the early part of the First World War. It shows a young girl telling the Kaiser that she wants to dedicate a flower to him.

Plains of Abraham during the Battle of Quebec during the Seven Years War and died doing so, became household names and not distant, out-of-reach, aristocrats.

Another side-effect was the emergence of satirical counter arguments which questioned official policy and ridiculed the attitudes and behaviour of many of the previously exalted worthies.

William Hogarth and other British satirists gave vent to the frustrations and incredulities of a more questioning population during this period. Although they were subsequently more famous for their novels, writers, such as Daniel Defoe, who, in February 1704, began his weekly, the *Review* – a forerunner of both the *Tattler* and the *Spectator*, and Jonathan Swift, the most influential contributor between November 1710 and June 1711 of the *Examiner*, which started life in 1710 as the chief Conservative political mouthpiece, both contributed to a growing climate of cynical observation. What electorate there was at this time still had to be convinced that their country was on the side of right.

The Seven Years War had seen the age-old colonial struggle between the British and French empires spread across two continents, extending from Europe to North America, where the westward expansion of the British colonies conflicted with the interests of France and ultimately melded with the grievances of American colonists that led to the American Revolution. Benjamin Franklin drew and published the first political cartoon in the colonies in 1747. His woodcut leaflet *Plain Truth*, depicting a kneeling man praying to Hercules who is sitting in the cloud, an allegory of 'Heaven helps him who helps himself', told the American colonists to defend themselves against the Indians without British help. Franklin's subsequent 1754 cartoon of a snake chopped into pieces, advised the colonies to 'join or die', to unite against their common foe, further encouraging sedition.

When, in the spring of 1798, twenty years after the end of the American War of Independence and the loss of the colonies, General Bonaparte's 'Army of England' massed along the Channel coast of France, the House of Commons again called the country to arms. Anti-Napoleon propaganda abounded in Britain and caricatures by the names of James Gillray and George Cruikshank flooded not only the British market but influenced German and French anti-Napoleonic sentiment in occupied territories as well. In Britain such satire not only aroused patriotism it raised awareness against possible French invasion, and drove enrolment in the army or navy and many towns raised volunteer groups of infantry and cavalry. This invasion crisis ended with Nelson's victory over the French Fleet, graphically depicted by Gillray who published caricatures showing John Bull eating the French ships, and a badly punished and bruised Napoleon, with a wound on his chest, labelled Nelson.

In July 1853 Tsar Nicholas's occupation of territories in the Crimea previously controlled by Turkey's Ottoman Empire encouraged Britain and France to declare war in an attempt to halt such Russian expansionism. The Crimean War was one of the first wars to be documented extensively in written reports and photographs, most notably by William Howard Russell, who wrote for *The Times* newspaper, and the photographer, Roger Fenton, whose images brought the reality of war into the living rooms of ordinary civilians. In his reports of the battles and especially of the Siege of Sevastopol, Russell said 'Lord Raglan is utterly incompetent to lead an army' – this was the first time such divisive comment about Britain's military commanders had appeared in the press. Revealing the sufferings of the British Army during the winter of 1854, his accounts even upset Queen Victoria who described Russell's writings as 'infamous attacks against the army which have disgraced our newspapers'. Lord Raglan complained that Russell had revealed military information potentially useful to the enemy. But coupled with the observations of Mary Seacole and Florence Nightingale, the correspondent's reports that British soldiers were dying of cholera and malaria motivated a public outcry and led to resignations in government.

This revolution in the ability of newspapermen and social commentators to file up-to-the-minute reports was largely facilitated by the electric telegraph and was a foretaste of modern war. It is also an early example of how the media could influence public opinion in the way TV showing images of body bags of dead GIs being unloaded from cargo aircraft returning from Vietnam in the late 1960s encouraged the United States to pull out of that costly war.

By the time of the South African, or Second Boer War, which began in October 1899 and continued until May 1902, developments in communications technology had further improved so that newspapers were able to keep their readership in Britain up to date with the twists and turns of the bloody conflict taking place 5,500 miles away. British householders read of the underhand hit and run tactics of the Boer fighters of the semi-independent South African Republic (Transvaal) and the initially, at least, scarlet-clad ranks of British soldiers. Soon Tommy Atkins adopted many of the methods of his adversary and readers discovered that British troops had swapped their high-visibility tunics for more discreet khaki uniforms and had gradually became better

Britain and France were confident that the Entente Cordiale agreements they'd signed on 8 April 1904 would see them safely through the war.

'To Willie with Compliments – Our grand artillerymen like to address a shell before they fire it. This shell, being one of the biggest size, is addressed to the biggest Hun.'

equipped to deny the rebellious claims of their volunteer enemy. Anxious Britons greedily consumed any news from South Africa, and news of the relief of Mafeking on 18 May 1900 was so deliriously received it encouraged street parties and public celebrations the likes of which had never before been seen.

As the tide of the war gradually favoured the British, thousands of Boer families were forced into concentration camps, leading to the death of more than 25,000 Boer women and children as well as 20,000 native Africans. The biggest scandal of the war, the camps began to influence British public opinion; the *Manchester Guardian* blamed the deaths on British brutality while pro-government newspapers such as *The Times* argued that they were caused by poor hygiene on the part of the Boers. Altogether nearly 30,000 whites died in the concentration camps, more than twice the number of fighting men, on both sides, who died in battle.

In 1906 the Boers were granted self rule and in 1910 the Union of South Africa was formed. Ironically, many Boer generals fought alongside their British comrades during the Great War and it was during this conflict that Britain used every aspect of modern communications to get its message across both in terms of inspiring new recruits to the armed services but also to reassure the public at home that their men were fighting the good fight on the side of might and right. Interestingly, like it had done successfully during the South African War, when it demeaned and denigrated the rebels and families of the breakaway provinces, accusing the Boers of brutish and underhand methods and their women folk of ignorance and stupidity, Britain also placed significant emphasis on atrocity propaganda as a way of mobilising public opinion against Germany during the First World War. The 'Hun' was depicted as a beast, a despoiler of women and a murderer of children.

However, although a well-established press stood by as a ready vehicle to communicate such government propaganda and the new picture palaces could project newsreels to eager audiences sitting slack jawed as they watched footage of our boys at the front, at the war's outbreak Britain lacked any official propaganda agencies. Britain's discovery that, on the other hand, Germany had a very active one and was vigorously employing it to communicate its side of the story to neutral countries, the most important of which was the United States of America, encouraged the urgent development of a specialist department, the War Propaganda Bureau, which though operating from a new home, Wellington House, a former insurance office located in Buckingham Gate, London, was under the direct supervision of the Foreign Office.

In August 1914 David Lloyd George, then Chancellor of the Exchequer, was given the task of establishing the new organisation and he appointed the writer and fellow Liberal MP Charles Masterman to head it. In turn Masterman invited twenty-five leading British authors to Wellington House to discuss ways of best promoting the country's interests during the war. These included such luminaries as William Archer, Arthur Conan Doyle, Arnold Bennett, John Masefield, Ford Madox Ford, G.K. Chesterton, Henry Newbolt, John Galsworthy, Thomas Hardy, Rudyard Kipling, Gilbert Parker, G.M. Trevelyan and H.G. Wells. Painters of the stature of Francis Dodd and Paul Nash were also asked to work with the Bureau, the main objective of which was to encourage the United States to enter the war on the British and French side. As a consequence, exhibitions of paintings and lecture tours were organised in the United States establishing unique links between aesthetes, writers and other influential creative minds from either sides of the Atlantic. Drawing on an extensive network of the most important and influential figures in the London arts scene, Masterman devised the most comprehensive arts patronage schemes ever to be supported in the country.

Before the Unites States joined the fray the combined armies facing the Germans and Austro-Hungarians proved a not inconsiderable obstacle to the Kaiser's ambitions.

Full of highly emotional drawings created by the Dutch illustrator Louis Raemaekers, early in 1915 the Bureau produced its first significant publication, the *Report on Alleged German Outrages*. Documenting atrocities both actually and allegedly committed by the German Army against Belgian civilians, this pamphlet achieved exactly what was intended and changed British attitudes towards Germans and Germany. No longer was Germany the culturally sophisticated home of Beethoven and Mozart, it was now the breeding ground of barbarians.

Masterman was also the prime mover behind *Nelson's History of the War* and from February 1915 this monthly magazine was published in twenty-three editions. Author

As intended, Raemaekers' skilfully drawn cartoons conjured precisely the emotions of hatred against the supposedly barbaric enemy.

John Buchan, of *The Thirty-Nine Steps* fame, headed the production and it was printed by his publisher, Thomas Nelson. Incidentally, Buchan was given the rank of Second Lieutenant in the Intelligence Corps and provided with the necessary documents to write the work.

After January 1916 the Bureau's activities were subsumed under the office of the Secretary of State for Foreign Affairs. After the success of the initial trials with artists like Dodd and his brother-in-law, artist Muirhead Bone, in 1917 arrangements were made to send other artists to France. Ill-health forced one of them, society painter John Lavery, to stay in the British Isles and paint pictures of the home front but, despite this, he was nearly killed by a Zeppelin during a bombing raid!

Alongside Wellington House, two other organisations were established by the government to deal with propaganda. The first was the Neutral Press Committee, which was given the task of supplying the press of neutral countries with information relating to the war and was headed by G.H. Mair, former assistant editor of the *Daily Chronicle*. The second was the Foreign Office New Department, which served as the source for the foreign press of all official statements concerning British foreign policy.

In February 1917 the government established a Department of Information and John Buchan was promoted to Lieutenant-Colonel and put in charge of it. Masterman, however, retained responsibility for books, pamphlets, photographs and war art, while T.L. Gilmour, the first secretary of the National Savings Committee, was charged with encouraging patriotic citizens to buy war bonds, was responsible for telegraph communications, radio, newspapers, magazines and the cinema.

In early 1918 it was decided that a senior government figure should take over responsibility for propaganda and on 4 March Lord Beaverbrook, owner of the *Daily*

In my opinion Ludwig Hohlwein is the greatest of all poster artists. This superb example is designed to raise funds in aid of German prisoners of war and civil detainees.

Express newspaper, was made Minister of Information. Masterman was subsequently placed in a subordinate position beneath him as Director of Publications, and John Buchan became Director of Intelligence. Lord Northcliffe, owner of *The Times* and the *Daily Mail*, was put in charge of propaganda aimed at enemy nations, while Robert Donald, editor of the *Daily Chronicle*, was made director of propaganda aimed at neutral nations. In February 1918, following the announcement of this reorganisation, Lloyd George was accused of creating this new system only to gain control over Fleet Street's leading figures.

Propaganda was not the government's only concern of course. Getting the message across was one thing. Preventing certain information from circulating, censorship, was quite another and just as important. Little more than a week before hostilities broke out in 1914, Winston Churchill, then First Lord of the Admiralty, announced in the House of Commons the setting up of a press bureau with the dual task of censoring press reports and of issuing to the press what he said would be 'all the information relating to the war which any of the Departments of State think it right to issue'. Throughout the war the various provisions of the Defence of the Realm Act (DORA) specified the matters for which publication was an offence. Mostly these related to the number and disposition of troops and any operational details which might jeopardise future strategy.

Feeding Britain's new propaganda machinery and those similar departments in each of the other belligerents was an army of some of the greatest artists and illustrators in the world.

Perhaps one of the earliest and most famous images of the Great War is Alfred Leete's poster of Kitchener – 'Your country needs you!'. Field Marshal Horatio Herbert Kitchener had won fame in 1898 for winning the Battle of Omdurman and securing control of the Sudan, becoming 'Lord Kitchener of Khartoum'. As Army Chief-of-Staff and later Commander-in-Chief in the Second Boer War he had played a key role in suppressing Boer forces. At the start of the First World War, Lord Kitchener became Secretary of State for War, a Cabinet minister, and immediately went about organising the largest volunteer army that Britain had ever raised.

Alfred Leete's iconic graphic first appeared as a cover illustration for *London Opinion*, one of the most influential magazines in the world, on 5 September 1914. Alfred Ambrose Chew Leete later contributed regularly

'Vive les Suffragettes'. This endearing postcard could only have been produced in France because although the Women's Social and Political Union (WSPU) had more or less agreed a truce with Lloyd George's government, in Britain the vote for women was still a very sensitive topic.

Perhaps one of the most famous posters of all time – Alfred Leete's iconic recruiting poster depicting Lord Kitchener first appeared in September 1914 and was singlehandedly responsible for encouraging thousands of men to flock to the colours.

to publications such as *Punch* magazine, the *Strand Magazine* and *Tatler*, and was well-known for his advertising posters for brands such as Rowntrees, Guinness and Bovril, and the Underground Electric Railways Company (the London Underground). But there's no doubt that he will be ever remembered for his drawing of Kitchener.

Other notable British posters and their creators included Bernard Partridge, whose stirring 'Take Up the Sword of Justice' was a rallying cry for recruits to Kitchener's army.

Sir Frank William Brangwyn RA learned some of his creative skills in the workshops of William Morris, and the Anglo-Welsh artist, painter, watercolourist, virtuoso engraver and illustrator worked steadily into the 1950s; he was knighted in 1941.

Although Brangwyn produced over eighty poster designs during the First World War, he was not an official war artist. His poster of a Tommy bayoneting an enemy soldier – 'Put Strength in the Final Blow: Buy War Bonds' – caused deep offence in both Britain and Germany. Allegedly, even the Kaiser himself is said to have put a price on the artist's head after seeing the image. Brangwyn's 1915 poster for the National Fund for the Welsh Troops is typical of the artist's combination of graphic and illustrative techniques.

Many other British artists contributed to the nation's war effort, providing stirring designs for posters in particular. Other notable posters include 'Song to the Evening Star' by F. Ernest Jackson, 'Their Home! Belgium, 1918' by T. Gregory Brown and a striking one by an anonymous artist from the army's publicity department: 'Young men of Britain! The Germans said you were not in earnest. "We knew you'd come – and give them the lie!" Play the greater game and join the football battalion.'

After he was invalided out of the army due to an injury while in the trenches, Paul Nash, one of Britain's greatest artists, who came to real fame during the Second World War, joined the other artists sent to the front in 1917 to record the carnage there. Nash's modernist painting *A Howitzer Firing* emphasises the role and destructive potential of artillery, suggesting the damage modern technology could inflict on human flesh.

Other artistic giants, such as Sir William Orpen and Eric Kennington, were also engaged as official war artists alongside Nash.

During Orpen's visit to the Western Front he produced drawings and paintings of privates, dead soldiers and German prisoners of war, many of which were used on posters and postcards by the Ministry of Information. Orpen's most famous works, however, are his large paintings of the Versailles Peace Conference which captured the political machinations of the assembled statesmen. He presented over one-hundred

'Hello Blighty!', No. 1 Observation Group, BEF postcard. It reads: 'Compliments of the season to you and best wishes for the New Year. Cheerio! Bert'. A Christmas card from 1917. The smiling Tommy was unaware that 1918 would deliver a renewed German offensive.

of his original artworks to the British government on the understanding that they should be mounted in simple white frames and kept together as a single body of work. They are now in the collection of the Imperial War Museum in London.

Like Nash, Eric Kennington had been invalided out of the army early in the war. He served as an official War Artist from 1916 until 1919 and would do so again during the Second World War. Kennington's first one-man show of *The Kensingtons at Laventie* at the Goupil Gallery 1916 caused a sensation. The artist had actually served in the 13th Battalion, The London Regiment, popularly known as 'The Kensingtons', and this magnificent painting actually depicts men from his own platoon and even includes a self-portrait. Kennington painted this tribute to his comrades after he was invalided out of the army in 1915.

The fine canvases of oil painters, though catching a mood and often, in an almost subversive way, revealing the inequities of the suffering of ordinary soldiers at the front, could only really be seen in art galleries or on the occasions when they travelled the nation to drum up contributions to national savings and war bonds. The art that most affected public opinion and reached the widest audience was that of the posterist.

Together with Alfred Leete's famous portrayal of Kitchener back in 1914, possibly the other single most memorable poster of this period was the work not of a well-known artist but of a now little-remembered one, E.V. Kealey. 'Women of Britain Say – Go!', a 1915 recruiting poster depicting a mother, daughter and young son watching soldiers march off to war. Created for the Parliamentary Recruiting Committee, and printed in London, this poster was more than a patriotic call to arms. Showing a defenceless mother and her two young children bravely home alone while the local menfolk, their protectors, march off to war, this emotive design was more than enough to inspire even the most reluctant recruit to enlist. After the war Kealey continued designing similarly striking posters but his commissions came now from the burgeoning travel trade, cruises to Africa and the exotic Orient and the like, rather than official commissions.

French illustrators provided equally stirring designs to support their country's war effort. Auguste Roll's stirring 1916 poster showing a French nurse tending a sick soldier and '*On les aura!*' ('We'll Get Them!') by Jules-Abel Faivre, published the same year to raise money for the second government defence-loan drive and showing a much more vigorous Poilu charging forward rifle in hand as he encourages his comrades to follow, garnered enormous public support.

A graduate of the Paris School of Fine Arts, Charles Fouqueray was a master of lithography and used his talents to design a fine series of war posters. In one of them, '*Le Cardinal Mercier Protege la Belgique*' ('Cardinal Mercier Protects Belgium') he portrayed the famous Catholic defender of Belgium, who, in the role of the shepherd protecting his flock, denounced the German occupation and especially the burning of the great Library of Louvain. Fouqueray also had a distinguished career as a mural painter and as a prolific illustrator for magazines and journals such as the *Graphic* and *Illustration*.

Another memorable poster, 'The French Woman in War-Time', by Georges Émile Capon, shows three women engaged in supporting the war effort by each either nursing young children, toiling on the farm or working in a factory at the lathe. Originally designed to promote a government film produced to encourage women to leave the comfort of home behind and do 'their bit' for the good of France instead, Capon's illustration soon enjoyed wider distribution.

Adolphe Willette's poster '*Journée du Poilu. 25 et 26 Décembre 1915*' ('Day of the French soldier') depicts a Poilu's Christmas leave from the front. One of the great artists of the belle époque, Adolphe Léon Willette is today best remembered for his lithographs illustrating the *chansonniers* of Montmartre, the solitary poet singer-songwriters who performed their own songs at the famous cabaret Le Chat Noir. In 1906, Willette achieved the highest honour for a French artist when he was appointed Chevalier de la Légion d'honneur.

Born in 1871, Jules Marie Auguste Leroux was a professor at the École nationale supérieure des Beaux-Arts in Paris for thirty years, a jury member of the committee of French Artists Society, an art teacher at the Academy de la Grande Chaumiere, and a knight of the Légion d'honneur. Despite his exalted position midst the higher echelons of Parisian Beaux-Arts, Leroux was not above creating posters in support of his nation's war effort. The one he produced in support of war loans raised by the Comptoir d'escompte de Paris, a now long-gone bank founded in response to the financial shock caused by the revolution of February 1848, command particularly high prices among collectors.

Though it did not get embroiled in fighting until 1917, from early in the war the United States had leaned towards the Allied course and was especially unsympathetic to the German invasion and subjugation of Belgium. Even before Congress approved America's entry on the side of the Allies American artists and illustrators had been heavily involved producing arresting graphics and when it became pretty clear that the United States would be drawn into the conflict, American artist and illustrator Joseph Pennell observed: 'When the United States wished to make public its wants, whether of men or money, it was found that art – as the European countries had found – was the best medium.'

And after news of the alleged German atrocities in Belgium reached the United States, numerous posters bearing the image of the 'Hun' were repeatedly employed to arouse public animosity towards the enemy.

The Wilson government's Division of Pictorial Publicity employed over 300 of the most prominent illustrators of the time to help with the propaganda efforts. Among them were artists such as C.B. Falls, E.H. Blashfield, Joseph Pennell, Howard Chandler Christy, Joseph Leyendecker, Jessie Willcox Smith and L.N. Britton.

James Montgomery Flagg's memorable poster of Uncle Sam: 'I Want You for the US Army', is as striking as Leete's poster of Kitchener.

Perhaps the most famous American poster of the First World War was created by James Montgomery Flagg. Originally published as the cover for 6 July 1916 issue of *Leslie's Weekly*, with the title, 'What Are You Doing for Preparedness?', Flagg's portrait of 'Uncle Sam' went on to become one of the most famous posters in the world. More than 4 million copies were printed between 1917 and 1918, as the United States mobilised and sent its 'dough boys' to the far-off trenches in Europe.

A member of the first Civilian Preparedness Committee organised in New York in 1917, Flagg contributed nearly fifty works to support the United States war effort. Because of its overwhelming popularity, Flagg's 'Uncle Sam' image was used again in the Second World War.

Other prominent artists working to support the United States' propaganda machinery included Ellsworth Young, the noted landscape painter who was also a prolific supplier of illustrations to book and magazine publishers. Featuring a menacing silhouette of an armed Prussian soldier, spiked Pickelhaube on his head and carrying off his 'war bounty', a screaming maiden, his famous poster, 'Remember Belgium', produced in support of American bonds, caused a sensation.

Dutchman Louis Raemaekers' cartoons were picked up for distribution by the British government in a series of propaganda pamphlets. The campaign was so effective, the Germans used their influence in the Netherlands to have Raemaekers tried for 'endangering Dutch neutrality'. British Prime Minister David Lloyd George was so impressed by his work that he persuaded him to go the United States where his drawings were syndicated by Hearst Publications in an effort to enlist American help in the war. In 1917 United States President Theodore Roosevelt paid the artist a striking compliment saying: 'The cartoons of Louis Raemaekers constitute the most powerful of the honorable contributions made by neutrals to the cause of civilization in the World War.'

Although of German decent, Adolph Treidler was another prolific artist working in support of the American war effort from 1917. Before this he illustrated numerous covers and also provided advertisement work for publications such as *McClure's*, *Harper's*, the *Saturday Evening Post*, *Scribner's* and *Woman's Home Companion*. His wartime propaganda posters in the First World War portrayed Women Ordnance Workers, otherwise known as WOWs, in munitions plants for the United War Work Campaign. Later on he also created wartime propaganda posters in the Second World War.

Vojtěch Preissig was a Czech typographer, printmaker, designer, illustrator, painter and teacher who had studied in Prague at the School of Applied Industrial Art before the war but moved to the United States as an art instructor. He designed a number of posters for the American government but is perhaps best known for one in particular, a striking graphic of a naval gun crew in action beneath the heading: 'Find the range of your patriotism by enlisting in the Navy'. Preissig return to his native Czechoslovakia in the 1930s and following the Nazi invasion of his homeland he joined the Czech resistance. The artist was arrested in 1940 for doing graphic design work for *V boj*, a magazine of the resistance that had been outlawed by German authorities. He died in 1944 in Dachau concentration camp.

Numerous other American artists and illustrators made enormous contributions to their nation's war effort but I have space to make mention of only one more and will single out Henry Raleigh for his 1918 poster promoting United States government bonds for the Third Liberty Loan. 'Halt the Hun!' features an American soldier restraining a German one from harming a woman and child, both of whom are cowering before the Teutonic giant. Like Raemaekers, Raleigh appealed to the sentimental side of his audience every time.

The Central Powers also possessed an abundance of artistic talent of course. In Germany painter Paul Plontke created an especially striking poster in 1917. '*Fur die Kriegsanleihe*!' ('For the War Loan!') showed a cherub holding a German Army helmet filled with coins and beseeching the viewer to contribute.

Otto Lehmann's poster '*Stutzt Unsre Feldgraunen*' ('Support our Field Greys. Rend England's might – subscribe to War Loans'), published in Cologne early in the war, is a strikingly descriptive example of the high quality of German graphic design so lauded by the post-war book *War Posters. Issued by Belligerent and Neutral Nations* (see below).

Viennese painter, illustrator, industrial designer and graphic artist Erwin Puchinger was a major component of the Austrian art scene and a friend and contemporary of Gustav Klimt, among others. Puchinger worked in London, Prague and Paris but during the war he was obliged to support his nation. His famous 1915 war-loan poster depicting a classical image of a knight defending a woman and child from the spears of unseen attackers reflects the influence of the Vienna Secession, of which he was a major part.

Other notable designers include Oswald Polte, whose sentimental poster entitled 'Collection of gold and jewels for the Fatherland – Pomeranian Jewel and Gold Purchase Week, 30 June 1918 – 6 July 1918', depicting a hausfrau offering up her jewellery collection, contrasts vividly with Ludwig Hohlwein's very graphic depiction of a powerful German soldier in full kit eating from his mess tin. Captioned 'Preserves Strength and Energy', both the striking simplicity and excellent drawing and the not so subtle double entendre are typical of the excellent designs to come from the Central Powers.

There are a couple of other great German artists worth mentioning and whose posters, if you can find them, are of particularly high value. F.K. Engelhard created many, especially striking posters. '*Nein! Niemals!* (No! Never!)' shows a kepi-wearing French soldier greedily grabbing out at German territory across the Rhine. The irony of such horror that anything like this could happen to the Fatherland was not lost on Belgians, whose neutrality had been so cruelly ignored by Germany in 1914. In fact, it wasn't only British and French news agencies that were filling newspapers with usually untrue stories of German atrocities. In 1914 the German Wolff Telegraph Agency caused a sensation among German readers when it wired a story about a French doctor who had allegedly been involved in an attempt to infect a well at Metz with plague and cholera bacilli. Also produced towards the end of the war and entitled 'Anarchie', depicting a giant knife-wielding King Kong-like ape stalking the streets, was another equally striking poster from Engelhard. This was created at the time of the German revolution in 1918 and the poster's subtitle, 'Misery and Destruction follow Anarchy', left the reader in little doubt about the likely results of an authoritarian collapse and the rise of communism in Germany. As we know, the ferment of these times gave voice to National Socialism and the rise of Hitler. Austrian artist Roland

Krafter put a more positive spin on Germany's collapse in November 1918 as his fine poster 'The Troops Home-Coming for Christmas', showing upstanding German troops marching across the border with laurels in their *Stahlhelms* and carrying pillowcases full of presents, so clearly illustrates.

Hungary, Germany and Austria's major ally, also provided the Central Powers with a number of fine artists who supported their nation's propaganda machinery to stunning effect.

After studying art in Berlin, Paris and London, Mihaly Bíró, who was born in Budapest in 1886, returned to Hungary and ultimately became famous for his social protest posters in support of the Hungarian revolutionary movement within which he became political poster commissar of the Hungarian Socialist Republic in 1919. Before this, in 1918 as the Austro-Hungarian Empire was collapsing and being torn up by French and Serbian forces while Russian Communist troops also looked likely to enter the country in support of Béla Kun's new Soviet Republic, the world's second, Bíró produced a striking artwork suggesting the calamity of a Russian invasion. After the overthrow of the government, Bíró moved to the United States, but returned to Hungary in 1947 and died in Budapest the following year.

Another Hungarian poster artist, George Kürthy, had a far more traditional, illustrative, yet primitive, almost 'peasant art' style. His graceful line drawings, to me very reminiscent of the work of English artists Aubrey Beardsley, can be seen decorating many of Hungary's war-loan posters during the 1914–18 conflict. As the war progressed and the effect of the Allied stranglehold on raw materials and other imports into occupied Europe began to be felt, the need for Austria-Hungary to look to its citizens for financial support became all the more critical.

In Britain, when the war finished, almost all of the propaganda machinery was dismantled. There were various interwar debates regarding British use of propaganda, particularly atrocity propaganda, most of which was found to be baseless. Commentators such as the politician Arthur Ponsonby, a member of the Union of Democratic Control, a British pressure group formed in 1914 and opposed to military influence in government, were active in refuting government claims against the Central Powers (Germany, Austria-Hungary and Turkey). In 1928 Ponsonby's book, *Falsehood in War-Time: Propaganda Lies of the First World War*, was published, exposing many of the alleged atrocities as either lies or exaggeration. Some modern commentators argue that one effect of Ponsonby's revelations was reluctance in Britain to believe the stories of Nazi persecution during the Second World War until the Allied armies were confronted with the awful realities of the Holocaust and the terror of Nazi reprisals against civilians, which proved such stories to be true. In Germany, however, military commanders such as Erich Ludendorff, who with his superior Paul von Hindenburg had more influence on Germany's strategy than the Kaiser himself, suggested that British propaganda had actually been instrumental in his country's defeat. Adolf Hitler echoed this view, and when they assumed power the Nazis later adopted many of the techniques used by British propagandists during the 1914–18 war.

Now part of Bloomsbury Publishing Plc, British publisher A&C Black had a rich and independent history since it was founded in 1807 by Adam and Charles Black in Edinburgh. In 1851, the firm bought the copyright of Walter Scott's *Waverley* novels for £27,000. Famous as the publisher of *Who's Who* since 1897, in 1902 it published P.G. Wodehouse's first book. Since then A&C Black's extensive backlist has encompassed many books on visual arts, glass, ceramics and printmaking. Little wonder then that immediately after the cessation of hostilities in 1919 this publisher was to produce one of the best, illustrated reference books about war posters. The introduction to *War Posters. Issued by Belligerent and Neutral Nations 1914–1919*, selected and edited by Martin Hardie and Arthur K. Sabin (A&C Black Ltd, London, 1920), an 80pp. hard-back book littered with superb full-colour and half-tone plates, is illuminating:

> The poster, hitherto the successful handmaid of commerce, was immediately recognised as a means of national propaganda with unlimited possibilities. Its value as an educative or simulative influence was more and more associated. In the stress of war its functions of impressing an idea quickly, vividly, and lastingly, together with the widest publicity, was soon recognised. While humble citizens were still trying to evade a stern age-limit by a jaunty air and juvenile appearance, the poster was mobilised and doing its bit.
>
> Activity in poster production was not confined to Great Britain. France, as in all matters where Art is concerned, triumphantly took the field, and soon had hoardings covered with posters, many of which will take a lasting place in the history of Art. Germany and Austria, from the very outset of the War, seized upon the poster as the most powerful and speedy method of swaying popular opinion. Even before the War, we had much to learn from the concentrated power, the force of design, and the economy of means, which made German posters sing out from a wall like a defiant blare of trumpets. Their posters issued during the War are even more aggressive; but it is the function of a poster to act as a 'mailed fist', and our illustrations will show that, whatever else may be their faults, the posters of Germany have a force and character that make most of our own seem insipid and tame.
>
> Here in Great Britain the earliest days of the war saw available spaces everywhere covered with posters cheap in sentiment, and conveying childish and vulgar appeals to patriotism already stirred far beyond the conception of the artists who designed them or the authorities responsible for their distribution.* This perhaps, was inevitable in a country such as ours. The grimness of the world-struggle was not realised in its intensity until driven home by staggering blows at our very life as a nation.
>
> ---
>
> * While this is being written, our authorities are again placarding our walls with indifferent posters showing the advantages of life in the Army as compared with the 'disadvantages' of civil life, and embodying an undignified appeal to Britons to join the Army for the sake of playing cricket and football and seeing the world for nothing!

The preface beginning the section specifically dealing with British posters includes the following passage:

Shortly after the War began, an 'Exhibition of German and Austrian Articles typifying Design' was arranged at the Goldsmith's Hall, to show the directions in which we had lessons to learn from German trade-competitors as to the combination of Art and economy applied to ordinary articles of commerce. The walls were hung with German posters, and one felt at once that while our average poster cost perhaps six times as much to produce, it was inferior to its German rival in just those vital qualities of concentrated design, whether of colour or form, and those powers of seizing attention, which are essential to the very nature of a poster.

While we have had individual poster artists, such as Nicholson, Pryde, and Beardsley, whose work has touched perhaps a higher level than has ever been reached on the Continent, our general conception of what is good and valuable in a poster has almost been entirely wrong. The advertising agent and the business firm rarely get away from the popular idea that a poster must be a picture, and that the purpose of every picture is to 'point a moral and adorn a tale'. They seldom realise that poster art and pictorial art have essentially different aims. If a British firm wishes to advertise beer, it insists on an artist producing a picture of a publican's brawny and veined arm holding out a pot of beer during closed hours to a policeman; or a Gargantuan bottle towering above the houses and dense crowds of a market-place; or a fox-terrier climbing on to a table and wondering what it is 'master likes so much' – all in posters produced at great expense with an enormous range of colour. The German, on the other hand – there was an example at the Goldsmiths' Hall – designs a single pot of amber foaming beer, with the name of the firm in one good spot of lettering below. It is printed at small cost, in two or three flat colours; but it shouts 'beer' at the passer by.

However the editors conceded that 'Our British war posters are too well known and too recent in our memory to require any lengthy introduction or comment,' adding:

The first official recognition of their value to the nation was during the recruiting campaign of 1914. The Parliamentary Recruiting Committee gave commissions for more than a hundred posters, of which two and a half million copies were distributed throughout the British Isles. Hardly one of the early posters had the slightest claim to recognition as a product of fine art; most of them were examples of what any art school would teach should be avoided in crude design and atrocious lettering. Among the best and most efficient, however, may be mentioned Alfred Leete's 'Kitchener'. But if one compares Leete's head of Kitchener, 'Your Country Needs You', with Louis Oppenheim's 'Hindenburg', the latter, with its rugged force and reserve of colour, stands as an example of the direction in which Germany tends to beat us in poster art.

It is not surprising that following the carnage of the Great War, when nearly 16 million died and a further 21 million were wounded most individuals looked forward to peace and benevolent technological development, shunning militarism and arms manufacture.

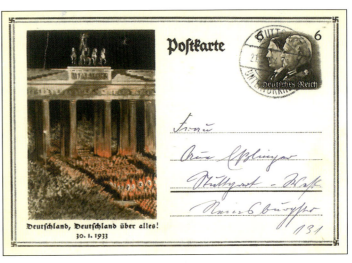

'Deutschland, Deutschland über alles'. A German postcard from January 1933, a period when Hitler still had to share power with President Hindenburg.

Japan had been at war since 1931 when it invaded Manchuria.

The future promised new homes with electric lighting and modern sanitation. In Britain 'Garden' cities were planned, featuring modern schools, hospitals, parks and playing fields. While totalitarian nations like Germany, Italy and Japan rearmed and argued that a nation's future well-being depended on a strong military, other countries either sought to shelter behind supposedly impregnable fortifications such as France with its hi-tech Maginot Line or the security of negotiation, peace bought by treaty, such as those negotiated by the so-called appeasers like Britain's Prime Minister Neville Chamberlain. The Americans on the other hand, the only major power inadvertently to profit from the war, sought to isolate themselves from the quarrels of the old order, concentrating instead on further expanding their mighty industrial and commercial base.

In 1915, a year after the Union of Democratic Control had been established, British liberal leaders had formed the League of Nations Society in an effort to promote a strong international organisation that could enforce the peaceful resolution of conflict. Later that year the League to Enforce Peace was established in the United States, striving for similar goals. These and other pacifistic initiatives helped to change attitudes and went some way towards the formation of the League of Nations, the covenant for which was signed at the Paris Peace Conference in June 1919.

As attitudes towards militarism changed numerous organisations joined the clarion call for an end to war. These included the War Resisters' International, the Women's International League for Peace and Freedom, the No More War Movement and the Peace Pledge Union (PPU). The League of Nations also convened several disarmament conferences in the inter-war period, the most significant of which was the Geneva Conference.

Revulsion of war was widespread in 1920s Britain, a nation mourning the loss of the flower of its youth. Novels and poems about the futility of war and the destruction of brave young souls on the threshold of life, forced into battle by misguided old fools, were published on a regular basis. Erich Remarque's *All Quiet on the Western Front* is perhaps the most famous story and was made into a successful film by director Lewis Milestone. Other books which had a significant effect on the consciences of all right-thinking citizens included *Death of a Hero* by Richard Aldington and *Cry Havoc* by Beverley Nichols. A debate at the University of Oxford in 1933 on the motion 'one must fight for King and country' captured this change of mood when the motion was resoundingly defeated.

Another novel which was translated into a blockbuster movie at this time was *Things to Come*, a work of science fiction by H.G. Wells, published in 1933, which Alexander Korda lavishly shot in Britain in 1936. Set in the fictional British city of 'Everytown', the film's narrative spans the years 1940 to 2036. The story begins by showing the discomfort felt by successful businessman John Cabal (Raymond Massey) who cannot enjoy Christmas Day 1940 because of news about a possible war. When conflict does come the depictions of aerial assault, bombing and gas attack are terrifying and went a long way to encouraging the public's acceptance of the British government's policy of appeasement in order to avoid such horrors.

In fact the appeasement policy of British Prime Minister Neville Chamberlain's government in the late 1930s wasn't of course simply a reaction to public sentiment or a symptom of his heartfelt hatred for war. He felt a duty to try, as much as he could, to do what the League of Nations had palpably failed to do – thwart aggressors by the use of negotiation rather than military might. Though it had been established to mediate in territorial quarrels, the League had stood idly by when, in September 1931, Japan, a member of the League of Nations, invaded northeast China and established a new territory, Manchukuo.

The League's policy of international cooperation and collective resistance to aggression, the policy of 'collective

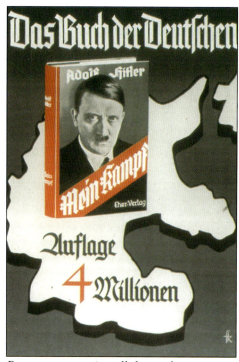

Poster encouraging all those who believed in the rebirth of a new Germany under the leadership of Adolf Hitler to purchase the party's bible, Mein Kampf.

In Britain there were also books about Hitler, not all of them hagiographies.

By the mid-1930s, with war looking inevitable, the Territorial Army was found to be woefully under strength and recruitment became a priority.

The Nazis took great comfort from the fact that there was considerable support for their claims upon the German-speaking Sudeten region of Czechoslovakia. An editorial in The Times *on 7 September 1938 even called for it to be returned to Germany.*

security' was further tested and found to be wanting in 1935 with Italian dictator Mussolini's invasion of Abyssinia (Ethiopia) and again in 1936 when Hitler sent German forces into the previously demilitarised Rhineland. Even though the Führer's officers had orders to withdraw if they met French resistance, the League did nothing.

Similarly, *Anschluss*, the political union of Austria with Germany, achieved through annexation by Adolf Hitler in 1938, when the 8th Army of the German *Wehrmacht* crossed the Austrian border, met no resistance and was indeed greeted by cheering Austrians.

However, the real crisis came in 1938 and involved Czechoslovakia, or more properly Nazi claims on the largely German-speaking Sudeten part of that country, dismembered from the Reich at Versailles. In September, Chamberlain flew to Berchtesgaden, the Führer's Bavarian holiday home, to negotiate directly with Hitler, in the hope of avoiding war. Demanding that the Sudetenland should be absorbed into Germany, Hitler convinced Chamberlain that refusal meant war. The British and French governments urged the Czech president to agree and in a stroke Czechoslovakia lost

800,000 citizens, much of its industry and its mountain defences in the west. Landing back at Croydon aerodrome, Chamberlain claimed he had secured 'Peace For Our Times' and the British, who had begun handing out gas masks and practising ARP (Air Raid Precautions), could breathe a sigh of relief. The Air Ministry, which had secretly been asking the Prime Minister to wait until 1939 before he went to war, also exhaled – there was still time to build the modern Spitfires they knew were essential to securing air superiority above Britain.

Many, of course were horrified at yet another example of democracy's weakness in the face of bellicose militarism. In February 1938, Foreign Secretary Anthony Eden resigned from the government, telling the House of Commons:

> I do not believe that we can make progress in European appeasement if we allow the impression to gain currency abroad that we yield to constant pressure. I am certain in my own mind that progress depends above all on the temper of the nation, and that temper must find expression in a firm spirit. This spirit I am confident is there. Not to give voice to it is I believe fair neither to this country nor to the world.

In answer to Eden's resignation, backbencher Winston Churchill, one of the lone voices who, throughout the 1930s had warned against German rearmament and Nazi ambition, told the Commons:

> The resignation of the late Foreign Secretary may well be a milestone in history. Great quarrels, it has been well said, arise from small occasions but seldom from small causes. The late Foreign Secretary adhered to the old policy which we have all forgotten for so long. The Prime Minister and his colleagues have entered upon another and a new policy. The old policy was an effort to establish the rule of law in Europe, and build up through the League of Nations effective deterrents against the aggressor. Is it the new policy to come to terms with the totalitarian Powers in the hope that by great and far-reaching acts of submission, not merely in sentiment and pride, but in material factors, peace may be preserved. A firm stand by France and Britain, under the authority of the League of Nations, would have been followed by the immediate evacuation of the Rhineland without the shedding of a drop of blood; and the effects of that might have enabled the more prudent elements of the German Army to gain their proper position, and would not have given to the political head of Germany the enormous ascendancy which has enabled him to move forward. Austria has now been laid in thrall, and we do not know whether Czechoslovakia will not suffer a similar attack.

It should not be forgotten that as a backdrop to the truly momentous events mentioned above, between July 1936 and April 1939 the bloody Spanish Civil War proved a further challenge to European peace and served as a useful testing ground for much of Hitler's new weaponry, especially his *Luftwaffe* – many of the German Condor Legion pilots who flew in support of the nationalist General Franco's rebellion would see

I think this is one of the most interesting pieces of wartime ephemera the collector could possess. Though dropped over Britain by the thousand, Hitler's 'Last Appeal to Reason' is also one of the rarest items – the majority which floated earthward were retrieved and used as loo paper!

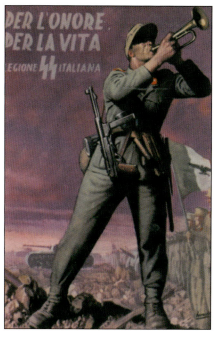

'Per L'onore Per La Vita Legione SS Italiana'. *Italian recruiting poster for the admission into Germany's Waffen SS. Of the 15,000 men who volunteered for service only 6,000 were considered suitable enough to meet the exacting standards required.*

'Mightier Yet!' *This leaflet compares production in April 1940 with that of June and explains that everything has improved. 'Dangerous times lie ahead of us. Glorious days, too. Germany is now up against the British Empire. For attack and for defence, the Empire is tremendously strong. It grows stronger as its free people's fight, arm and work.' Ministry of Information, 1940.*

action against the RAF in the Battle of Britain. Similarly, volunteers to the International Brigade which supported the elected, republican government, notably Britain's Tom Wintringham and America's 'Yank' Levy, learned valuable lessons in guerrilla fighting which would prove of enormous value to the Home Guard and Churchill's super-secret Auxiliary Units.

In fact, several organisations already existed to publish and distribute these new learnings among Britain's regular and more clandestine forces. The largest and most well-known was His Majesty's Stationery office (HMSO), owned and operated by the British government, which came into being during the 1780s when the British Parliament undertook an audit of expenditure and discovered that the government used too much paper. As a result an official stationer accountable to the Treasury was established and continued to grow with the consequence that independent contracts ceased, the last of which was terminated in 1800.

At the outbreak of the First World War in 1914, the Treasury was forced to recall

all gold coinage to finance war preparations and the government directed the Stationery Office to arrange for the printing, on penny stamp paper – the only secure quality stock available – of one pound and, later, 10 shilling notes. The war put incredible strains on the Stationery Office and although wartime shortages forced bureaucrats to reduce the amount of printed items they had previously relied upon, orders for millions of ration books and public notices cancelled out the benefits of such economies.

By the mid-1930s, the Stationery Office itself employed more than 3,000 people, this dramatic increase in its capacity and capabilities was put to good use when, by the end of the decade, the threat of another European war encouraged the government to prepare, in secret, numerous handbooks and leaflets advising the public about what to do in the event of attack from the air and, especially, about the nation's preparations for dealing with chemical warfare, poison gas delivered by enemy bombers. In fact HMSO supervised the printing of 78 million ration books and hundreds of thousands of instruction manuals on everything from cooking to air raids. The threat of invasion, the potential evacuation of all government operations from London and the autumn night Blitz in 1940 encouraged HMSO to establish a second press facility in Manchester.

Pre-war RAF recruitment poster by Norman Keane.

The nation's official stationer wasn't the only publisher of information and advice. Many private firms produced an abundance of useful handbooks and pamphlets, many of them officially sanctioned.

In Britain, Gale & Polden probably rank as the most prolific producer of information during both world wars. In 1868 James Gale opened a bookshop near Brompton Barracks at Chatham, on the Medway in Kent. Soon after investing in a printing press he won lucrative contracts to supply the Headquarters of the Chatham Military District, among them the annual publication of the Garrison Directory. Together with a variety of important naval and army establishments, HMS *Victory* was built there, Chatham was also the home of the Royal Engineer Establishment, renamed the School of Military Engineering in 1868.

'Come and help with the Victory Harvest' (artist unknown). Come ye land girls all.

James Gale's first book, *Campaign of 1870–1: The Operations of the Corps of General V. Werder* by Ludwig Lohlein, was published in 1873 and his company soon expanded. In 1875 he employed two apprentices, one of whom, 16-year-old Thomas Ernest Polden, was instrumental in introducing a range of improvements into the production side of Gale's business. Polden was soon made senior partner and went about extending the company's distribution network throughout garrisons and dockyards across the Home Counties and eventually throughout Britain. Expansion was such that on 10 November 1892 the company was incorporated as Gale & Polden Ltd.

By the turn of the twentieth century Gale & Polden had relocated to Aldershot, then the largest British Army base in Great Britain. Things continued on the up and up and in 1916 Gale & Polden was even granted a Royal Warrant. A huge proportion of the handbooks used by British soldiers, sailors and airman during the First World War originated from Gale & Polden's Aldershot factory. Even a major fire at the factory in 1918 achieved little more than disruption with the effect that when another major war loomed at the end of the 1930s, Gale & Polden were in an excellent position to supplement HMSO with official publications. By the late 1950s Gale & Polden had acquired a number of smaller printing firms, including larger rivals such as their main competitor in Aldershot, John Drew Ltd. In 1963 Gale & Polden was taken over by the Purnell Group, which in 1964 merged with another printing company, to form the new British Printing Corporation (BPC), the largest printing company in Europe. When Robert Maxwell gained control of BPC in 1981, naming his new company Maxwell Communications, Gale & Polden was finally closed.

Until it was bloodied in the Battle of Britain during the summer of 1940, and then very quickly withdrawn from the campaign, the Junkers Ju-87 Stuka reigned supreme above the unfolding battlefields of Europe. This book, published by Berlin's Verlag Herman Hiller in 1941, is packed with colour illustrations about every aspect of this infamous aircraft.

Though Gale & Polden seem to have benefitted most as far as picking up business HMSO might have been expected to have produced themselves either at their London or Manchester print works, several other publishers benefitted from total war. Among them, Key, Bernards and Nicholson & Watson did particularly well. Interestingly, the latter house was once home to the late Graham Watson, a British literary agent who represented such literary giants as John Steinbeck and Gore Vidal. After joining Nicholson and Watson in 1934, a publishing firm co-founded by his elder brother and financed by their father, in 1947 Graham Watson moved to London literary agency Curtis Brown, as head of its American book department. He worked there for thirty years, the last fifteen as managing director, representing a total of forty authors which together with American giants also included British luminaries like Daphne du Maurier, Randolph Churchill, John O'Hara and C.P. Snow.

Founded in 1909, *Flight* (now *Flight International*) the British produced global aerospace weekly and the world's oldest continuously published aviation news magazine, was another publisher of specialist information which appeared as wartime paper restrictions allowed to keep enthusiasts up to date with developments in aircraft design and performance. Similarly, the *Aeroplane* (now *Aeroplane Magazine*), which first appeared in 1911, was *Flight*'s great rival. Between them these publications met the insatiable demand for recognition handbooks of the sort devoured by 'air mad' school boys and used by those employed on observation duties, most notably the volunteers of the Observer Corps, an organisation established in 1925 to keep a lookout for enemy aircraft and which, as a result of its role during the Battle of Britain, was awarded the 'Royal' prefix in April 1941.

It is just as well that Britain possessed the machinery to communicate with its concerned citizenship, keeping nervous civilians informed, albeit with the official government approved line, about developments that threatened another European war.

Popular history records that British Prime Minister Neville Chamberlain once again backed down in front of Nazi aggression during the Munich Crisis of September 1938. However, we now know that the government was simply playing for time and that Chamberlain's repeated appeasement wasn't the result of a lack or mettle but an expedient delaying tactic which bought his country time to rearm and make the necessary adjustments to its economy to go onto a war footing. Nevertheless, as early as April 1939, five months before Britain declared war with Germany, the government began to get its propaganda ducks in a row, or at least attempted to.

During the early spring the reborn, but still as yet secret, Ministry of Information commissioned a series of public information posters for use in the event of another European war. Sent to the printers in August, within weeks, budgeted at a cost of £20,600, nearly 4 million posters were printed, distributed and stocked in warehouses in time to be put into use immediately war was declared on 3 September 1939.

An interesting piece of British propaganda aimed at Portugal, its oldest ally. Neutral during the Second World War, Portugal traded with both the Allies and the Axis and was a focus for espionage by both sides. The message here lampoons Goering's boast that no bombs would every fall on the Ruhr and then goes on to remind the reader that in 12 months the RAF has bombed the region 530 times.

Though undoubtedly produced with the best intentions, this first batch of British home-front propaganda posters, each sporting bold sans-serif type reversed out in white on a plain signal red background arranged beneath a white monarch's crown, proved a disaster. The public considered one design in particular, centred type arranged in five lines one on top of the other, reading: 'Your courage Your Cheerfulness Your Resolution WILL BRING US VICTORY', patronising and laced with the same old class-ridden ironic rhetoric that many assumed was a thing of the past. Though readers liked the red background, thinking this a cheerful and positive colour, the emphasis on the repeated 'Yours', underlined each time for additional significance, simply meant that the working class would once again carry the burden of front-line fighting or working long hours in the factories if they were engaged on the home front. Many observers thought that 'US' stood for the ruling elite. It would be the same old, same old as far as suffering was concerned.

Curiously, one piece of publicity produced as part of this quickly cancelled and now long-forgotten campaign has become very much part of the cultural fabric of twenty-first-century Britain – the rediscovered 'KEEP CALM AND CARRY ON' poster.

In 2000, one of the owners of Barter Books, Stuart Manley, was going through a box of dusty old books bought at auction when at the bottom of the pile he discovered a curious piece of folded paper. Upon opening and flattening the item, what looked like an old war-time poster was revealed to Stuart. He and his wife Mary liked it so much they decided to frame it and proudly display it in their shop above the till. It went down so well with customers, many of whom enquired whether they could purchase copies, that Barter Books decided to run-off and sell facsimile copies.

The 'Keep Calm and Carry On' poster was the third of three designs commissioned before the fighting actually started. Together with 1 million impressions of the 'Your Courage . . . Will Bring Us Victory' design, nearly 600,000 versions of a similar poster simply reading 'Freedom is in Peril' were printed.

Of the now ubiquitous 'Keep Calm' poster, Dr Bex Lewis (PhD, FHEA, PCP), Research Fellow in Social Media and Online Learning at Durham University and who has done a great deal of research into the provenance of early British propaganda posters, has written:

> Although some may have found their way onto Government office walls, the poster was never officially issued and so remained virtually unseen by the public – unseen, that is, until a copy turned up more than fifty years later in that box of dusty old books bought in auction by Barter Books.
>
> The Ministry of Information commissioned numerous other propaganda posters for use on the home front during the Second World War. Some have become well-known and highly collectable, such as the cartoonist Fougasse's 'Careless Talk Costs Lives' series. But we will probably never know who the graphic artist was who was responsible for the 'Keep Calm' poster, but it's to his or her credit that long after the war was won, people everywhere recognize the brilliance of its simple timeless design and still find reassurance in the very special 'attitude of mind' it conveys.

In February 2012, while I was researching this book, an article in the *Daily Mail* newspaper began: 'A collection of "Keep Calm and Carry On" posters that are believed to be the only surviving originals in Britain have emerged on the Antiques Roadshow.' Apparently, the posters uncovered on the *Roadshow* at St Andrews University were given to Moragh Turnbull, from Fife, by her father William, who served as a member of the Royal Observer Corps. The feature continued:

> Mr Turnbull was given about 15 to put up close to his home but by the time he received them, the threat of a German invasion had waned. He kept them rolled up in an elastic band at his home before passing them on to his daughter – who only realised their true value after taking them to an Antiques Roadshow event. Roadshow expert Paul Atterbury told Miss Turnbull that she was 'probably sitting on the world's only stock' of the famous posters – and they are worth

several thousand pounds. Mrs Turnbull told the presenter: 'I may keep hold of the posters for a few years and sell them for a pension fund.'

Because the government was concerned about being seen to limit civil liberties in a way their Fascist enemies took for granted, the new Ministry of Information did not formally exist until 4 September 1939, the day after hostilities commenced. However, since 1935 the Committee of Imperial Defence, established in 1902 to create a strategic vision defining the future roles of Britain's arms of service, had been busy putting the building blocks in place. When it did emerge from concealment the department's functions were threefold: news and press censorship; home publicity; and overseas publicity in Allied and neutral countries.

Four Ministers headed the MOI in quick succession: Lord Hugh Macmillan, Sir John Reith and the restored Duff Cooper (the most public critic of Neville Chamberlain's appeasement policy inside the Cabinet, he had resigned the day after the 1938 Munich Agreement) before the Ministry settled down under Brendan Bracken in July 1941. Supported by Prime Minister Winston Churchill and the press, Bracken remained in office until victory was clear.

The Home Publicity Division (HPD) was co-ordinated by Kenneth Clark, director of the National Gallery, and Harold Nicolson, husband of Vita Sackville-West. Nicolson also served as Churchill's official censor. Interestingly, Kenneth Clark was also responsible for the successful relocation and storage of most of Britain's finest paintings. We have him to thank for the fact that they all survived the London Blitz. The Home Publicity Division undertook three types of campaigns, those requested by other government departments, specific regional campaigns and those it initiated itself. The General Production Division (GPD), managed the printing, producing work in as little as a week or a fortnight, when normal commercial practice might require three months.

Through the Home Intelligence Division (HID), the MOI collected reactions to general wartime morale and, in some cases, specifically to publicity produced. In fact, the government often turned to Mass Observation, a project to study the everyday lives of ordinary people in

It wasn't just those on the home front who were subjected to a barrage of posters telling them what and what not to do. Those in the armed services received their fair share too. This poster reminds anti-aircraft gunners to make sure they knew the particular recognition signals used to identify friendly aircraft on any given day.

Formed in 1925, the Observer Corps was awarded the title prefix 'Royal' by the King in April 1941, in recognition of service carried out during the Battle of Britain.

Britain, established in 1937 by the anthropologist, journalist, soldier and, well, polymath Tom Harrisson, with filmmaker Humphrey Jennings and the poet-cum-sociologist Charles Madge. The authorities first found Mass Observation useful during the abdication crisis of 1936, when King Edward VIII decided to marry divorcée Wallis Simpson and forsake the throne. The views of the man in the street proved invaluable to the government's appreciation of public opinion. Actually, in 1939 Mass Observation was one of the most vocal critics of the Ministry of Information's initial series of posters.

Fortunately, the series of posters which replaced the expensively pulped initial outlay of the Ministry of Information were received far more favourably. Created by the *Punch* cartoonist Cyril Bird, pen name, 'Fougasse', who gave his time freely for such government commissions, the 'Careless Talk Costs Lives' campaign is an example of the best in British publicity. To this day it is still used as an example of the perfect combination of matter of fact copy writing teamed with appealing illustrations. The message might have been deadly serious but the execution was entertaining and people looked at these posters and took the message on board. Humour got the point across. A careless comment on a bus or in an Underground train might, just might, be over heard by an enemy agent and a bit of innocent chit-chat about the destination of a loved one returning to his regiment from leave might result in disastrous consequences.

By the late 1930s Britain possessed a well-established graphics industry, developed to support the growth in consumerism and an emerging market eager to purchase the various mass-produced labour saving mechanical devices which ranged from toasters, vacuum cleaners and washing machines at one end to automobiles at the other. The new MOI was able to comb through the cream of the crop of this burgeoning creative industry and contract the best designers available.

Together with 'Fougasse', other notable graphic designers working in Britain at this time included Abram Games, F.H.K. Henrion, Herbert Tomlinson, Reginald Mount, Philip Zec, Harold Forster, Jan le Witt and the Pole George Him.

Sadly, though the authorities could call upon a network of some of the best creative talent around, sometimes the concepts they asked them to execute fell far short of the mark. Following the debacle of the retreat from Dunkirk, a potential disaster which the British Army only narrowly avoided, yet even though most of the troops were plucked from the occupied continent they had left their best weapons and equipment in France, the powers that be assumed the Allied collapse must be the result of enemy subterfuge when, of course it was simply the reward the *Wehrmacht* deserved for employing the modern tactic of blitzkrieg. Convinced that the French Army was defeated by an insidious fifth column of spies and defeatists, the British government's next big poster campaign was designed to put an end to defeatist talk, if it existed at all, and gossip that might help the enemy. On the theme of the 'Silent Column', the new campaign featured the rather two-dimensional characters of Miss Leaky Mouth, Mrs Glumpot and Mr Knowall – none of them to be trusted.

This campaign was posted in public areas at the same time as a wave of prosecutions took place under the auspices of the draconian Regulation 18B of the Defence (General) Regulations 1939, which allowed the internment of people suspected of being Nazi sympathisers and the suspension of habeas corpus, which, dating back to the Magna Carta required that a person under arrest had to be brought before a judge or jury before he or she was sentenced. Given that ordinary citizens were being told that the fight was against authoritarian totalitarianism and to preserve their democratic freedom, this campaign touched a raw nerve. In his diary Harold Nicolson confided that 'the Ministry of Information was in disgrace again'.

As mentioned earlier, the Ministry of Information really found its feet under the governance of Brendan Bracken, the Irish-born businessman and Tory Cabinet minister who after the war was responsible for the merger of the *Financial News* into the *Financial Times*, creating the financial daily we know today. Churchill appointed him as his parliamentary private secretary soon after the outbreak of the Second World War and Bracken replaced Duff Cooper as Minister of Information on 21 July 1941.

Bracken's publishing experience – he had joined Eyre & Spottiswoode in 1923 and in 1925 became a director of the publishing company – was a real advantage. He also edited the *Financial News*, the *Banker* and the *Practitioner* before being promoted to managing director of the *Economist* in 1928.

Although he argued against either appealing to public sympathy or lecturing the masses as if they were children, saying the former made them furious, the latter resentful, he wasn't beyond criticism himself for his forthright view about how things should be done. One of his employees, Eric Blair, later George Orwell, who worked under Bracken on the BBC's Indian Service, customarily referred to Bracken by his initials, B.B., the same as those used for his character Big Brother in *Nineteen-Eighty-Four*, his post-war book warning of the dangers of an authoritarian state. Orwell resented wartime censorship and doubted the need to manipulate information, something he felt Bracken's office managed with a Machiavellian hand.

But, to stay on course every ship needs a firm hand on the tiller and as we shall see throughout the pages of this book Bracken managed to supervise a series of very successful campaigns which in their small way went some way to supporting Britain's war effort. We've the combined talents of the Ministry of Information to thank for giving us phrases such as 'Dig For Victory', 'Cold's

The Soldiers' and Sailors' Families Association was founded in 1885 by James Gildea. In 1919, after the RAF was formed, it became a charity and changed its name to the Soldiers', Sailors' and Airmen's Families Association (SSAFA).

Issued by the National Savings Committee and printed by His Majesty's Stationery office (HMSO), this poster showed prospective savers what their contributions were helping to support.

and Sneezes Spread Diseases', 'Go To It!' and 'Don't be Fuel-ish' and these messages resonated across the ages.

It should not be forgotten that while Britain's authorities were girding themselves to face a war they had avoided for so long, there were still vocal splinter groups who continued to oppose another European war, especially one hard on the heels of a conflict that had wrought such calamity upon the Continent and its constituent populations, and also those who actively supported the kind of totalitarianism, fascism, which was proving so popular in Italy and Germany.

The main players upon this stage included people such Gerard Vernon Wallop, 9th Earl of Portsmouth, better known as Viscount Lymington. He edited *New Pioneer* magazine from 1938 to 1940 and founded the British Council Against European Commitments in 1938, with William Joyce. Joyce, better known as 'Lord Haw-Haw', was an Irish-American fascist politician who famously broadcast Nazi propaganda to the United Kingdom during the Second World War and was hanged for treason at Wandsworth prison for his treachery when, contrary to his pronunciations, the Allies proved victorious.

The English politician Sir Oswald Mosley began his career as a Conservative at the end of the First World War before switching his allegiance to the Independent Labour party in 1924. After his first wife, Lady Cynthia Curzon, died in 1933 Mosley married his mistress, Diana Mitford. The ceremony took place at Joseph Goebbels' Berlin home in 1936 and Adolf Hitler was one of the many guests who attended. This is, perhaps, less surprising when one considers that three years earlier Mosley had abandoned traditional British politics to establish the British Union of Fascists (the BUF, which included the notorious Blackshirts among its membership) and urged for closer association with Nazi Germany despite Hitler's steady acquisition of sovereign territory for incorporation into the Third Reich. Mosley was interned in 1940 and the BUF was proscribed.

Other far right organisations included the British People's Party (BPP), founded in 1939 by ex-BUF member and Labour Party politician John Beckett. The BPP had its roots in the journal *New Pioneer*, which Beckett edited and which was effectively the mouthpiece of the British Council Against European Commitments.

The National Socialist League (NSL), English Array, League of Loyalists and English Mistery (an organisation in favour of bringing back the feudal system and which wanted to return leadership to the English aristocracy) were equally active on the fringes of British politics as Britain teetered on the precipice of another world war.

At this time Britain abounded with politicians, each with profound but essentially polarised opinions. Among them Katharine Marjory Stewart-Murray, the Duchess of Atholl, an aristocrat and Scottish Unionist Party politician, argued against totalitarian regimes and in 1931 published *The Conscription of a People* – a protest against the abuse of rights in the Soviet Union. She followed this with *Searchlight on Spain*, about the Spanish Civil War, and her support for the Republican side in the conflict earned her the nickname the 'Red Duchess'.

English diplomat, author, diarist and politician Sir Harold George Nicolson was the husband of writer Vita Sackville-West. He was also briefly in partnership with Sir Oswald Mosley, joining Mosley's so-called New Party in 1931, even editing the party newspaper, *Action*. However, Nicolson ceased to support Mosley when the latter formed the British Union of Fascists the following year. Despite his earlier proclivities, Nicolson remained a friend of Winston Churchill, supporting the lone voice's frequent calls for rearmament. Indeed, in 1940 Nicolson became Parliamentary Secretary and official Censor at the Ministry of Information in Churchill's 1940 wartime government of national unity, serving under Duff Cooper.

Other prominent members involved in the anti-war debate at the time included American Helmuth Engelbrecht (author of *Merchants of Death* and *Revolt Against War*), Sir Richard Acland (*Unser Kampf*), Philip Noel-Baker (*Hawkers of Death*), E.O. Lorimer (*What Hitler Wants*) and W.A. Sinclair (*The Voice of the Nazi*).

However, with the advent of the Second World War pacifist sentiments in the democracies declined. The communist-controlled American Peace Mobilisation even halted its anti-war activism once Germany invaded the Soviet Union in 1941. The great philosophical pacifist Bertrand Russell claimed defeating Adolf Hitler and the Nazis was a unique circumstance where war was *not* the worst of the possible evils. His so-called 'relative pacifism' gave a green light to military action. H.G. Wells, too, changed his mind. After the Armistice in 1918 he had joked that the British had suffered more from the war than they would have done if they had capitulated to Germany and agreed terms at the start. In 1941 he supported fighting the Nazis to the end, arguing that a large-scale British offensive on the Continent of Europe was necessary to destroy Hitler once and for all. Albert Einstein wrote: 'I loathe all armies and any kind of violence; yet I'm firmly convinced that at present these hateful weapons offer the only effective protection.'

In the introduction to *Years of Wrath* (1949), David Low's collection of 300 of his best cartoons, the New Zealand-born political satirist and caricaturist who lived and worked in Britain for many years, wrote:

> In these pages Hitler emerges as a man of fallacies and miscalculations, the instigator of unspeakable horror and abomination. As the years roll on, the poets and dramatists may make myths and legends out of him, as they frequently do about the characters of history – especially war-mongering characters – and present him to posterity, not as a vicious muddle-head, but as a picturesque, lonely hero posing against a background of the Alps at Berchtesgaden. And then other fools may be tempted to follow his example. If this volume can contribute in the very smallest degree to preventing that, the author will be well content.

It's little wonder that cartoons such as Low's one dating from 13 May 1940, which showed a jack-booted figure of death standing before a pile of corpses in Belgium next to Hitler saying: 'I did it to assure your destiny', a reference to the Führer's recent proclamation: 'The fight which begins to-day will decide the destiny of the Germans for a thousand years', earned the author an entry into the Nazi's infamous 'Black Book', the 'Sonderfahndungsliste G.B.' ('Special Search List G.B.'), a list of Britons to be arrested in the event of a successful invasion of Britain by Germany!

In the seminal 1941 publication *Modern Publicity in War*, John Gloag, a prominent English writer in the fields of design and architecture who had served with the Welsh

Guards during the First World War, and was invalided home after suffering gas poisoning, wrote:

> A democracy does not dream of war, it thinks of trade. It is concerned with the manufacture and sale of commodities; it looks after its markets and its traffic, and gives to its citizens a wide though unequal measure of prosperity, a material standard of living incomparably higher than their grandfathers enjoyed a century ago, and, in Britain, a minimum guarantee against starvation . . . Napoleon's gibe about 'the nation of shop keepers' has never been really resented by the people it was supposed to wound. He was only a soldier with a swelled head who knew nothing about business . . . Even when war starts, trade in our democracy is still a primary concern . . . The slogan that steadied commercial morale, although it may have retarded recruitment in 1914, was 'business as usual'.

Gloag went on to expand on his thoughts about the importance of commercial and state propaganda and advertising in wartime by adding:

> Propaganda, as a weapon for use against the enemy, was not organised until later in the war, although Major-General Sir Ernest Swinton had arranged as early as October 1914 for 25,000 copies of a leaflet addressed to German soldiers to be dropped by the Royal Flying Corps behind the enemy lines. Airborne propaganda was considerably older than the aeroplane; in the Napoleonic wars Lord Cochrane had pamphlets dropped from kites towed by the brig Pallas when cruising along the French coast . . . The part British propaganda played in weakening the resistance of the civil population in Germany has been recognised, and even admired as a technical performance, by Nazi specialists in propaganda. This British campaign against civilian morale has been imitated, with characteristic variations in the form of appeal, by the propaganda organisation directed by Dr Goebbels . . . This time we enjoy a full awareness, not only of what we are fighting, but for what we are fighting. Wisely planned, informative propaganda has crystallised our understanding of Britain's

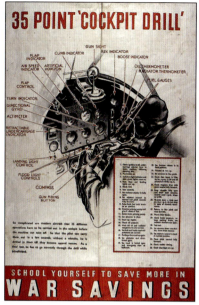

This War Savings poster purported to show savers what the inside of the cockpit of a modern RAF fighter looked like. The old-fashioned bead sight was certainly not state of the art technology . . .

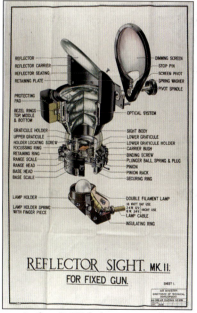

. . . in fact RAF fighters were fitted with reflector gun sights of the type shown in this then top-secret Air Ministry poster.

mission as an Empire. We know now that we have shouldered a world responsibility. We are more than trustees of liberty; we are its last defenders.

In his book *The Posters That Won The War*, American author Derek Nelson echoes Gloag's sentiments:

Posters tend to simplify matters. They don't give us essays or closely reasoned debates, they give us slogans. Posters for war bonds, recruiting and industrial production dominate any selection. Some posters take less tangible ideas as their subject. They deal, sometimes symbolically, with such things as democracy and religion, in a way that may sound peculiar to modern ears. Archibald MacLeish wrote in *The American Cause* in 1941: 'To mobilize planes only or armies only, forgetting our purposes as a democratic people, interrupting our history, neglecting the realisation of our won hopes, is to invite disaster.' These stirring pronouncements were an intrinsic part of the experience of the war, which was once again aimed at making the world safe for democracy.

In his follow-up tome, *The Ads That Won The War*, Nelson expanded on the same theme.

Wartime ads contained images of aircraft and combat that were as accurate as any painting or illustration of the time. Spurred and focused by official agencies such as the Office or War Information and such volunteer groups as the War Advertising Council, the ads blended patriotism with propaganda. Sometimes they were sensitive, and at other times they were blunt. They ranged from strikingly effective to corny and silly. In searching for truth and objectivity, students of war will find that ads offer a wealth of material for study. Wartime advertising was also controversial; there were full-blown arguments about whether it should even be permitted. But the ads remained popular. Surveys found that soldiers liked looking at the ads because the pretty girls, morale-boosting tableaux, and other vivid pictures reminded them of life back home . . . Ultimately, what sets the ads of the war apart isn't their character or their

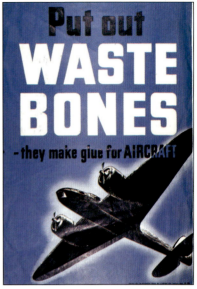

'Put Out Waste Bones' – they were not only used for glue in aircraft manufacture but also in munitions, the glycerine derived from animal waste being used in Dynamite.

A successor to ARP, the Civil Defence Corps (CDC) was established in Great Britain in 1949 to take control in the aftermath of a nuclear attack. It was stood down in 1968.

themes or their slogans. Wartime ads were more than 'tin to win' campaigns and candy bars from home, just as the war was more than tactics and manoeuvres and new kinds of fighter aircraft. The wartime ads unabashedly reflected what people accepted as the meaning of the war: preserving democracy and a way of life.

'We Can Do It!', an American wartime propaganda poster produced by J. Howard Miller in 1943 for Westinghouse Electric, was an inspirational image to boost worker morale. Similar to Britain's 'Keep Calm and Carry On' poster, this now famous American design was actually little seen during the Second World War, being rediscovered in the early 1980s and widely reproduced in many forms since, often simply called 'Rosie the Riveter' and used to promote feminism and other political issues. The image even made the cover of the *Smithsonian* magazine in 1994 and was fashioned into a United States first-class mail stamp in 1999.

As is it had been in the First World War, Germany's propaganda machine worked at full pelt during the second. But this time, rather than Oberstleutnant A.D. Deutelmoser, who ran Germany's *Kriegspresseamt* (War Press Office), formed in 1915 under the General Staff to centralise censorship as well as information output, and was later head of the nation's propaganda bureau, Paul Joseph Goebbels was in control of propaganda. One of Adolf Hitler's closest associates and most devout followers and Reich Minister of Propaganda in Nazi Germany from 1933 to 1945, Goebbels was the very definition of evil genius.

Under his supervision the full panoply of available media was put under state control and employed to do the Nazis' bidding, extoling the virtues of Adolf Hitler while abominating the very presence of Jews, communists, gypsies and homosexuals. Goebbels made a virtue out of hate and forced every German to be complicit in the Nazi's warped practices.

Like they did in Britain and the nations of the other belligerents, many of the German designers who supported their nation's propaganda machinery during First World War resumed similar work in the Second World War, there being only a twenty-year gap in between. However, specific mention must be made of two designers in particular whose work will be forever linked with the rise and rise of the Nazi party and the German war effort during 1939–45.

The first, Ernst Rudolf Vogenauer, was born in 1897. After the First World War, he worked as a poster designer and a book illustrator, but he also designed banknotes, postage stamps, wooden toys and ceramics. He is perhaps remembered today as the artist behind the numerous postage stamps the Nazis introduced, many of them prominently featuring Hitler.

However, the work of the second artist, Ludwig Hohlwein (1874–1949), was both more prolific and graphically groundbreaking. Until 1906 Hohlwein, from a privileged childhood and born into a prominent family, trained and practised as an architect after which he switched to poster design. Hohlwein's adaptations of photographic images were based on a deep and intuitive understanding of light and shade and how form is illuminated. The ultra-graphic high tonal contrasts within his illustrations, a dazzling combination of silhouette, interlinked shapes of flat colour and superb drawing, have proved an inspiration for countless designers since. His work also influenced many of his contemporaries during the war, even across warring divides.

Greatly influenced by the Beggarstaff Brothers, British artists Sir William Nicholson and James Pryde, the collaborative partnership active in poster design in the late 1890s, by the mid-1920s an exhibition of his posters in New York had introduced him to the advertising industry in the United States, and very soon he already had 3,000 advertisements under his belt and had become one of the best-known German commercial artists of his time. In Germany he produced posters for Audi, Bahlsen, BMW, Daimler Benz, Erdal, Ernemann, Görtz Shoes, Kaffee Hag, Kulmbach, Leitz, Lufthansa, Marklin, MAN and Henkel. His posters for the 1936 Olympic Games are fine examples of his craft.

After accepting commissions from the Nazi regime, he joined the Nazi Party in 1933 and designed posters for the NSDAP, the Nazi People's Welfare, the Winter Relief Fund. After the war Hohlwein established a studio in Berchtesgaden, the location of Hitler's Bavarian Alpine retreat which, after renting it from 1928, in 1933 he purchased outright from the proceeds of his book *Mein Kampf*. Hohlwein died in Berchtesgaden in 1949, and the burnt out shell of Hitler's 'Berghoff' was demolished by the Bavarian government in 1952.

The National Hospital Service Reserve (NHSR) was founded in 1949 and staffed by volunteer doctors and nurses and first-aiders. The NHSR was part of civil defence, the emphasis of which shifted to coping with the aftermath of a nuclear attack. The NHSR closed in 1968 when the civil defence services were disbanded.

CHAPTER 2

The Home Front

Those left at home in Britain during both world wars were never as remote from the action as were previous generations of non-combatants; the folks who remained by the fireside awaiting news of loved ones during the Napoleonic Wars, the Crimean campaign or against the Zulu or Boer in southern Africa. This had partly to do with vastly improved communications, which permitted fighting men to write home, sending postcards and letters on a fairly regular basis. But it also enabled journalists to file newspaper reports – and photographers to accompany said dispatches with either prints or exposed film. All of these developments combined to reveal the true reality of warfare to those at home.

But there was, of course, another fundamental reason why civilians were now better informed about modern war: in the twentieth century those on the home front were often right on the front line.

British civilians were first subjected to total war in December 1914, when the German High Seas Fleet shelled Scarborough, Hartlepool and Whitby, an attack resulting in 137 fatalities and 592 casualties, many of whom were civilians, and then again when German aircraft attacked Dover.

These early raids were pinpricks. Though Dover Castle and the port were the main targets, the puny Taubes and Friedrichshafen floatplanes being unable to carry a significant bomb load did little damage, many of the bombs crashing into back gardens of private dwellings or harmlessly in open spaces. However, as *The Times* reported:

'I try to forget you', a First World War postcard.

> One German airman on Christmas Day was more venturesome. Under cover of a dense fog, he eluded the watches on the coast as far as Sheerness, and there was lost sight of. He was next seen flying over Gravesend, and was, forced to turn, with a British-'biplane in pursuit, towards the North Sea, running the gauntlet of a heavy fire from anti-aircraft guns at different points.

It transpired that the pilot, Lieutenant von Prondzynski, ended up over Dover and, at a height of 5,000ft, leant over the padded edge of his cockpit combing and proceeded to heave his single bomb over the side, before releasing his grip and letting it fall. The pilot was about 400yd short of his target, Dover Castle, and succeeded in planting his bomb in the garden of the adjoining rectory. It made a crater about 4 or 5 ft deep, smashed some windows and knocked the gardener, Mr James Banks, out of the tree he was pruning.

But, even though these early air raids and the sinking of RMS *Lusitania* off Ireland in May 1915, which claimed 1,198 lives, were modest harbingers of what total war was to deliver in later years, enemy attacks on the British mainland still amounted to the deaths of only some 5,000 civilians during the First World War. Furthermore, when one compares the 1,500 British civilian deaths during the winter of 1917–18, the worst period for air raids with over 100 German attacks launched against the mainland, with the 750,000 British soldiers killed while on active service, the true impact of the war against the civilian populace is put in true and sobering perspective.

Worse, much was worse was to come, and during the Second World War a combination of conventional night bombing and, from June 1944, attacks by cruise (VI) and ballistic (V2) missiles amounted to over 60,000 civilian fatalities in Britain with thousands more survivors badly wounded or made homeless.

In both world wars, generally, the civilian populations at home suffered psychological rather than physical assaults.

First, of course, families were never sure of the whereabouts or indeed the mortal existence, of spouses, fathers or sons and this wearing uncertainty was a constant burden that played on the minds of adults at home or in the factories or children at school, anxious to hear that daddy was safe.

There was also constant unrelenting psychological pressure applied to non-combatants in more subtle, insidious ways. Men who had not joined up, either because they were retained at home in reserved occupations that were crucial to the war effort or because they were either too young, too old or medically unfit for military service carried a burden of guilt and the stigma of being a coward, possessing low moral fibre. Women, even if they were fully occupied managing a home, looking after children or perhaps an elderly or infirm relative, felt that they weren't pulling their weight. To avoid such accusations of complacency many women somehow managed to survive long hours on the shop floor or munitions factory, or as so many did as early as 1915 by taking over jobs made vacant by men heading for the front, and driving trams and buses to keep society on the move.

While they might not have faced the mortal dangers of the men at the front, civilians at home experienced their own kind of barrages – the daily, incessant bombardment of official notices telling them what to think and how to

'It's a puzzle for a woman', a First World War postcard.

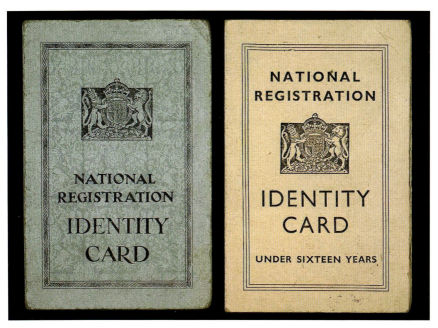

The National Registration Act 1939 established a National Register which began operating on 29 September 1939 and introduced a system of identity cards for adults and children with the requirement that they must be produced on demand or presented to a police station within 48 hours.

act. Whether it was one of the earliest British government communications designed to prick the consciences of so-called shirkers – a poster featuring an accusing John Bull, all top hat and tails and union flag waistcoat, stood in front of a row of new khaki-clad recruits, who, with outstretched arm and pointing finger, asks: 'Who's Absent? Is It You?' or one from the Auxiliary Royal Air Force in the 1940s: 'Castles of the Air. Man the Walls! – Join a Balloon Barrage Squadron' – the message was clear. Everyone was in it together.

When war was declared in August 1914, in Britain, and indeed throughout Europe, there were street celebrations everywhere and a mood of optimism prevailed. Most people were sure the war would be over by Christmas. Asking for 100,000 volunteers, the government was both surprised and delighted to receive 750,000 new recruits in just a month.

Fought between 5 and 12 September 1914, the Battle of the Marne was viewed as a miracle because it resulted in an Allied victory against the German Army, and effectively ended the German push towards the outskirts of Paris. However, it required a counterattack of six French and one British field armies along the Marne River to persuade the enemy to retreat. The Germans weren't pushed back too far and still occupied a chunk of France and all of Belgium. It was the beginning of four years of trench warfare on the Western Front. The early optimism at home soon dissolved and it became obvious that there would not be a quick victory.

The government could not hide the fact that many thousands of men had been killed or severely wounded. The return of wounded soldiers to London rail stations late at

'Watch me make a fire-bucket out of 'is 'elmet' – one of Bruce Bairnsfather's many 'Old Bill' postcards from the First World War.

night did nothing to detract from the knowledge that casualties were horrendous.

As if being witness to such tragedy as seeing the flower of their youth returning so severely damaged – at least the lucky ones returned, however mangled – those at home suffered other privations.

Inflation was one obvious consequence to which the isolation of total war and the unrestricted U-boat warfare subjected Britain's economy. Poorer families soon discovered they could no longer afford the increased prices for basic food staples. Unlike during the Second World War when it was introduced in 1940, in the First World War, despite the shortages, rationing was only brought in by the government in February 1918 when a fixed allowance for sugar, meat, butter, jam and tea was introduced. British Summer Time was also established, providing more daylight working hours than before.

To ameliorate the effects of rationing *The Win-The-War Cookery Booky,* 'published for the food economy', was available on bookshelves in 1918 priced at a very reasonable 2*d*. 'Eat one pound less bread per week than you are eating now' was emblazoned across the cover and inside a variety of cheap and easy recipes showed cooks how to supplement their diets. Recipes inside this very helpful and popular book included Surrey Stew, Fish Sausages, Parkin and Barley bread, incorporating all kinds of ingredients, except wheat. Rationing was beginning to take a hold but it worked and prevented marauding U-boats from starving Britain out of the war.

Other shortages at home had a dramatic effect on the troops in the front line. The shell crisis of 1915, which revealed that there simply were not enough munitions reaching the troops and, often, what shells did arrive turned out to be duds, encouraged Lloyd George as Minister of Munitions to be critical of Chief of Staff Lord Kitchener. The upshot was that Kitchener's reputation never recovered and that Lloyd George

'Passed by Censor' (received from HMS ship, no charge raised) envelope posted from HMS Folkestone, 1915.

Contents of the envelope above. The letter is from an officer aboard HMS Folkestone who, writing to his mother, not only asks her for 'a couple of thin Aertex Cellular vests and pants, a couple of suits of thin pyjamas', but goes on to explain that he has been mentioned in French despatches and even nominated for the Croix de Guerre! Such items are not only very collectable they also make an invaluable contribution to the historical record.

assumed the role of Prime Minister after the fall of Asquith's government, a direct result of the scandal. Another result of the increased demand for war munitions meant that factories worked round the clock and, for the first time, women took over jobs traditionally occupied by men.

The combination of long hours and raw recruits to such a demanding and hazardous job inevitably meant that accidents happened – safety sometimes being compromised in place of speed and quantity of manufacture. The worst factory accident was at Silverton in the East End of London. On 19 January 1917, the munitions factory exploded and 69 people were killed and over 400 injured. Extensive damage was done to the area around the factory.

Passed in August 1914, the Defence of the Realm Act (DORA) allowed the government to take over the coal mines, railways and shipping. Fortunately, the pragmatic endeavours of hardy Welshman Lloyd George enabled the government to work closely with the trade unions to avoid strikes. But with so many males leaving to join the army traditionalists had to accept that with a reduced workforce women were needed to do many jobs that had previously been the province of men.

Emmeline Pankhurst's Women's Social and Political Union (WSPU), the 'Suffragette' movement in Britain that lobbied for the vote for women, earned new respect by limiting their militant actions in favour of supporting the war effort. As a result an amnesty was granted for WSPU prisoners and, in recognition for them keeping their side of the bargain, well before the war ended, on 6 February 1918, the Representation of the People Act was passed, enfranchising women over the age of 30. Women over 21 didn't achieve the vote until 1928. But just as it had at the front, where the war threw working class lads alongside the middle class and even aristocrats, the twain never likely to ever have met in 'civvie street', the First World War had a massive effect on the role of people at home. Regarding women, especially, it both enfranchised them politically and socio-economically. Things would never be the same again.

We will never know just how the ordinary civilians who had thrown themselves so wholeheartedly into supporting the war effort during the 1914–18 conflict felt when confronted by an official poster, aimed at men who had still managed to avoid the draft (conscription having been introduced with the Military Service Act of 1916), showing an enormous Zeppelin hovering above St Paul's and featuring the headline: 'It is far better to face the bullets than to be killed at home by a bomb. Join the army at once and help to stop an air raid. God Save the King.' This poster might have finally encouraged malingerers to join up but I'm sure it didn't do much for the morale of those rushing to catch a tram to the shell factory or, indeed, those women who were now driving them.

This postcard, 'Pals!', showing a Tommy and his trusted mount appears all the more poignant following the success of Michael Morpurgo's successful novel War Horse.

Surviving air raids during the First World War was largely left in the hands of providence, Air Raid Precautions not being officially organised until the late 1930s and based on the dread predictions of 'experts' who simply multiplied the effective bomb loads and high-explosive capacity of the First World War biplane bomber aircraft and their puny ordnance with the greatly increased capabilities of streamlined monoplanes with cavernous bomb bays. When the likelihood of poison gas and incendiaries being delivered alongside high-explosive bombs was added to the mix, it is not surprising that it wasn't until long after 1918 that protection from such attacks was given official priority. Despite this, at the beginning of the Second World War those civilians without gardens into which they could bury corrugated iron Anderson shelters were forced to seek refuge in Underground stations, there being no official communal shelters available at the outbreak of hostilities.

During the First World War air-raid shelters were largely improvised. In Ramsgate, for example, caves and tunnels in the chalk cliffs were employed as shelters for several thousand people. They would be reused in the Second World War. That's not to say there weren't any purpose-built refuges to help civilians shelter from the aerial storm emanating from Zeppelins and Gothas. In Cleethorpes, Lincolnshire stands the oldest surviving air-raid shelter in Britain. It was constructed in April 1916 by Joseph Forrester, a chemist and local councillor, who built it from reinforced concrete with walls half a metre thick. The structure is 4m wide and 5m deep, and consists of a single room with two entrance lobbies. At some point, it was turned into a garage, and as such it survives, a legacy of the first strategic bombing campaign in history.

The First World War was a revelation. Not just because of the extent of the slaughter but also because it was the first time civilians were exposed to the full fury of modern war and, crucially, because it saw the products of the Industrial Revolution and mass production turned to such an evil purpose as killing on a grand scale. Little did they, or the general officers who commanded them, know, but the Tommies who went over the top along the Somme in July 1916, facing rows of machine guns, were really steadily advancing towards unrestricted machine tools. They were walking towards malevolent lathes and milling machines which, spewing bullets in place of swarf, had had their guards removed and simply went about automatically killing and mutilating anyone who got in the way.

Lessons were learned from all this horror. One of them, of course, was to try to avoid repeating it. But, as we know, this was not to be. Fortunately, when, to the consternation of most right-thinking people, it became obvious that another war was unavoidable, the authorities had amassed enough data to enable them to provide civilian populations with the wherewithal, at least, to prepare themselves for a resumption of war on the home front.

It is from the Second World War, and the build-up to that conflict, that the majority of official leaflets and posters were produced and survive to this day.

Although it didn't exist during the First World War, the Air Raid Precautions (ARP) organisation which was created in Britain in 1924 almost links this conflict with the Second World War. It certainly charts the growing neurosis and fear that another war with its fleets of fast heavily armed bombers would lay cities to waste and signal the end of civilisation.

Italian Giulio Douhet published his influential *Command of the Air* in 1921 and his main argument supported the general fear that modern war planes would prove unassailable. In 1932 the Conservative Stanley Baldwin, then Lord President of the Council in Ramsey MacDonald's National Government, famously used the phrase 'The bomber will always get through' in a speech

Delightful First World War postcard emphasising how much had changed in so little time as young men swapped civilian clothes for khaki.

This postcard makes exaggerated and cruel comment about those soldiers involved in logistics behind the front line enjoying far better rations than those at the front.

before Parliament entitled 'A Fear for the Future'. Baldwin argued that, regardless of air defences, sufficient bomber aircraft will always survive in sufficient numbers to press on their attacks and destroy cities.

In 1938 the Air Ministry predicted 65,000 casualties a week – in the first month of war the British government was expecting 1 million casualties, 3 million refugees and the majority of the London laid to waste. In the same year the Socialist biologist J.B.S. Haldane wrote *A.R.P. (Air Raid Precautions)* addressed to 'the ordinary citizen, the sort of man and woman who is going to be killed if Britain is raided again from the air'. Haldane intended it to be a scientific counter argument to all the fantastical predictions prevailing at the time. With chapters entitled, 'The Technique of Mass Murder', 'Keeping Bombers Away', 'The Government's Precautionary Measures', 'Protection Against High Explosive Bombs' and 'Gas Proof Bags For Babies', it made pretty chilling reading but the authorities quickly adopted many of its principles.

Home Secretary Samuel Hoare was naturally closely involved with the progress of government Air Raid Precautions in Britain. Answering a question about the nation's defences against enemy air attack in a debate in the House of Commons in May 1938, he said:

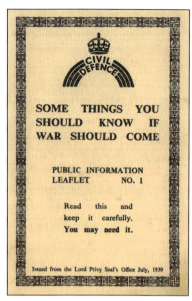

'Some Things You Should Know If War Should Come', Public Information Leaflet No. 1 issued as early as July 1939.

> By the Regulations made under the Air-Raid Precautions Act, the duty of providing such shelters as are necessary is placed upon the local authorities. My hon. Friend is aware that I have asked authorities to conduct a survey of the problem in their areas, so that they may ascertain the number of persons likely to be exposed in the streets and the numbers who are in houses in which additional protection cannot be given. I have also asked them to make a survey of the accommodation available in their area which, with some adaptation in peace-

Stanley Baldwin had famously claimed that the night bomber would always get through. The first thing most people feared was their homes being razed by enemy bombs.

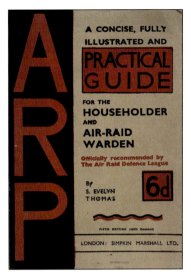 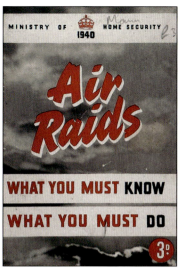 

Officially recommended by the Air Raid Defence League, established early in 1939 to bring all ARP workers together into one organisation, this ARP Practical Guide sought to equip householders with all the information they would require to cope with air attack.

'Air Raids. What You Must Know and What You Must Do' was issued in 1940 by the Ministry for Home Security.

Dating from 1 October 1938, the inaugural edition of Sir Edward Hulton's pioneering Picture Post magazine. First editions of any periodical command the highest prices among collectors.

A trio of petrol coupons dating from 1940. Petrol was the first commodity to be rationed upon the outbreak of war in September 1939.

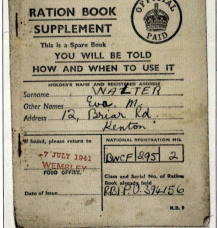

Ration Book Supplement, the householder's spare ration book, dating from 1941.

time, could be used as shelter accommodation in war-time, and I have more recently indicated the need of planning for a deep trench system in all open spaces in or near centres of population. When plans on these lines have been completed it will be possible for the local authority to see whether it is necessary to provide any specially constructed shelter accommodation.

Soon afterward the government published a booklet entitled *The Protection of Your Home Against Air Raids*. It was posted to every citizen and additional copies could be purchased for only a penny. Hoare penned the introduction headed 'Why this book has been sent to you'.

If this country were ever at war the target of the enemy's bombers would be the staunchness of the people at home. We all hope and work to prevent war but, while there is a risk of it, we cannot afford to neglect the duty of preparing ourselves and the county for such an emergency. This book is being sent out to help each householder to realise what he can do, if the need arises, to make his home and his household more safe against air attack.

The Home office is working with the local authorities in preparing schemes for the protection of the civil population during an attack, but it is impossible to devise a scheme that will cover everybody unless each home and family play their part in doing what they can for themselves. In this duty to themselves they must count upon the help and advice of those who have undertaken the duty of advice and instruction.

If the emergency comes the country will look for her safety not only to her sailors and soldiers and airmen, but also to the organised courage and foresight of every household. It is for the volunteers in the air raid precautions services to help every household for this purpose, and in sending out this book I ask for their help.

Section 1 of this useful but rather chilling little booklet was entitled 'Things To Do Now'. It contained advice about preparing a safe refuge in your home, ensuring that the blackout was observed ('In time of war all buildings will have to be completely darkened at night . . .'), tips on how to tackle fires and small incendiary bombs and how to deal with the new respirators (gas masks) that were about to be distributed. The authors were particularly concerned that householders looked after these contraptions which, they said had been:

Designed for you by Government experts and, though simple to look at, exhaustive tests have shown it to be highly efficient.
When not wearing the respirator, remember these rules:
1. Do not expose it to strong light or heat.
2. Do not let it get wet.
3. Do not scratch or bend the window.
4. Do not carry or hang the respirator by the straps.

Issued by the Ministry of Home Security.

WHAT TO DO ABOUT GAS

OTHER COUNTRIES LOST THEIR FREEDOM in this war because they allowed the enemy to create confusion and panic among their civilian population so that the movement of defending armies was impeded.

We are not going to allow that to happen here. It won't happen if we are all on our guard, prepared to meet anything the enemy may do.

He may use gas. THE DANGER IS NOT SERIOUS if you do the right thing, both NOW and when the time comes. If you do, this weapon will have failed and you will have helped to beat it.

Here are the things to know and do. Read them carefully and remember them well in case the day comes. Keep this leaflet and look at it again.

HOW NOT TO GET GASSED.
NOW

1. In your gas mask you have the best possible protection against gases that affect your lungs or your eyes. It is a sure defence if you use it properly and in time. Make sure your own and your children's gas masks fit and are in working order: your warden or A.R.P. post can tell you. Practise putting them on and get used to wearing them with confidence. Your life may depend on whether you can put your mask on quickly. Remember to take off your spectacles before putting on your gas mask.

2. CARRY YOUR GAS MASK ALWAYS, and have it handy at night.

3. To prevent the face-piece misting over, smear a little soap lightly on the inside once a week.

4. If your chemist has " No. 2 Anti-gas ointment " (price 6d.) in stock, buy a jar. Read the instructions on the jar and carry it always. This ointment is for use as a protection against the effects of liquid blister gas.

IF THE GAS RATTLES SOUND.

1. PUT ON YOUR GAS MASK AT ONCE, wherever you are, even in bed.
2. TAKE COVER. Get into any nearby building as soon as you hear the rattle. Go upstairs if the building is a tall one. Close all windows in your house.

Don't come out or take your gas mask off till you hear the handbells ringing the " Gas clear ".

NEVER LOOK UPWARDS—you may get a drop of liquid gas in your eyes.

COVER YOUR SKIN UP so long as you are out of doors—hands in pockets, collar turned up. Or if you have an umbrella, put it up.

IF YOU DO GET GASSED.
GAS OR VAPOUR. If you breathe any gas or vapour—

1. PUT ON YOUR GAS MASK AT ONCE.
2. KEEP YOUR MASK ON, even though you may still feel some discomfort.

The threat of chemicals (poison gas) being delivered from enemy aircraft hung like a sword of Damocles above the heads of British civilians throughout the Second World War in the same way that the 'A-bomb' threatened subsequent generations during the cold war.

To help enforce these regulations and offer advice about the best ways to protect their homes from air attack, civilians turned to the growing band of ARP Wardens who patrolled the blacked out streets. ARP Wardens were trained in basic fire-fighting and first aid, and could keep an emergency situation under control until the official rescue services arrived. In addition they helped to police areas suffering bomb damage and assisted bombed-out householders.

Stirring 'Your Britain Fight For It Now' poster by Frank Newbould who was assistant to the War Office's official war artist for posters, Abram Games.

'Grow Your Own Food' another poster from the genius that was Abram Games.

Nearly a million and a half volunteer wardens supported Air Raid Precautions during the war and almost all of them were unpaid part-time volunteers who also held day-time jobs. Far from being the grumpy little Hitlers portrayed in popular comedy, for ever bellowing 'Put That Light Out!' whenever they spotted a chink of light escaping from a living room window, they were really the unsung heroes of the home front. Initially, wardens were expected to be on duty three nights a week, but the frequency of their shifts increased as night bombing became more frequent.

During the Air Estimates debate in the House of Commons on 1 August 1939 British politicians reviewed the progress in Civil Defence, especially the provision of shelters for the civilian population, especially those who were without the space to erect Anderson shelters. Interestingly, part of the debate involved criticism of these constructions, Robert Boothby arguing that they were fragile and leaked. The subsequent Hailey Conference decided that providing deep shelters would lead to workers staying underground rather than staying on the surface and working when the all clear had been signalled. However, this policy was reversed in 1940 when most of the London Underground network was opened for use as overnight shelters and the construction of specialised communal deep shelters began.

The National Registration Act of 1939 established a National Register and everyone, including children, had to carry an identity (ID) card at all times to show who they were and where they lived. The identity card gave the owner's name and address, including changes of address. Each person was allocated a National Registration number and this was written in the top right-hand corner on the inside of the card. The local registration office stamped the card to make it valid. ID cards had to be produced on demand or presented to a police station within 48 hours.

Collectors should note that the earliest, buff-coloured cards are the rarest. Blue ID cards were introduced in 1943 and government officials had green ID cards. Members of the armed services had their own, unique identification cards. Children under 16 were issued with identity cards but they were to be kept by their parents. Identification was necessary if families got separated from one another or their house was bombed, and if people were injured or killed.

On the actual outbreak of war a small, blue, eight-page roll-fold leaflet entitled 'War Emergency Information and Instructions' was distributed to British householders. The text on the cover set the tone from the start: 'Pay no attention to rumours. Official news will be given in the papers and over the wireless. Listen carefully to all broadcast instructions and be ready to note them down.' The leaflet contained concise details about what to do regarding identity labels, during air raids and about the closing of cinemas, theatres and places of entertainment. It told readers about the need for evacuation from certain areas likely to be the scene of armed combat, about lighting restrictions, fire precautions and how to deal with incendiaries and about travelling on the road and railways. The authorities wanted to avoid arterial highways being blocked by civilian refugees – something they thought greatly aided the progress of blitzkrieg.

A further Abram Games classic – a famous recruitment poster for the ATS.

> You must not drive or cycle at night unless your lights are dimmed and screened in accordance with the regulations. You can get a leaflet giving details of these restrictions from any police station. No car or cycle will be allowed on the road at night until the lights have been dimmed in the way described in the leaflet. If you have a car use it very sparingly because the supply of petrol will be rationed immediately.

Citizens were told that from the first day of war day schools would be closed for a week and would only reopen upon the discretion of local authorities. They were also advised not to use the telephone unless there was an emergency.

> A speedy telephone service is vital for defence. You may be causing delay to very urgent calls. To meet the needs of defence operations it may be necessary to disconnect some telephones temporarily. Do not telegraph unless it is very urgent. Telegraph offices will also be dealing with official messages and your message may delay important telegrams.

There was also information for pensioners about the need to keep their pension and allowance books with them, especially if they moved away from home, in order to draw their pension. Similarly, those in receipt of other benefits, such as widows, orphans and those drawing Great War disability payments were advised to keep their papers in order so that they could 'cash the orders in them on the proper dates at a Post Office in their own district'.

People were told not to worry about food supplies because stocks of foodstuffs in the country were sufficient. However, the leaflet did allude to rationing:

> In order to ensure that stocks are distributed fairly and to the best advantage the Government are bringing into operation the plans for the organisation of food supplies which have already been prepared in collaboration with the food trades. Steps have been taken to prevent any sudden rise in the price, or the holding up of supplies. For the time being you should continue to obtain supplies from your usual shops. You should limit your purchases to the quantities which you normally require.

Section 15 summarised the general instructions and was intended to reassure a naturally very nervous populations:

> Carry your gas mask with you always.
> Do not allow your children to run about the streets.
> Avoid waste of any kind whether of food, water, electricity or gas.
> Obey promptly any instructions given you by the police. The special constables, the air raid wardens, or any other authorised persons and be ready to give them any assistance for which they ask you.

All of the above is quite chilling. This was reality. Goodness knows what people thought when they considered their futures. Certainly, what they did know was that in the last war Britain had suffered nearly 1 million casualties. Since then technology had developed exponentially. Just what the 'lights of perverted science', to paraphrase a later speech by Winston Churchill, might be able to inflict on cowering civilians now that aeroplanes flew higher and faster and could carry much larger bomb loads than ever before, was doubtless something that kept many people awake at night.

The authorities were, of course, aware of all this and were sensitive to the people's insecurities. In an effort to reassure the electorate the last couple of paragraphs of the War Emergency instruction leaflet were printed in block capitals:

> DO NOT TAKE TOO MUCH NOTICE OF NOISE IN AN AIR RAID. MUCH OF IT WILL BE THE NOISE OF OUR OWN GUNS DEALING WITH THE RAIDERS.
> KEEP A GOOD HEART: WE ARE GOING TO WIN THROUGH.

Although food rationing had first been introduced to Britain in 1918, when Germany's U-boat campaign began to have a dramatic effect on the nation's imports, it was more widely applied and lasted much longer when introduced in January 1940, during the Second World War. With Britain depending on imports for 70 per cent of its food each year this was hardly surprising.

To buy rationed items, each person had to register at chosen shops, and was then

Issued by the Ministry of Information in co-operation with the War Office and the Ministry of Home Security

Beating the INVADER

A MESSAGE FROM THE PRIME MINISTER

IF invasion comes, everyone—young or old, men and women—will be eager to play their part worthily. By far the greater part of the country will not be immediately involved. Even along our coasts, the greater part will remain unaffected. But where the enemy lands, or tries to land, there will be most violent fighting. Not only will there be the battles when the enemy tries to come ashore, but afterwards there will fall upon his lodgments very heavy British counter-attacks, and all the time the lodgments will be under the heaviest attack by British bombers. The fewer civilians or non-combatants in these areas, the better—apart from essential workers who must remain. So if you are advised by the authorities to leave the place where you live, it is your duty to go elsewhere when you are told to leave. When the attack begins, it will be too late to go; and, unless you receive definite instructions to move, your duty then will be to stay where you are. You will have to get into the safest place you can find, and stay there until the battle is over. For all of you then the order and the duty will be: " STAND FIRM ".

This also applies to people inland if any considerable number of parachutists or air-borne troops are landed in their neighbourhood. Above all, they must not cumber the roads. Like their fellow-countrymen on the coasts, they must " STAND FIRM ". The Home Guard, supported by strong mobile columns wherever the enemy's numbers require it, will immediately come to grips with the invaders, and there is little doubt will soon destroy them.

Throughout the rest of the country where there is no fighting going on and no close cannon fire or rifle fire can be heard, everyone will govern his conduct by the second great order and duty, namely, " CARRY ON ". It may easily be some weeks before the invader has been totally destroyed, that is to say, killed or captured to the last man who has landed on our shores. Meanwhile, all work must be continued to the utmost, and no time lost.

The following notes have been prepared to tell everyone in rather more detail what to do, and they should be carefully studied. Each man and woman should think out a clear plan of personal action in accordance with the general scheme.

Winston S. Churchill

STAND FIRM

1. What do I do if fighting breaks out in my neighbourhood?

Keep indoors or in your shelter until the battle is over. If you can have a trench ready in your garden or field, so much the better. You may want to use it for protection if your house is damaged. But if you are at work, or if you have special orders, carry on as long as possible and only take cover when danger approaches. If you are on your way to work, finish your journey if you can.

If you see an enemy tank, or a few enemy soldiers, do not assume that the enemy are in control of the area. What you have seen may be a party sent on in advance, or stragglers from the main body who can easily be rounded up.

Imagine the shock of receiving a leaflet such as 'Beating the Invader' through your letterbox today! 'Stand Firm!' and 'Carry On!' urged Prime Minister Winston Churchill.

provided with a ration book containing coupons. The shopkeeper was provided with enough food for registered customers. Customers had to take ration books with them when shopping, so the relevant coupon or coupons could be cancelled.

The first commodity to be rationed was petrol, immediately war began in September 1939. In January 1940 this was followed by the rationing of bacon, butter and sugar and subsequently by meat, tea, jam, biscuits, breakfast cereals, cheese, eggs, lard, milk, canned and dried fruit and, by 1942, almost every foodstuff except vegetables and bread.

To encourage citizens to supplement their diets by growing their own food the government initiated the 'Dig for Victory' campaign and urged the public to use any spare land available to grow vegetables – parks and even golf courses were turned over to the common good.

The government also distributed 10,000,000 leaflets showing householders how to turn their lawns and flower beds into productive agricultural land and further encouraged people to keep an allotment. The campaign was so successful that it is thought to have been the catalyst for nearly 1,500,000 allotments. It wasn't just about cabbage and potatoes, civilians were also encouraged to keep wildlife. Most who did husbanded chickens, ducks and rabbits, but others kept goats and even pigs, which were very popular because they thrived on kitchen waste. 'Pig Clubs' were started for collecting food leftovers in big bins to feed the pigs.

Children were especially entertained by Doctor Carrot and Potato Pete, two cartoon characters who featured on 'Dig for Victory' posters, although perhaps they were less enamoured with Woolton pie, the dish made entirely from vegetables which was popularised by Lord Woolton, the Minister of Food in 1940. Neither, I'm sure, were they great fans of 'curried carrot' or 'carrotade' – a sweetened drink based on, you guessed it, the humble carrot.

By 1943, allotments in Britain produced over a million tonnes of vegetables.

At the outbreak of the Second World War all males aged between 18 and 41 were asked to register so that the authorities could direct any men not engaged in vital war work, in 'reserved occupations', as required into the army, navy or air force. By February 1942 more than 3,500,000 men had been called up and some 250,000 women wore the uniform of the Women's Auxiliary Services – the Auxiliary Territorial Service (ATS), the Women's Auxiliary Air Force (WAAF) or the Women's Royal Naval Service (WRNS).

Ernest Bevin, co-founder and general secretary of the powerful Transport and General Workers' Union from 1922, had in 1940 been made Minister of Labour in Churchill's war-time coalition government. Bevin squeezed the most out of the British labour supply, massively reinforcing the workforce with a minimum of strikes and disruption.

Mabel Lucie Attwell's career as an illustrator began at the turn of the twentieth century and she is rightly famous for her illustrative work in Alice in Wonderland, The Water Babies *and* Peter Pan. *She also illustrated dozens of postcards during both world wars and they are now very collectable. The two seen here date from the Second World War period.*

'Come into the Factories' poster by Philip Zec, encouraging women into war industry for the good of the nation.

'Back Them Up' by Ron Jobson. After leaving Camberwell School of Art, where he had won a scholarship aged 13, he joined the War Artists and Illustrators Studio. After the war Jobson worked in publishing advertising and illustrated for clients including one that's dear to my heart, Airfix.

'Dig on for Victory' poster by Peter Fraser.

'Let Us Go Forward Together', the iconic Ministry of Information photo-montage poster featuring Winston Churchill.

'The Life-Line is Firm Thanks to the Merchant Navy', a 1942 poster by Charles Woods.

'Keep Mum – She's Not So Dumb!' by Harold Forster. Interestingly, this was in the same vein as the previous 'Be Like Dad, Keep Mum' poster which outraged Labour MP Dr Edith Summerskill, a feminist and one of the founders of the Women's Home Defence Unit, where women who could shoot, wanted to defend their homes but were ineligible for the Home Guard turned to after the Fall of France in 1940.

Bevin was the prime mover behind the Registration of Boys and Girls Order, 1941 and posters detailing the provisions of this new Act of Parliament were posted in public places for all to see. It read:

Notice to boys born between 1st February, 1925 and 28th February, 1926, both dates inclusive. Requirement to register on 28th February, 1942

Boys who live more than six miles from a Ministry of Labour and National Service Office, or suffer from some permanent incapacity, may fill up a registration form on the day prescribed and post it to a Ministry of Labour and National Service Office. Forms for this purpose may be obtained on request from a Ministry of Labour and National Service office.

Penalties

Any boy who fails to register in accordance with the foregoing requirements is liable, on summary conviction, to imprisonment for a term not exceeding three months or to a fine not exceeding £100 or both. There are heavier penalties on conviction on indictment.

Despite their wishes, perhaps, for a job in the armed services, the Ministry of Labour's official urgings saw nearly 48,000 so-called Bevin Boys, chosen at random, perform vital but largely unrecognised service in Britain's coal mines. More than 10 per cent of those young men conscripted were to see service at the coal face rather than on the battlefield. It is, however, an undoubted fact that such war service was every bit as vital to the war effort as those young men aged between 18 and 25 who went to sea, wore khaki in the British Army or joined the RAF.

From 1938 onwards British civilians had been inundated with a deluge of instructions about almost anything. What to do in the event of air raids, how to participate in the war effort and even how to enjoy themselves. To keep an eye on their reactions and gauge public morale in general the government tapped into an existing organisation, Mass Observation (MO), established in 1937, by Tom Harrisson, Humphrey Jennings and Charles Madge – 'a project to study the everyday lives of ordinary people in Britain', 'an anthropology of ourselves' (see Chapter 1). In gathering its research, MO more or less spied on the average man and woman in the street.

'The Navy Thanks You' poster by Pat Keely, a prolific posterist who also produced work for London Transport, Southern Railway and the Post Office.

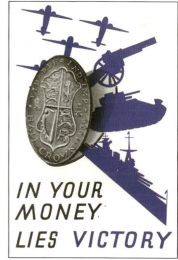

'In Your Money Lies Victory. We civilians have as important part to play in the war as the Navy, the Army or the Air Force. It is for us to provide them with money. Purchase saving certificates.', extract from this leaflet issued by the Post Office Savings Bank.

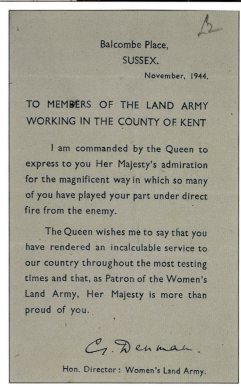

Collecting original letters together with any official documents such as log books like the examples shown here belonging to Flying Officer J.R. Whelan, a Blenheim pilot with 18 Squadron (BEF) in France, adds gravitas to any anthology.

During the Second World War Balcombe Place became the headquarters of the Women's Land Army. Having been an active supporter of the Suffragette movement before and during the First World War, in the Second World War its owner, Lady Gertrude Mary Denman, was Director of the Women's Land Army.

Balcombe Place,
SUSSEX.
November, 1944.

TO MEMBERS OF THE LAND ARMY WORKING IN THE COUNTY OF KENT

I am commanded by the Queen to express to you Her Majesty's admiration for the magnificent way in which so many of you have played your part under direct fire from the enemy.

The Queen wishes me to say that you have rendered an incalculable service to our country throughout the most testing times and that, as Patron of the Women's Land Army, Her Majesty is more than proud of you.

G. Denman.

Hon. Director: Women's Land Army.

'War Weapons More Money'. For each belligerent nation the cost of modern warfare proved prohibitive and national funds needed to be supplemented by contributions from the body publics. War savings and war bonds schemes abounded and many were designed by the cream of the commercial art industry, as these two leaflets so ably illustrate. Issued by the Post Office Savings Bank.

Professor Dorothy Sheridan MBE has worked with the Mass Observation papers since 1974, both as archivist and then Director of the Archive at the University of Sussex. I had the good fortune to meet her when I used the archive while researching my book *A Nation Alone* in the late 1980s. Professor Sheridan has also written a number of excellent anthologies about the organisation. In one of them, *Wartime Women*, she collated numerous reports which reveal precisely how women, the great majority of whom endured hardships such as rationing and the terrifying uncertainty of coping with night bombing, made sense of the disadvantages they now faced.

Norfolk resident Muriel Green worked at her family's garage in 1940 and kept a record throughout which she shared with Mass Observation and upon which, along with hundreds of other returned questionnaires and essay submissions, the organisation was able to assess the true state of British morale and consequently help the government adjust policies which might affect the well-being of the civil population.

Ms Green's entry for 31 January is particularly revealing and provides us with an excellent idea of just how tough life was during the first winter of the war:

> We have run out of coal. We have no garage fire and are burning wood in the house. We have had no meat this week, as the butcher has not come. He had hardly any last week. A customer bought us two rabbits on Monday so we are not starving, but lots of people, my great aunt among them, have had no meat. Ever so many have had no coal all the week. Arnold shot us two pigeons in the wood opposite.

The First World War had brought about massive changes to the social fabric of Great Britain and women had assumed a much more important role within society.

And families were left in no doubt about whose future they were fighting and saving for.

While this period could hardly be said to have seen women's status change in a massive way, the impact of the Suffragette struggle and that organisation's acquiescence to government appeals for calm and co-operation during the conflict did garner some results and this period could be seen as the birth of women's liberation. Similar social evolution occurred during the Second World War, with women not just taking over some of the roles traditionally held by men in the workplace, for example at the lathe and even operating forges, but also adopting habits that were previously the preserve of menfolk, such as drinking in pubs.

Mass Observation's archives are full of numerous recordings of discussions with and about women and public houses. One pub landlord, from Fulham in London, had this to say:

Freelance illustrator Phillip Boydell allegedly created the famous 'Squander Bug' while in bed with influenza.

> Yes, the war has made a great deal of difference; I don't mind girls drinking in the bar alone or otherwise. Usually when they come in alone, they don't go out alone, but who am I to criticise – my job is to sell the liquor and be pleasant to customers, not to be nosey about their coming and goings.

With the announcement of Hitler's death on 1 May 1945, it was obvious that the war in Europe was about to come to an end. On 7 May the Mass Observation entry of Amy Briggs, a nurse in Leeds, encapsulated the general feeling (Victory in Europe, or VE, Day, a public holiday, would take place on 8 May):

> What a day! It hardly seems possible that it was only this morning that I got up! There has been a steady crescendo of excitement, and the lack of any official announcement only added to the chaotic conditions. At the 3p.m. news broadcast, there was a report from the German radio that they surrendered unconditionally this morning, but SHAEF [Supreme Headquarters Allied Expeditionary Force] has said nothing. Now this really is something; the office is buzzing with excited, facetious chatter. A woman clerk comes in and we tell her the news: 'Six years I've sat in this chair waiting to hear that, and <u>now</u>, when it comes, I have to be out of the room!'

British citizens weren't only expected to make do with less they were also expected to reuse and repair what they already had. When clothes rationing was introduced in May 1941, ration books contained only sixty-six clothing coupons and they had to last for a year. Although people still had to pay for clothes, one dress also required eleven coupons and the right number of coupons had to be handed over each time a garment was purchased.

In 1943 the MOI published a handy little booklet, *Make Do and Mend*, which suggested a whole variety of ways individuals could spruce up their wardrobes and add new life to existing, often tired and unfashionable, garments.

Hugh Dalton, the Labour Party economist who served in Churchill's wartime coalition Cabinet first as Minister of Economic Warfare from 1940–2 when he established the Special Operations Executive, and was later a member of the executive committee of the Political Warfare Executive, was, by 1943 President of the Board of Trade and wrote the forward to *Make Do and Mend*:

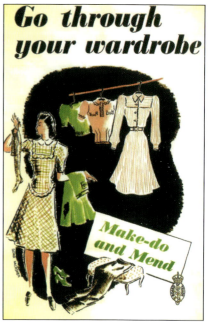

> First I would like to thank you all for the way in which you accepted clothes rationing. You know how it has saved much needed shipping space, manpower and materials, and so assisted our war effort.
>
> The Board of Trade Make Do and Mend campaign is intended to help you to get the last possible ounce of wear out of all your clothes and household things. This booklet is part of that campaign, and deals chiefly with clothes and household linen.
>
> No doubt there are as many ways of patching or darning as there are of cooking potatoes. Even if we ran to several large volumes, we could not say all there is to say about storing, cleaning, pressing, destroying moths, mending and renovating clothes and household linen.
>
> But the hints here will, I hope, prove useful. They have all been tested and approved by the Board of Trade Make Do and Mend Advisory Panel, a body of practical people, mostly women, for whose help in preparing this booklet I am most grateful.

With rationing severely restricting the availability of new fabrics, those who wanted a new outfit simply had to learn how to 'Make Do and Mend' with whatever materials they could find at home. This famous poster was designed by Donia Nachshen, who was from a Jewish family and born in Russia. She studied at the Slade School of Fine Arts, London. Nachshen was a book illustrator for publisher John Lane and also designed posters for the Post Office.

Though sometimes patronising and full of sexist gender stereotyping ('Clothes have simply got to last *longer* than they used to, but only the careful women can make them last *well*.'), the *Make Do and Mend* booklet was full of good intentions. It helped households deal with a range of vexing issues including 'The Moth Menace', 'Binding for Frayed Edges', 'Worn Underarms', 'Too-short Blouses' and 'Too-tight Underwear'.

The CC41 utility label, meaning 'Controlled Commodity', was designed by

Reginald Shipp, a London-based commercial artist whom The Board of Trade awarded a personal prize of £5. His logo appeared on clothing from 1942 and lasted, amazingly, until 1952. Clothes bearing the CC41 label were cut to avoid wasting cloth so pleats, embroidery and unnecessary folds were a definite no-go. There were no turn-ups on trousers either, an item of clothing which the *Make Do and Mend* booklet addressed thus: 'Trousers. Fold carefully in their proper creases every night. Sew a piece of tape or odd piece of material or leather inside the bottom of each leg where the shoe rubs, to prevent it wearing thin.' In fact Hansard records that during a debate in the House of Commons on 16 March 1943, the subject of trouser turn-ups, or rather the lack of them, was actually debated in government. Mr Edmund Radford, the MP for Rusholme in Manchester, asked Hugh Dalton, President of the Board of Trade, if:

> In view of the wide dissatisfaction with the austerity clothes regulations, whether he will consider the advisability of conferring with practical representatives of the bespoke tailoring trade, as distinct from the manufacturing interests, with a view to amending the regulations, thereby making them more practical and thus removing the serious irritation they are causing to professional and business men in particular?

Despite numerous more pressing issues a Cabinet minister was bound to deal with, Hugh Dalton found time to answer Mr Radford's question with careful consideration:

> These regulations were introduced in May, 1942, after consultation with the trade. Their purpose was to effect a substantial economy in shipping space, materials and labour, and in this they have succeeded. The need for such economies is even more urgent now than it was ten months ago, and I could not agree to any amendment of these regulations which would diminish their effectiveness in this respect. Subject to this condition, I shall be glad to consider any representations which the trade may wish to make.

Radford then thanked Dalton for being prepared to receive representatives of the bespoke tailoring trade and asked him whether the austerity regulations were originally intended to apply only to utility clothing and not to non-utility: 'Is it not a fact that trousers with turn-ups wear longer than non-turn-ups?' Dalton's answer was immediate but revealed not a little of the irritation he must have felt given that, although Britain could at last see light at the end of the tunnel having won the Second El Alamein the previous November, there was still a long way to go.

> No, Sir. There was never any limitation of these regulations for utility clothing. Turn-ups are a very debatable subject. I do not accept the view of my hon. Friend, and I would like to let him know that on the turn-ups regulations alone millions of square feet of cloth have already been saved. The Services have no turn-ups, nor do many hon. Members of this House who take particular care of their tailoring.

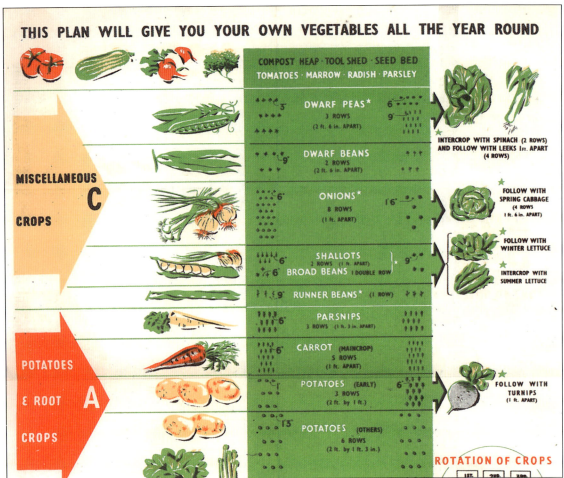

This leaflet explained that by following a plan householders could cultivate and enjoy fresh vegetables all year round.

Together with the numerous official publications raining down on the average citizen either from billboards or received in the post, as well as the covert snooping of Mass Observation pollsters during the Second World War, both twentieth-century conflicts saw a popular increase in kinds of literature driven by public desire and interest rather than official nannying.

Apparently, the first postcard can be dated to Austria in 1869 and they arrived in Britain a year later. Presumably this wasn't receipt of the one posted in Austria!

It was the Paris Exhibition of 1889, held on the hundredth anniversary of the storming of the Bastille, which really saw this message of communication take off in a big way. With nearly 6,500,000 visitors attending in just 6 months one can imagine the number of stories people who went there wanted to share, and they did this via the postcard. In 1894 Britain's Post Office finally approved of the private publication of postcards and a cheaper, ?d stamp was introduced specifically for such missives. The divided back postcard, with clearly defined areas for address and message was introduced in 1902.

During the Edwardian period postcards became a veritable craze, not just because people found them a useful way of keeping in touch – the email of the time, but because they enjoyed building collections. In fact, postcard albums really replaced photographic albums in popularity. Consequently, when war was declared in 1914 and thousands of British troops marched off to France, postcards proved the ideal way for them to keep in touch.

Embroidered silk postcards, 'silks', proved particularly popular at this time. Local French and Belgian women embroidered different motifs onto strips of silk mesh which were sent to factories for cutting and mounting on postcards. These motifs often featured sentimental messages of love and adoration but also, equally often, regimental badges and colours.

There was a lighter side to Air Raid Precautions, as this postcard demonstrates.

Postcards were often published as a series, perhaps each separate card bearing a single verse from a popular song of the time. Many featured faithful spouses longingly waiting for the return of their men folk. Some depicted wives stoically urging their men on to final victory. On the other hand some revealed just what the men were fighting for and revealed what might happen if the barbaric Hun arrived in Britain and rampaged through isolated homesteads, devoid of men to protect the vulnerable women and children living there. Some inevitably depicted the alleged barbarities inflicted on the innocent people of Belgium by advancing German troops. Many simply showed the devastation the war had wrought on the towns and villages of Flanders.

Publishers like Raphael Tuck and Charles Rose printed new postcards by the thousand and supported the efforts of artists such as Louis Wain, Donald McGill, Tom Browne, James Bamforth and Mabel Lucie Attwell. However, perhaps the most famous artist of the First World War period is Bruce Bairnsfather, who before the war had illustrated advertising posters for products such as Lipton Tea, Players Tobacco and Beechams powders. During the war Bairnsfather served as an officer in the Royal Warwickshire Regiment alongside such people such as Captain Bernard Montgomery and Lieutenant A.A. Milne.

Bairnsfather had actually taken part in the famously unofficial Christmas truce of 1914 and was subsequently censured for his actions, narrowly avoiding court martial. However, it is for the drawings of life on the Western Front, and in particular the creation of that veteran soldier Old Bill, published from 1915 in the *Bystander* magazine as 'Fragments from France', for which he will be forever remembered. Postcards featuring Old Bill and surviving vintage copies of 'Fragments from France' now command high prices which the hundredth anniversary of the war have only pushed even higher.

During the Second World War many of the artists and illustrators who had established themselves some twenty years earlier found a ready market for their work once again, Mabel Lucie Attwell notably among them. Indeed, her beautifully illustrated postcards now command some of the highest prices.

In relative terms, certainly in the first few years of the Second World War, far fewer British men were on active service overseas than had been the case during the 1914–18 conflict. Other than French postcards mailed by the men of the BEF during the winter of 1939/40 and images of the Sphinx, Pyramids, the port of Alexandria and Cairo street scenes from soldiers in the Middle East (the beleaguered troops in Burma had rather more on their mind than postcards), there aren't as many vintage examples from this period as there are surviving from the Great War.

However, Kenneth Clark and his colleagues on the War Artists Advisory Committee (WAAC) ensured that art remained a priority at home. Clark also won the blessing of the trustees of the National Gallery for a series of free public concerts by Dame Myra Hess who organised what would turn out to be some 1,700 lunchtime concerts spanning a period of 6 years, starting during the London Blitz. Clark even managed to persuade the Home Office and Ministry of Works to grant the concerts dispensation from the ban on public gatherings. 'The sooner we can start the better', he wrote, 'As this is the period when people are beginning to feel the want of nourishment for mind and spirit and it would be a great thing for the National Gallery to give a lead.'

The WAAC was also the prime mover behind a painting which, like Dame Myra's musical talents, was also exhibited at the National Gallery. Charles Ernest Cundall's epically large canvas *Withdrawal from Dunkirk* was painted in June 1940, barely a month after the famous maritime evacuation of ¼ million men of the BEF. Cundall's painting rapidly

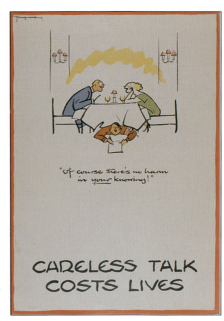

Hitler eavesdropping in one of Cyril Kenneth Bird's (Fougasse) famous 'Careless Talk Cost Lives' posters. The artist was seriously injured at the Battle of Gallipoli during the First World War but had a very successful career with the British press and with magazines, including the Graphic *and* Tatler.

'Let's Go – Wings For Victory' poster from 1943.

become a popular propaganda image of British endurance and like so many other famous images became a popular subject for postcard publishers.

At the time of writing a series of articles in the press revealed that British postcards had an eager following in Nazi Germany, where they were used to help Hitler plan his proposed invasion, Operation Sea Lion, and referred to by *Luftwaffe* planners selecting high-profile targets in the British Isles. The *Daily Mail* Online reported the following:

> A collection of English seaside postcards collected by German tourists before the Second World War confiscated by Hitler and used to plan the Nazi invasion of Britain have recently been unearthed. The black and white images of coastal beauty spots were originally taken home by families as mementoes of their visit to the island. After the outbreak of war in 1939 the German military machine collected thousands of the postcards as Adolf Hitler plotted to conquer Britain.

Together with postcards, the find also included a selection of booklets full of specific details which might be of help to the invader. Max Haslar, of London-based Drewcatts auctioneers who were preparing to sell the collection, said (as quoted in the *Daily Mail* Online):

> These briefing booklets were printed in preparation for Operation Sealion, the German invasion of Britain which thankfully never came to pass. This is probably the most extensive collection of these booklets to come up at auction. They were used by the German military and the *Luftwaffe* during the war and illustrate places and road junctions in the UK that German intelligence thought should be attacked as part of the British invasion.

Certainly it is known that from April 1942, starting with Exeter, *Luftwaffe* planners used copies of Germany's famous Baedeker travel guide to plan a series of *Vergeltungsangriffe* (retaliatory attacks) on English cities in response to the bombing of the German city of Lübeck the previous month. The so-called 'Baedeker Blitz' would see raids on Norwich, Exeter, Bath, York and Canterbury, leaving 1,637 civilians dead, 1,760 injured and more than 50,000 homes destroyed.

This little booklet (front and back cover shown) explained how the United States was sending men and materials to help Britain in time to launch a concerted second front in Europe.

Whether a miner at the coal face, a fire-watcher on the lookout for stray incendiaries or a housewife running a rationed household – everyone on the home front was in it together. As these five cards so ably put it: 'To Blast the hopes of Hitler! It all depends on me.'

Collecting cigarette cards was as popular during the Second World War as postcard collecting had been during the First World War. Like vintage postcards, cigarette cards now command high prices. And, like postcards, their value is higher if they are in good condition and not stuck into albums. However, unlike with postcards, the major publishers of cigarette cards produced albums specifically for collectors to paste their cards into. Although each card had a description about its illustrated face specifically printed on the card's reverse, this was repeated in the album, immediately below the position where the individual card was to be stuck, which naturally encouraged owners to glue their cards into position. Although the cards, usually published in sets of fifty, looked much better when placed in position in their specific albums and were naturally much easier to study, they have a far higher value if they are mint and loose.

Manufacturers including John Player and Sons, Ardath, W.A. & A.C. Churchman, Gallaher, W.D. and H.O. Wills among others published sets with titles such as 'Life in the Royal Navy', 'It All Depends on Me', 'The RAF at War', 'Army Badges', 'Air-Raid Precautions', 'Aircraft of the Royal Air Force' and 'Life in the Services', all of which proved very popular and encouraged purchasers greedily to smoke successive packs of cigarettes in order to get that last elusive card and complete their sets.

Information printed on the backs of cigarette cards was obviously not particularly up to date and showed wartime developments in pretty generic terms. There were, of course, the newspapers, and although the MOI, housed in the University of London Senate House and upon which Orwell based the Ministry of Truth in *Nineteen-Eighty-Four*, had the power to censor the press it rarely did. The Home Office could fall back on the Emergency Powers Act, which made it illegal to disseminate information that might harm operational security, but, again, this stricture was rarely enforced as, after the event, the damage would probably already have been done.

So, newspapers were largely left alone. However, as broadsheets were only read by the cognoscenti, press articles didn't have a massive readership. With so many people visiting the cinema on a regular basis, the best method for conveying news, and official propaganda, was via the newsreels, which were a feature of every programme.

Women might not be able to operate eight Browning machine guns but they could 'Serve in the WAAF with the Men who Fly'. In fact dozens of women pilots were in command of unarmed fighters and bombers in the Air Transport Auxiliary (ATA).

Saving and recycling waste paper isn't an entirely modern innovation, and sensible householders where actively engaged in reprocessing more than seventy years ago.

Initially, short documentaries were made and filmed by the GPO film unit, a subdivision of the UK General Post Office. This organisation was established in 1933 and took over the responsibilities of the Empire Marketing Board Film Unit, which had been set up in the mid-1920s by the Colonial Secretary Leo Amery to promote intra-Empire trade with its slogan 'Buy Empire'. At first the GPO Film unit produced documentary films mainly related to the activities of its parent, the GPO.

One of its most famous films is Harry Watt's and Basil Wright's 1936 production *Night Mail*, which features music by Benjamin Britten and poetry by W.H. Auden.

In 1940 the GPO Film Unit became the Crown Film Unit, under the control of the Ministry of Information. The Crown Film Unit produced a mixture of information heavy shorts as well as longer documentary films and many of what we now know as docudramas. Its audience was not restricted to the general public in Britain but to those living abroad. In fact, the Crown Film Unit continued to produce films, as part of the Central Office of Information (COI), until it was disbanded in 1952.

Pathé, Movietone and Gaumont were the principal privately owned producers of newsreels.

Charles Pathé and his brothers founded the Société Pathé Frères in Paris in 1896, adopting the national emblem of France, the cockerel, as the trademark for their company. French Pathé began its newsreel in 1908 and opened a newsreel office in Wardour Street, London in 1910.

During the First World War, Pathé's *Animated Gazettes* began to give traditional newspapers a run for their money, and often beat their press competitors to a scoop. By 1930, British Pathé was covering news, entertainment, sport, culture and women's issues through programmes including the *Pathétone Weekly*, the *Pathé Pictorial*, the *Gazette* and *Eve's Film Review*. Associated British Picture Corporation (ABPC) acquired British Pathé in 1937 and in 1940, Warner Bros in the United States bought a large holding in the firm.

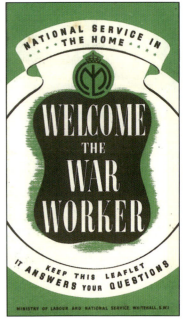

Those unable to leave their home and contribute in National Service as factory workers or fire-watchers, for example, could still do useful war work from home, as this leaflet explained. In total war everybody did their bit.

Poster explaining how householders could seek shelter and compensation if their homes were damaged in a raid.

  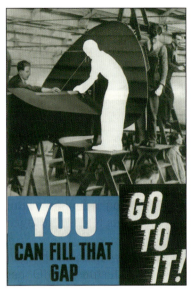

Another classic Abram Games poster graphically emphasising that the more crops grown at home the fewer vital spaces required in the holds of ships to transport foodstuffs to Britain.

'This is a War of Machines' national savings leaflet explaining that in modern war it was the duty of citizens to provide their armed forces with the best equipment – and that this cost money.

With so many able-bodied men away on active service it was vital that the factories and foundries were staffed by capable workers. This leaflet explained how those exempt from fighting could participate in industrial production.

British Movietone News, a subsidiary of US Corporation Fox Movietone News, released newsreels in Britain from 1929 to 1979. Leslie Mitchell, the first commentator for the new BBC Television Service when it began transmissions on 2 November 1936, was also a commentator for British Movietone News. In September 1939, Mitchell and other Movietone editorial staff were evacuated to Denham, although they returned to Soho Square soon after. Mitchell worked for Movietone throughout the war, and was also commentator on *War Pictorial News*, which began production in 1940.

The third major player in the late 1930s and throughout the war years was Gaumont-British News. Originally dealing solely in photographic apparatus, the company began producing short films in 1897 to promote its own cameras and film projectors. In 1914, however, Léon Gaumont's Cité Elgé studios in La Villette, France were the largest in the world. Gaumont dominated the motion-picture industry in Europe until the outbreak of the First World War in 1914. Gaumont also constructed London's Lime Grove Studios, used by the BBC prior to its move to the TV Centre at White City in the 1960s.

Together with newspapers and the newsreels the public also referred to a series of regular magazines to keep up to date with the progress of the war and developments at home, such as items about new fashion trends or Hollywood celebrities – anything in fact to take their minds off the drudgery of rationing and the bleakness of the blackout.

Picture Post, essentially Britain's equivalent of the American illustrated magazine *Life*, was founded in 1938. From the start *Picture Post* adopted a liberal and distinctly anti-fascist stance. From 1940 the legendary journalist and picture editor Tom Hopkinson took over as editor, previously he had worked on *Weekly Illustrated* and *Lilliput* magazines. Most famous for the quality of its photo-journalism, under Hopkinson's auspices, the very human photographs of luminaries, such as native Londoner Bert Hardy, were given priority. In only its second month the magazine was selling 1,700,000 copies per week. This is one reason why so many of these fantastic publications survive to this day and are inexpensive and accessible to collectors.

Picture Post pulled no punches. As early as 1938 its picture story, 'Back to the Middle Ages', exposed the reality of life in Nazi Germany, and revealed the dark character of the Reich's leaders Adolf Hitler, Joseph Goebbels and Hermann Göring. It is amazing that *Picture Post*'s publisher and owner, the Conservative party member Sir Edward G. Hulton, tolerated Hopkinson's left-wing views, which always took precedence over stories from the right wing of British politics in the magazine.

In January 1941 *Picture Post* published its 'Plan for Britain' which proposed minimum wages throughout industry, full employment, child allowances, a national health service, the planned use of land and a complete overhaul of education. 'Plan for Britain' was an influential forerunner to the 1942 report *Social Insurance and Allied Services* (known as the *Beveridge Report*) which served as the basis for the post-Second World War welfare state.

It is comforting to learn that while the war was very far from over, Britain's administrators were confidently looking to a better and more prosperous life for their citizens post-war.

Published in December 1942, the *Report of the Inter-Departmental Committee on Social Insurance and Allied Services*, to give the *Beveridge Report* its proper name, set out to tackle what its author considered the five 'giant evils' of modern society: squalor, ignorance, want, idleness and disease. Beveridge proposed widespread reform to the system of social welfare to address these issues, famously saying: 'All people of working age should pay a weekly National Insurance contribution. In return, benefits would be paid to people who were sick, unemployed, retired, or widowed.' The notion of free health care to all citizens and universal child benefit given to parents was revolutionary. The Labour Party's election victory in 1945 saw many of Beveridge's reforms implemented and on 5 July 1948, the National Insurance Act, National Assistance Act and National Health Service Act came into force, and Britain's welfare state was born.

Britain's wartime government didn't just consider the social welfare of its citizens it also thought long and hard about where and how its population would live in a presumably victorious country once the fighting had ended. With large areas of the urban environment devastated by enemy bombing, such considerations were of vital significance if those fighting men returning from active service were going to live in a land fit for heroes.

As early as January 1940 the government convened a Royal Commission on the Distribution of the Industrial Population which was required to inquire into the 'causes which have influenced the present geographical distribution of the industrial population

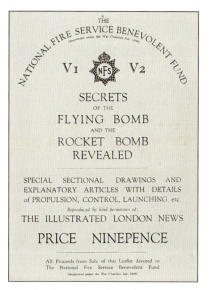

In 1927 Procter & Gamble purchased Oxydol, a laundry detergent created in 1914 by Thomas Hedley Co. of Newcastle upon Tyne. Before WW2, Oxydol, now an international brand, was the sponsor of America's Ma Perkins radio show - the first soap opera!

Front page of a four page flyer for the Secrets of the Flying Bomb exhibition held in Leicester Square in 1945. Showing how the 'various automatic devices controlled the robots in flight' this exhibition helped Londoners come to terms with both the pulse-jet powered V-1 Buzz Bomb, or Doodlebug, the first proper cruise missile, and the far more terrifying supersonic ballistic V-2 rocket.

Germany fired 9,521 V-1 bombs on southern England and although around half were destroyed by anti-aircraft fire or RAF fighters an estimated 2,754 people were killed by them, with 6,523 wounded. Over 5,000 V-2s were fired on Britain but only 1,100 reached their target. Nevertheless they killed 5,475 people and wounded another 16,309.

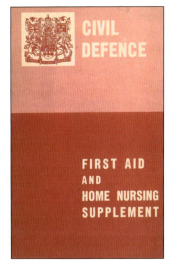

Civil Defence First Aid and Home Nursing Supplement. *The fear of a sinister death delivered from the air which so troubled people in the 1930s returned to haunt them in the 1950s during the nuclear standoff between East and West. 'It is estimated that first aid might have to deal with 20,000 casualties following an air burst of a nominal atomic bomb . . .' began the introduction to this Commonwealth booklet.*

of Great Britain and the probable direction of any change in that distribution in the future'. It was to consider what social, economic and even strategic disadvantages arose from the concentration of industries or of the industrial population in large towns or in particular areas of the country and then to report what measures, if any, should be taken in the national interest to remedy this and planning deficiencies.

The Commission published findings which among many other recommendations decided that there should be continued and further redevelopment of congested urban areas, where necessary the decentralisation or dispersal both of industries and industrial populations from such areas and appropriate diversification of industry in each division or region throughout the country. It argued that:

> The continued drift of the industrial population to London and the Home Counties constitutes a social, economic and strategical problem which demands immediate attention. The Central Authority should examine forthwith and formulate the policy or plan to be adopted in relation to decentralization or dispersal from congested urban areas in connexion with such issues as garden cities or garden suburbs, satellite towns, trading estates, further development of existing small towns or regional centres, etc. In all cases provision being made for the requirements of industry and the social and amenity needs of the communities, the avoidance of unnecessary competition, and the giving of due weight to strategical considerations. Without excluding private enterprise municipalities should be encouraged to undertake such development, if found desirable on a regional rather than on a municipal basis, and they should be assisted by Government funds, especially in the early years. All existing and future Planning Schemes should be subject to the Central Authority's inspection with a view to possible modification.
>
> The Government should appoint a body of experts to examine the questions of compensation betterment and development generally.

On 15 August 1942 Lord Justice Scott's Committee on Land Utilisation in Rural Areas was published. It considered: 'The conditions which should govern building and other constructional development in country areas consistently with the maintenance of agriculture, and in particular the factors affecting the location of industry, having regard to economic operation, part time and seasonal employment, the wellbeing of rural communities and the preservation of rural amenities.' The Committee concluded that if no centralised authority directed planning, industry and its necessary supporting housing would continue to be established on the peripheries of Britain's existing great population centres leading in particular to the still greater growth of London and Birmingham. It argued that the current drift of population to the towns could be countered by improving housing and general living conditions, and so equalising economic, social and educational opportunities in town and country. The improvement of rural housing and amenities would be a key factor in balancing things out and ensuring that those living in rural communities enjoyed actually quite basic facilities such as electricity and piped water, which those in urban areas had begun to take for granted.

The following month Mr Justice Uthwatt's Expert Committee on Compensation and Betterment published its final report which analysed the subject of the payment of compensation and recovery of betterment in respect of public control of the use of land, and the payment of compensation on the public acquisition of land, advising what steps should be taken to prevent the work of reconstruction after the war from being prejudiced. Uthwatt's Report viewed post-war reconstruction as the rebuilding of war-devastated areas combined with the modernisation of such areas so that they met the requirements of modern living.

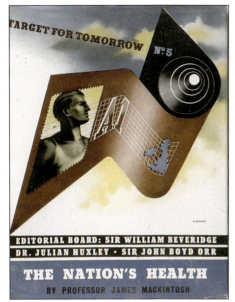
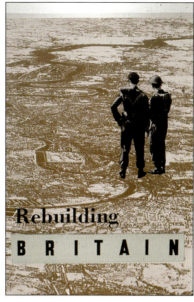

Rebuilding Britain. *The Greater London Plan which had been formulated in 1944 and the New Towns Act which came on to the statute books in 1946 conspired to change the face of post-war Britain.*

'Targeting Tomorrow, No. 5, The Nation's Health'. *The establishment of the National Health Service immediately after the Second World War was seen by many as a fitting reward for the sacrifices working class people had once again made for their country.*

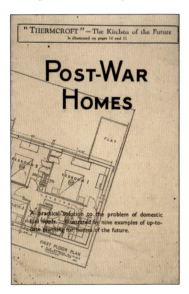

'Homes Fit For Heroes!' *That was the promise to returning soldiers after the Great War. The landslide victory for Clement Attlee's Labour government in July 1945 brought similar promises but this time new houses were constructed with vigour.*

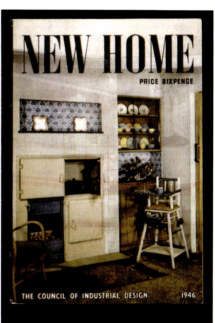

The Council of Industrial Design's New Home *brochure, 1946.*

Best known for the post-war re-planning of London – he published the County of London Plan in 1943 and the Greater London Plan in 1944, Sir Patrick Abercrombie originally trained as an architect, becoming Professor of Town Planning at University College London. His legacy also remains in the modern rebuilding of cities such as Plymouth, Hull, Bournemouth and Bath as well as award-winning architecture in Dublin.

In 1945, the former Director General of the BBC, Lord Reith, was appointed chair of the government's New Towns Committee, established to consider how best to repair and rebuild urban communities after the ravages of the Second World War. Recommending the construction of new towns planned by development corporations supported by central government, the New Towns Act of 1946 was the result of the Committee's deliberations. Basildon, Crawley, Stevenage, Cwmbran, East Kilbride among other new conurbations in Great Britain soon evolved from drawing board schematics into the reality of bricks and mortar.

While committees and town planners published report after report containing their visions of a better Britain and improved communities for the body public which had toiled so long to preserve its national identity, some people wanted simply to pick up where they had left off in 1939 and return to familiar homes and streets. To some, of course, their once familiar streets looked very different. Rows of terraced houses now revealed the occasional gap, like a missing tooth, where a dwelling had been levelled by bomb blast. Many were forced to seek new homes.

Fortunately the government had an expedient answer to the sudden shortage of homes – the supposedly temporary prefabs, kit houses that could be assembled in days rather than months. There were Airey Houses, designed by Sir Edwin Airey, to the Ministry of Works Emergency Factory Made (EFM) housing programme's plan, which featured frames of prefabricated concrete columns reinforced with tubing recycled from military vehicles, with walls consisting of a series of ship-lap-style concrete panels. Along with Airey Houses there were also numerous of the more familiar single-storey rectangular prefabs which consisted of steel or aluminium panels fixed to a timber or steel frame; simple dwellings of the kind originally envisaged by Winston Churchill and committed to legislation with the passing of the Housing (Temporary Accomodation) Act 1944.

Strategy for Survival. First Steps in Nuclear Disarmament. A Penguin Special *by Wayland Young (1959). 'This is a book for clear-minded people tired of hot air who seek a practical guide to the desperately urgent problem of nuclear warfare.' The son of the politician Edward Hilton Young, 1st Baron Kennet, and the sculptor Kathleen Scott, née Bruce, widow of Captain Scott of Antarctic fame, Young served in the Royal Navy during the Second World War, then began a career as a journalist, writer and Labour politician.*

Between the years 1945 and 1951, when the programme officially ended, 156,623 prefab houses were constructed. Envisaged to last just ten years, the author quotes an article published in the *Daily Mail* in 2011, sixty years after they were constructed, about Britain's last surviving prefab estate at Catford, South London: 'Plonked on top of pre-plumbed concrete slabs, these homes could be built in a day by teams of German and Italian prisoners-of-war who were in no hurry to return home, come the peace.'

Some people returned to homes that although they

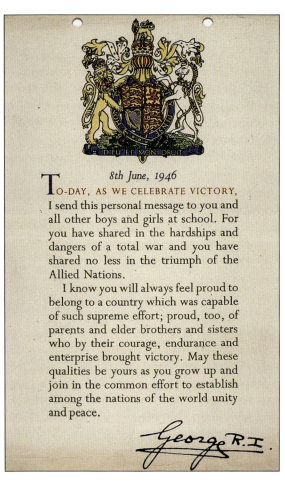

In June 1946, this letter from King George VI celebrating victory was sent to every school child in Britain.

were structurally sound and had not been demolished by either the *Luftwaffe* or the local authority's wrecking ball, were in need of urgent maintenance and repair. Fortunately, early in the war, the War Damage Commission had directed the passing of the War Damage Act 1941. This legislation provided for the payment of compensation for war damage to land and buildings throughout the country, with repairs being carried out by local authorities or private contractors.

All this new and temporary accommodation was all very well, but no sooner had rebuilding begun when the future security of householders in Britain was once again jeopardised by political developments in Continental Europe. This time the enemy wasn't Nazi Germany but a former ally, Soviet Russia.

Harking back to pre-Second World War government leaflets such as *The Protection of Your Home Against Air Raids* from 1938, the 1963 publication *Advising the Householder on Protection against Nuclear Attack* was the culmination of nearly fifteen years of nuclear arms proliferation since the Soviet Union detonated 'First Lightning', their first nuclear test weapon, at Semipalatinsk, and began to challenge the United States' predominance in this field. Published by the Home Office and the Central Office of Information (COI), *Advising the Householder on Protection against*

Nuclear Attack contained guidance for the public and the emergency services on what to do in the event of a nuclear attack. Although warning was given about the tremendous danger of the heat and blast generated by an atomic weapon, fall-out, 'the dust that is sucked up from the ground by the explosion and made radioactive in the rising fireball' was described as the insidious killer. The guide was full of chilling advice such as this:

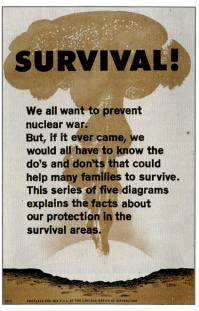

> If you have been caught out-of-doors, take off your outer garments and leave them outside the fall-out room; brush your remaining clothes and wash exposed parts of the body before going to shelter. This would help get rid of any fall-out dust you may have picked up outside. Give shelter to anyone caught without protection near your home.

Of course, householders would need a pre-prepared fall-out room within which to seek refuge in the first place and were advised to be prepared to stay in it for at least a week. An idea of how difficult it might actually be for the average family and, perhaps, an unknown stranger or two if the householders had been considerate enough to heed the publication's advice and given last-minute shelter to individuals caught outside without protection, can be ascertained when one considers this paragraph about sanitation:

All the best intentions of those who planned to build a better Britain were jeopardised by the threat of a nuclear holocaust between former allies but now cold war adversaries as this leaflet prepared for the Women's Voluntary Service (WVS) by the Central Office of Information (COI) makes graphically clear.

> You could not rely on being able to use your W.C. There might not be enough water to flush it or the sewerage system might be damaged. Keep the following items in the fall-out room or within easy reach outside the door: Large receptacles with covers and with improvised seats for use as urinal, and for excreta. Ashes, dry earth, or disinfectant toilet paper. Clean newspapers, brown paper or strong paper bags (to wrap up food remains and empty tins). Dust-bin with well-fitting lid. For pets keep a box of earth or ashes.

Numerous similar leaflets and more technical, restricted pamphlets produced for the armed forces and emergency services were accompanied by a series of public information films called *Civil Defence Information Bulletins*. Designed to be broadcast in a state of emergency, the most notorious of these appeared in Peter Watkins' controversial BBC production *The War Game*, a programme that was found to be so disturbing it was soon banned.

The reader might be interested to learn that my good friend Peter Donaldson, who recently retired as BBC Radio Four's much-loved and long-serving chief continuity announcer, was, as he calls it, 'the voice of doom' and recorded the announcement which heralded the 4-minute warning before atomic bombs struck Great Britain! Peter's frightening monologue began thus:

> This is the Wartime Broadcasting Service. This country has been attacked with nuclear weapons. Communications have been severely disrupted, and the number of casualties and the extent of the damage are not yet known. We shall bring you further information as soon as possible. Meanwhile, stay tuned to this wavelength, stay calm and stay in your own house.
>
> Remember there is nothing to be gained by trying to get away. By leaving your homes you could be exposing yourself to greater danger . . .

With Home Office permission, in October 2008 the BBC published the complete script of this ominous recording on their website and it has since been made available to the public via The National Archives.

Protect and Survive, the final government leaflet explaining what to do if the cold war suddenly turned hot, was, reluctantly, formally published in May 1980. Since the Soviet invasion of Afghanistan the previous year and the increasingly hostile relationship between East and West, *The Times* newspaper had been inundated by numerous letters asking about the precise details of the government's civil defence arrangements. The public disquiet even forced the Minister of State at the Home Office, Leon Brittan, to tell Parliament that:

> This was not a secret pamphlet. There was no mystery about it. It had been available to all local authorities and chief police and fire officers. It had not been published for the simple reason that it was produced for distribution during a grave international crisis when war was imminent. It was calculated that it would have the most impact then.

However, following the public interest the government made the leaflet available, but printed relatively few copies. The consequence is that this is now one of the most rare documents from the period of the nuclear arms race and a must-have for collectors.

Mikhail Gorbachev's ascendancy to the post of General Secretary of the Communist Party of the Soviet Union in 1985 and then as the country's head of state in 1988 saw dramatic changes within the USSR. Gorbachev's urgent introduction of *glasnost*, or 'openness', to the machinery of state ultimately led to disaffected republics going their own way and, remarkably, in 1991 the total collapse of the Soviet Union. The partial dismantling of the Berlin Wall in 1989 and its complete removal in 1990 had already witnessed a dramatic thawing of the cold war with the effect that in Britain, at any rate, the 1990 defence spending review *Options for Change*, foresaw the dismantling of much of the machinery that had endured since East–West nuclear stand-off began. One of the results was that the the Royal Observer Corps (ROC), the British civil defence organisation founded in 1925 and whose observers did such sterling work during the Battle of Britain, was formally stood down in December 1995.

The cold war was over and the threat of nuclear Armageddon was lifted at last.

CHAPTER 3

Entertainment

The communications revolution of the late Victorian age literally brought Britain together. Railways encouraged travel and opened up the nation, revealing much that was new to many. People made new acquaintances and got to know those who were previously strangers. More people read daily newspapers. These, and tours by professional variety acts who performed the same well-rehearsed routines in music halls across Britain, delivered shared experiences and encouraged a sense of community that spread far beyond the previous restricted village or county boundaries people had been used to for generations.

The electric telegraph and telephone further accelerated this inter relationship and made physical distance much less restrictive.

Everything got closer.

The Hero's Return, *a popular First World War* marche militaire *for the pianoforte by Valentine Hemery who was well-known for his 1909 composition* Sympathy. A song without words for Piano.

Whistling Tommies. Sketch for piano, *1917*. 'Frank Marsden' was really composer Ernest Reeves who published under a range of other pseudonyms including Fabian Scott, Allan R. Cameron, René Dubois, Paul Peronne, Leon Verré and even Gladys A. Wood!

This sense of nationalism and shared purpose was of course one of the main motivators behind Britons accepting the need to go to war both in 1914 and 1939 and also permitted them to join the military, either as volunteer recruits or accepting conscription.

The media and entertainment industries exploited this sense of togetherness by promoting patriotism; lionising celebrities and promoting their songs, skits and stage personalities. In the build-up to the First World War the music hall was the primary way a sense of patriotic community was engendered. In the Second World War it was radio and the cinema that encouraged people to rally round the flag.

What we now recognise as the music hall, a type of entertainment that had previously been confined to the back rooms of public houses, or in so-called 'song and supper rooms' and in seaside pleasure gardens which, to the consternation of the middle class, had gone more downmarket as workers flocked to them during high days and holidays, had by the mid-1850s, evolved into something more substantial, taking place in purpose-built auditoriums, often close to the boozers where they had started. Not surprisingly, a fairly bawdy atmosphere was maintained.

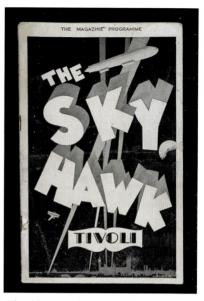

The Sky Hawk *was a 1929 American adventure film starring Helen Chandler, John Garrick and Gilbert Emery about First World War British aviator Jack Bardell battling German Zeppelin attacks over London.*

By 1870 415 fairly substantial halls, each complete with amenities for the professional performers and a range of catering facilities for the audience, had taken root across Britain. Performers often appeared on stage, going through the same act, at several venues each night (there were thirty-one music halls in London alone in 1870). Music-hall performers were the superstars of the age.

Soon, greater regulation, with its consequent public safety implications, as well as a restriction on licensing in certain premises pushed prices up. But music hall remained

Published right at the beginning of the war in 1939 and intended to offer ideas to cheer up the suddenly long dark evenings, proceeds from the sale of Howard Thomas's Brighter Blackout Book, *went to the* Daily Sketch *War Relief Fund.*

a big business, such that commercial organisations like Moss, Stoll and Thornton began to dominate and their 'Palaces' and 'Empires' the destination of choice for audiences looking for a good night out.

Regulation continued. Performers looked to protect their hours and wages by forming the Variety Artists' Federation and even organised the first music-hall strike. But in 1912, with the first Royal Command Performance, it was clear music hall had come of age and gained a level of respectability.

By the advent of the First World War music halls were operated more along the lines or regular theatres with food and drink banned from the auditorium.

The United States had developed a similar entertainment industry, though rather than the 'variety acts' of British music hall, Americans flocked to 'vaudeville'. Not dissimilar to its British cousins, vaudeville nevertheless developed from less bacchanalian traditions and generally aspired towards a more middle-class audience. By 1910 the rapid growth of cheap-price movie theatres in the United States had taken its toll on vaudeville and was about to develop into the massive industry we know today. In fact, one of the young variety stars of British music hall, Charlie Chaplin, a featured player with the Fred Karno Repertoire Company, moved there that same year and was offered his first part in a silent movie in 1912. Very soon Chaplin was to become, perhaps, the most famous man in the world and certainly one of the richest.

In Britain music hall proved the ideal mechanism to drum up support for the war effort and artists and composers threw themselves into rallying public support.

Two patriotic music-hall compositions kicked off the war in 1914.

Keep the Home-Fires Burning ('Till the Boys Come Home) was a combination of Welshman Ivor Novello's music and American Lena Ford's patriotic lyrics:

> They were summoned from the hillside,
> They were called in from the glen,
> And the Country found them ready
> At the stirring call for men.
> Let no tears add to their hardship,
> As the Soldiers pass along
> And although your heart is breaking,
> Make it sing this cheery song.

Your King and Country Want You ('We Don't Want to Lose You, but we think you ought to go') featured words and lyrics by Paul Rubens, the English author of some of the most popular Edwardian comedies. The latter was intended as a recruiting song for women and the profits from Ruben's famous creation were given to a fund for women with none other than Queen Mary as its patron.

Written by Jack Judge two years before the outbreak of hostilities, 'It's a Long Way to Tipperary' has nonetheless become one of the songs most associated with the Great War. Although songwriter and music-hall entertainer Judge performed his song on numerous occasions, it was Irish tenor John Francis Count McCormack who made it world-famous. It is best remembered for its chorus:

While you've a Lucifer to light your fag,
Smile, boys, that's the style.
What's the use of worrying?
It never was worthwhile, so pack up your troubles in your old kit-bag,
And smile, smile, smile.

'Pack up your troubles in your old kit-bag' was a 1915 classic penned by Welshman George Henry Powell, under the pseudonym George Asaf, with music by Felix Powell. Ironically, the song's lyricist was a pacifist and a conscientious objector whose conscription had to be imposed in 1916.

Songwriters and music publishers weren't averse to sentimentalism or a bit of emotional blackmail when targeting men for enlistment to the colours and naturally the authorities were 100 per cent behind their promptings.

In December 1915 'F.W. Ramsey', the pseudonym of Fred Douglas, the lead singer in a comedy duo called the 'Two Gilberts', performed 'All the Boys in Khaki Get the Nice Girls', a sentiment echoed the same year by the famous cockney singer Marie Lloyd when she intoned, 'I didn't like you much before you joined the army, John, but I do like yer cockie now you've got your khaki on.'

Entitled 'What did you do in the Great War, daddy?' and made famous by Tom Clare, the London-born music-hall singer who had already had a success with 'Who Bashed Bill Kaiser?', this piece was designed to prick the conscience of all those who had tried to avoid the call to arms and were, perhaps, even indulging in some black-market profiteering. How would they explain their lily-livered behaviour to their children when the fighting was over and the troops had come home?

Come and sit beside me, Daddy
Tell me the tale once more
I often asked you to tell me, Daddy
What you did in the great Great War?

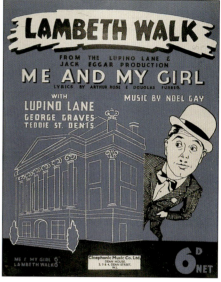

The Lambeth Walk, *a song from the 1937 musical* Me and My Girl, *has become synonymous with the 'Blitz spirit' of working class Londoners. In 1939 a film of the same name played to packed audiences.*

Made famous by Vera Lynn in 1939, We'll Meet Again *was a hit again in 1943 when the 'Forces' Sweetheart' played the lead role in a musical of the same name.*

As the war progressed and there was no hiding the casuality figures and the apparent deadly stalemate in the trenches, songs became less motivational, almost subversive.

Telling the story of three fictional soldiers on the Western Front suffering from homesickness and their longing to return home, 'Take Me Back to Dear Old Blighty' was written by Arthur Mills, Fred Godfrey and Bennett Scott, and was especially popular when it was first performed in 1916. Perhaps it was no coincidence that in July that year, on one day alone, 20,000 young men were killed as they battled through no-man's-land on the Somme.

The same year music-hall artiste Vesta Tilley had a hit with the song 'I'm Glad I've Got a Bit of a Blighty One' in which the hugely popular male impersonator played a soldier delighted to have been wounded and in hospital. 'When I think about my dugout,' she sang, 'where I dare not stick my mug out . . . I'm glad I've got a bit of a Blighty one.' The phrase 'a Blighty one' soon becoming the lingua franca in the British Army for a wound that would require hospitalisation back home.

However, despite the somewhat questionable sentiments of 'I'm Glad I've Got a Bit of a Blighty One', Tilley's popularity knew no limits during the First World War. Indeed, she and her husband ran a military recruitment drive and, dressed in the guise of characters like 'Tommy in the Trench' and 'Jack Tar Home from Sea', Tilley performed songs like 'The army of today's all right' and 'Jolly Good Luck to the Girl who Loves a Soldier'. Tilley soon earned the nickname 'Britain's best recruiting sergeant', and often at her shows young men were asked to join the army on stage there and then.

Costing the British an estimated 275,000 casualties against the German's 220,000, making it one of the war's most costly campaigns, the Battle of Passchendaele, the Third Battle of Ypres, took place on the Western Front between July and November 1917. The same year one of the most notorious of music-hall

Humours of ARP *by the cartoonist Giles was published in 1941 and followed by* Laughs With the Home Guard *and similar books about each branch of the forces. Now quite rare, you should expect to pay as much as £50 for a copy. Carl Ronald Giles was awarded an OBE in 1959 and died in 1995.*

Not to be confused with its modern soft-core porn incarnation, the original Men Only *actually dates back to 1935 when it was founded by C. Arthur Pearson Ltd as a pocket magazine. It was similar in format to the more famous* Lilliput *magazine which followed it in 1937.*

songs, 'Oh! It's a lovely war', was performed by Ella Shields, yet another male impersonator. Ms Shields was an American and performed there in vaudeville with her sisters until a talent scout lured her to the London stage in 1904. In 1910 she appeared at the opening night of the London Palladium and it was at this time that, like Vesta Tilley, she became a male impersonator.

In 1915 her British husband, William Hargreaves, wrote 'Burlington Bertie from Bow', a huge hit. Ella's moment came when she sang the words and music penned by John Long and Maurice Scott:

Oh it's a lovely war!
Up to your waist in water, up to your eyes in slush,
using the kind of language that makes the sergeant blush,
Who wouldn't join the army? That's what we all enquire.
Don't we pity the poor civilian sitting by the fire.

Published in 1943, Nice Types *featured the range of popular RAF characters created by Anthony Armstrong, the wartime pseudonym of Squadron Leader Anthony Armstrong Willis.*

In 1939, the irony of British soldiers marching back to Flanders fields to fight the Germans again little more than twenty years since the 'war to end all wars' had finished was not lost on those at home and especially not by the 'poor bloody infantry' who manned defensive positions a mere yards from the ones their father's had previously occupied. As the troops dug in, assuming a replay of the previous conflict but fearing a stalemate that would be made all the more terrible by what Churchill called 'the lights of perverted science', they nevertheless clung on to familiar things which reminded them of home. A particular tonic was visits to the front from film stars and popular musicians.

Despite getting into hot water with the suggestive lyrics of his 1937 song 'With My Little Stick Of Blackpool Rock', George Formby's cheeky-chappie demeanour made him hugely popular, especially with the troops of the British Expeditionary Force (BEF) shivering in the dugouts in France during the 'phoney war' of the winter of 1939–40.

Turned down by the army for having flat feet when he tried to enlist in 1939, Formby joined the Home Guard instead. He was the first big star to visit the BEF in France in 1940, and enjoyed a tremendous welcome from the troops. The newsreel recorded at the front in March and showing Formby entertaining troops there has become legendary. His performance of 'Imagine Me

The 1941 British documentary film Target for Tonight *about the crew of a Wellington bomber won an honorary Academy Award in 1942 and 'Best Documentary' by the National Board of Review in 1941.*

in the Maginot Line', while he played his faithful ukulele, displayed an empathy with the men which they never forgot.

> Hitler can't kid us a lot,
> His secret weapon's Tommy Rot,
> You ought to see what the sergeant's got!
> Down in the Maginot Line.

On 19 August 1943 George was back with the troops again, this time with the Entertainments National Service Association in North Africa. He also toured the battle fronts of Malta, Sicily, Gibraltar and Italy and in less than eight weeks had entertained a quarter of a million men.

Formby was in Normandy less than a week after D-Day. His visit made the front page of the *Daily Mail*, whose headline suggested that now George Formby was on hand to support Montgomery, the war was as good as won.

The Crazy Gang made their first appearance at the London Palladium in 1931. They made the most unlikely troupe of acts ever assembled on the stage for a single show. Comprising a pair of slapstick artists, an acrobatic high-wire act and a couple of comics who laced their jokes with schmaltzy songs, they seemed unlikely to hit the big time. But they did, and how. The Crazy Gang topped the bill for over thirty years, making their final appearances at the Victoria Palace Theatre in 1962.

Individually they were well-established acts before they came together in 1931 and each of their names headlined variety bills. Jimmy Nervo and Teddy Knox combined the agility of a high-wire act with an hilarious slow-motion wrestling performance and a spoof ballet display. Ten years older than the rest of the 'Crazies', Charlie Naughton and Jimmy Gold, a pair of slapstick comics famous for decades on the London pantomime scene, harmonised perfectly with Nervo and Knox. Charlie Naughton's mastery of the art of double-talk being something audiences never forgot.

The Crazy Gang of Bud Flanagan, Chesney Allen, Jimmy Nervo, Teddy Knox, Charlie Naughton and Jimmy Gold were a hit on the wireless and played to packed theatre audiences during the darkest days of the Second World War.

A mere old Penny purchased Cinegram No. 78 which was all about Alexander Korda's latest movie, Q Planes (Clouds Over Europe in the United States). *Starring Ralph Richardson, Laurence Olivier and Valerie Hobson, this action-packed spy film sees a mysterious foreign ship beaming a powerful ray at top-secret prototype aircraft and their crews to discover their secrets.*

In 1926, while touring with Florrie Forde, the famous Australian-born singer, best known for her rendition of 'Down At the Old Bull and Bush', comic Bud Flanagan met and teamed up with fellow funny man Chesney Allen. Though the pair's first inclination was to throw their combined talents into setting up a bookmakers, Flanagan and Allen's performances went down so well they were swiftly booked by Val Parnell for a debut at the Holborn Empire in 1929.

Although the Crazy Gang appeared to consist of pairs of variety acts who had each come together due to their obvious synergies, there was one 'lone wolf' in the troupe – juggler turned comic (often described by fellow comics as the funniest man in the world) – 'Monsewer' Eddie Gray.

Following their London Palladium debut the Crazy Gang found a regular home and began a popular residency, 'Crazy Week', at the Victoria Palace Theatre. They also made several films, starting with *O-Kay For Sound* in 1937, but are probably best remembered for their war-time film *Gasbags* in 1940. From the moment this movie began, with a senior officer inspecting the disposition and readiness of a local balloon barrage, only to discover that the one controlled by the Crazy Gang was being used to advertise the team's fish and chips businesses and was connected to the ground by a cable from which a series of pennants streamed promoting the various dishes on offer, audiences knew what they were in for.

'Hitler's Crazy Gang' may have been an apt epithet for the hard-line Nazis who surrounded Hitler and put his radical theories in to practice. It was no joke, however, to those in occupied Europe, especially Jews.

Ever popular, like George Formby the Crazy Gang took their turn to entertain the troops during wartime, appearing in Normandy only a few weeks after D-Day.

With so many people, men and women, serving in the regular or auxiliary forces, both at home and abroad, it was clear that something better than simply relying on the naturally biased services of theatricals like Val Parnell and Lew Grade to select and arrange variety bookings had to be organised. So in 1939 the Entertainments National Service Association (ENSA) was established.

One of the founders of ENSA was Basil Dean, the English actor, writer and producer/director of both theatrical and cinema productions who founded Associated Talking Pictures, which later became Ealing Studios and who worked closely with stars such as Gracie Fields and George Formby. Basil had all the necessary clout to run the government-sponsored body responsible for bringing live performances to the armed services.

The other prime mover behind ENSA was Leslie Henson, an English comedian, actor, and like Dean, a successful producer for films and theatre, and a film director. Born in London's Notting Hill Gate, Henson had made a name for himself as far back

Written by Ulster songwriter Jimmy Kennedy, while he was a Captain in the British Expeditionary Force during the early stages of the Second World War, We're Going to Hang out the Washing on the Siegfried Line *became a morale-booster during the Battle of France.*

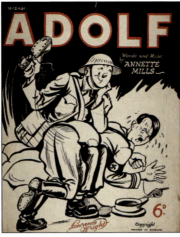

Published in 1939 and made famous by comedian Arthur Askey, Adolf *contained inspiring lyrics like, 'Adolf, you toddle off, and all your Nazis too! Or you may get something to remind you of the old red, white and blue!'*

I'm Sending You the Siegfried Line (To Hang Your Washing On) *was a popular 1939 composition, which, as things turned out, was a proposition which would take much longer to achieve than most Britons thought at this stage of the war.*

Good Night (got your torchlight?) *was the perfect accompaniment to the Blitz and published in 1941, by which time the blackout and regular night bombing had entered its second year.*

'The badge from your coat will be close to my heart. It will always remind me of you,' wrote Annette Mills, of string puppet 'Muffin the Mule' fame, and Horatio Nicholls (the nom de plume used by songwriter Lawrence Wright) in 1940 after allegedly seeing a woman who had been dancing with an officer at a club in Blackpool take a badge from his coat as a souvenir.

We're Gonna Have To Slap, The Dirty Little Jap, and Uncle Sam's the Guy who can do it *was first performed by Carson Miller a mere matter of days following Japan's surprise attack on Pearl Harbor. America's indignity and disgust is evident in lyrics such as: 'We'll skin the streak of yellow from this sneaky little fellow and he'll think a cyclone hit him when he's thru it. We'll take the double crosser to the old woodshed, we'll start on his bottom and go to his head, when we get thru with him he'll wish that he was dead.'*

as the Edwardian era and starred in silent films and musical comedies to huge public acclaim – he was famous for his bulging eyes, malleable face and raspy voice.

ENSA stars included Arthur Askey, Gracie Fields, Vera Lynn, George Formby, Tommy Cooper and Joyce Grenfell. In 1945 Sir Laurence Olivier and Sir Ralph Richardson were both made honorary lieutenants in the British Army and joined ENSA to embark on a six-week tour of Europe performing plays by William Shakespeare.

This was pretty apt because Olivier was fresh from the success of his 1944 British film adaptation of William Shakespeare's *Henry V*. With its moving score by none other than 'The' William Walton, the film was originally 'dedicated to the 'Commandos and Airborne Troops of Great Britain, the spirit of whose ancestors it has been humbly attempted to recapture.' *Henry V* won Olivier an Academy Honorary Award for an 'outstanding achievement as actor, producer and director in bringing Henry V to the screen'.

The first ENSA concert took place on 10 September 1939 in Surrey, while the last performance the organisation produced was in India on 18 August 1946. Even though there is no doubt that it lured the best performers, and paid them handsomely too, ENSA was not without its critics and sometimes deserved its soubriquet, 'Every Night Something Awful'.

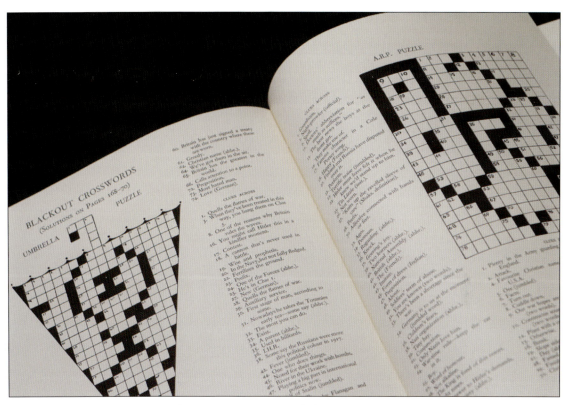

Full of innocent games – there was even one entitled 'Hitler's favourite game' which involved making a swastika out of playing cards! – at this stage of the war Blackout Puzzles *and* ARP Crosswords *seemed to promise shortlived interludes before normal service was resumed and peace came. Little did they know.*

Like the Brighter Blackout Book, 101 Things to do in War Time *(1940) was a noble attempt to offer alternatives to the boredom of sitting in the gloom of a blacked-out sitting room. Ideas ranged from knitting balaclava helmets for the navy to indoor croquet games!*

Although it's beyond the scope of this book, which is, of course, designed as a guide to the variety of wartime ephemera available to collectors and this narrative simply to provide background to the society and cultural influences that produced each piece, no mention of radio during the Second World War would be complete without mention of Tommy Handley.

It's That Man Again, more commonly known as *ITMA*, was a programme that ran from 1939 to 1949. The title refers to a contemporary expression concerning the ever more frequent news stories about Hitler in the lead-up to the Second World War, and specifically a headline in the *Daily Express* written by Herbert 'Bert' Gun, who coined the phrase. The acronym ITMA was adopted by Tommy Handley, a popular comedian who had served with a kite-balloon section of the Royal Naval Air Service during the First World War and went on to work in variety after the end of hostilities. Handley became a regular broadcaster on radio, and wrote many scripts himself. He later starred in the *ITMA* film in 1942 and in *Time Flies* in 1944. Such was the pressure of *ITMA* that the regular scripts required for this enormously popular radio show were written by the prolific Ted Kavanagh.

CHAPTER 4

Children

'Boy, 12, was youngest British soldier in First World War' read the shocking headline of an article by Julie Henry published in the *Daily Telegraph* newspaper on 31 October 2009. 'The child, said to be too short to see over the edge of a trench, was recalled by another under-age soldier, George Maher, who was only 13 when he was sent to the Somme during the First Wold War,' she wrote. Ms Henry went on to explain that when Mr Maher's real age was discovered – he had told a recruiting officer that he was 18 to enable him to join the 2nd King's Own Royal Lancaster Regiment in 1917 – he was hauled before an unsympathetic officer.

Mr Maher, who died aged 96 in 1999, had originally told his story to historian Richard Van Emden for his book *Veterans: The Last Survivors Of The Great War*. 'I was locked up on a train under guard, one of five under-age boys caught serving on

The Aeroplane *was founded in 1911 and is still going strong. Back in 1940 for only 2s the magazine's readers, many of them 'air minded' youngsters, could purchase a series of 'Aircraft Identification' supplements. This is the cover from the first in an extensive series published throughout the war years.*

the front being sent back to England,' he explained to the author adding, 'The youngest was 12 years old. A little nuggety bloke he was, too. We joked that the other soldiers would have had to have lifted him up to see over the trenches.'

Such was the fervour to join Kitchener's rapidly expanding army the moment war was declared in August 1914, a rush exacerbated by the widespread belief that it would be over by Christmas, that many red-blooded patriots feared they'd be left out of the fighting. Consequently, despite pretty clear regulations which stipulated that you had to be 18 to join the army and at least 19 before you could serve abroad, dozens of youngsters flocked to the colours in the hope that they might slip through the screening net and join up. A startling number of boys got away with lying about their age, recruiting officers were reluctant to quench the patriotic desire to do what was right for 'King and Country' and often allowed individuals to sign the enlistment form without requiring sight of birth certificates, and many officers, tasked with filling the ranks as quickly as possible, were perfectly happy to accept a recruit's word and did not demand to see written proof of age.

Another book by Richard van Emden, *Boy Soldiers of the Great War*, records that eighty-six boy soldiers aged 17 or under were killed on 25 September 1915, the first day of the Battle of Loos. This date is just one of countless days of bloody engagement between 1914 and 1918.

This page shows a classic three-view recognition silhouette of the RAF's Boulton Paul Defiant 1 turret fighter. Although the typed specification panel says that the Defiant gave a good account of itself over Dunkirk, in reality it proved inadequate against Luftwaffe *fighters and was quickly withdrawn from front-line duties.*

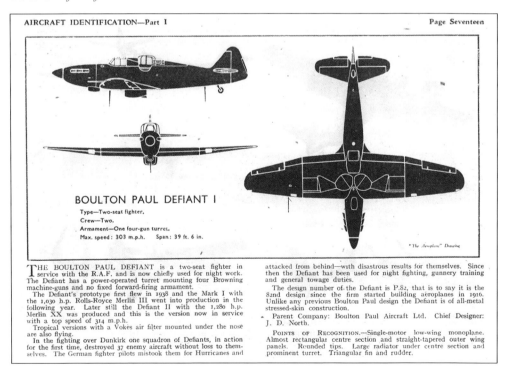

Other than the chance that they might end up in the trenches, many children suffered in another significant way. The First World War saw the biggest loss of fathers in modern British history – half a million youngsters lost their dads.

Children who went to France were forced to grow up fast but so were those who stayed at home. Donald Overall told the BBC News Channel that when still at a tender age his mother told him his father was dead and that he would now have to be the man of the house. 'I thought "mum, I'm only five years old",' Mr Overall recalled, 'But I had to stand up and be counted – and I did.'

It should also be remembered that those children whose fathers returned apparently fit and unharmed often discovered that their parent had changed in a frightening way, bearing the 'invisible' scars of shell-shock. Furthermore, adolescents were confronted by legions of grown-up men who had returned with very visible scars. Just how young imaginations dealt with being confronted by grown-ups with missing limbs or the sight of men who had lost both their legs dragging themselves along on primitive wooden platforms fitted with bicycle wheels or, if they were more affluent, seated in proper wheelchairs. Whether or not they had experienced this, the youngsters of this period grew up fast.

The minimum age for joining the British Army at the outbreak of the Second World War was still 18. After the horrors of the Great War, the 'war to end all wars', which left hardly a family in Britain unaffected, there was, not surprisingly, rather less of a clamour to join the ranks at the outbreak of another European conflict. Conscription rather than patriotism 'encouraged' most young men to take up arms.

But, like the generation before them, the children of 1939 were also forced to grow up fast. Evacuation was one of the literally divisive ways whereby youngsters were forced to come to terms with the realities of this new conflict.

In 1938, as Lord Privy Seal, in Neville Chamberlain's Cabinet, John Anderson, 1st Viscount Waverley, was put in charge of air-raid preparations. One of the things initiated was the development of a kind of air-raid shelter made of

'Boys Just the Book You've Been Looking For', the Aeroplane Instructional Drawing Book.

During the late 1930s British children enjoyed a steady diet of American science excitement on the wireless and during Saturday morning cinema. Their cousins across the Atlantic also got to see monthly magazines such as the best in the field Amazing Stories. *This edition dates from July 1940. Robert Fuqua's dramatic illustration on the cover depicts a scene from A.R. Steber's* When the Gods Make War.

prefabricated pieces which could be assembled in a garden. Bearing his name, he will forever be remembered for this life-saving contraption. It is less well known, however, that he was also responsible for drawing up preparations for evacuating civilians from areas at high risk of bombing. It should also be remembered that it wasn't just fear of bombs dropping from enemy aircraft that terrified people but also the thought that poison gas might also be similarly unleashed from the skies.

Planned for implementation by the Ministry of Health, the Government Evacuation Scheme was developed during the 'Munich Crisis' in the summer of 1938. The country was divided into zones, classified as 'evacuation', 'neutral' or 'reception', with priority evacuees being moved from the major urban centres and billeted on the available private housing in more rural areas.

Anderson's 'Operation Pied Piper,' which began on 1 September 1939, relocated more than 3.5 million people, of which about 800,000 were children. Further waves of official evacuation and re-evacuation occurred from the south and east coast in June 1940, when a seaborne invasion was expected, and from affected cities after the Blitz began in September 1940. The plan was put into action in September 1939. However, many returned home after a few weeks. Others stayed in the countryside for the rest of the war.

It is often forgotten that following the 1940 invasion scare and the night Blitz there were other evacuations. Living in Shepherd's Bush, West London, my maternal grandmother refused to let her children be evacuated unaccompanied in 1939. My mother, the eldest of three sisters stayed with her mother and siblings throughout the Blitz and beyond. However, after the first 'doodlebug', the infamous V1 pilotless flying bomb, struck London on 13 June 1944, only a week after D-Day, a further evacuation was implemented and the government acquiesced, allowed mothers to accompany evacuated children this time.

After assembling with her own mother and sisters, and her aunt and cousin, my mother and her familial group of evacuees got on a bus to London's King's Cross railway station where they boarded a train for Lancashire.

It was now time for the two families to assemble in another school hall, this time in Oldham, where the children were given cakes and soft drinks and there was tea and biscuits for mothers. Because my mother's group comprised an adult and three children, each less than 10 years of age, a potential handful, they were picked last. My mother recalls that her aunt and cousin were snapped up and went to a very nice home. Mother tells me that her group was eventually adopted by 'an old witch', apparently devoid of any redeeming

In contrast to the pulp fiction enjoyed by American youth, British boys had to make do with more wholesome fare such as Boy's Own Paper. *The cover depicts a mountain hiker – 'Have you ever thought of a mountain holiday?' Also inside, readers discovered that twins John and Melvin Roylance 'collected £700 all in aid of the Wings for Victory appeal!' Who needs ray guns?*

features. Indeed, I was told that all the money sent to his wife from my grandfather, a Bofors gunner serving with the Royal Artillery in Burma, was appropriated by the home owner. The only respite from a very strained environment came when one of the local men, who had been present at the reception hall when my mother's family arrived in Oldham, invited them to his nearby bungalow at weekends. According to my mother he, his wife and young son were 'a lovely family' and provided an oasis of warmth.

After six weeks my grandmother had had enough and scooping up her three daughters proceeded to return to London – just in time to experience the V2 ballistic rocket, a much deadlier threat which they endured in favour of being unwelcome guests in a stranger's home hundreds of miles away.

BOO-BOO the Barrage Balloon, *published by Raphael Tuck, London, 1943, one of the many illustrated books for children produced during the Second World War despite paper rationing. This is now a very rare book, with only a few being known to survive in private collections.*

Of course, as is the experience of the front-line soldier, fighter pilot or sailor, most of the time children experienced boredom rather than the terror of an enemy trying to kill them. Soldiers traditionally whiled away their free-time by fashioning so-called 'trench art' from bits and pieces of discarded military equipment, pilots retired to a local pub or the mess after the day's sorties have finished and sailors spent hours tattooing each other. Youngsters amused themselves by reading comics, playing games with their friends or by absorbing themselves in a solitary pursuit involving arranging serried ranks of lead soldiers or fashioning a model from scratch from either balsa, lime or box wood.

In a time before technology supplied 'fun' on tap – no television, no transportable recorded music, no computer games, no mobile phones (and not very many residential static ones either), no smart phones and apps – youngsters had to devise their entertainment for themselves. They did so with vigour and because a century or so ago children spent much of their time playing outside with very real friends, not virtual ones delivered via social media platforms, they were often healthier and socially more adept than their twenty-first-century counterparts.

One of the reasons children were expected to entertain themselves was because in the average home there simply was insufficient disposable income to buy toys.

Nevertheless, despite this, youngsters enjoyed themselves and because there was little or no traffic, the streets and roads were safe to play in.

These urban playing fields became the home for games of marbles. Boys were proud of their marble collections and would swap among themselves to build a collection of the size and colour variety they wanted.

Girls used sticks to beat wooden hoops along the pavement – the boys tended to prefer iron ones, which they ran alongside using a kind of large hook to keep the hoops going.

By their very nature paving slaps were found to be very useful for playing hopscotch and could easily be marked out with chalk. Girls generally favoured hopscotch and devised numerous variations of this innocent game which kept them entertained for hours.

About 2in long and about 1½in in diameter, wooden whipping tops fitted with metal pegs at the base and with grooved sides around which a length of string about two feet in length was wound, would be thrown onto pavements and with a brisk jerk the top was sent spinning on its peg. The winner was the boy or girl who kept a top spinning for the longest.

When this stirring edition of the weekly War Thriller *comic was published on 18 May 1940 the evacuation of the BEF from France was still a week from beginning and British schoolboys were still convinced that the Anglo-French armies would stand firm.*

Other popular outside activities at the turn of the last century included football, cricket and . . . skipping! Wealthier children could expect to play with superior quality skipping ropes containing ball bearing races in their turned wooden handles which prevented the rope from twisting out of shape as it swung round. Children playing in the streets outside tenements or in the new housing estates built to home factory workers made do with simple lengths of rope.

Playing 'Diabolo', not to be confused with the contemporary video game, was another enormously popular childhood pastime. A real product of the Industrial Revolution because the first examples employed discarded cotton reels from the mills, this activity involved keeping a wooden cylinder spinning by manipulating it on a length of cord tied to two sticks, each of which was held in the player's hands. The advent of early plastic moulding following the First World War saw this temporary expedient replaced with a synthetic piece, resembling two inverted egg cups joined at the base, the inward curve guiding the cord which propelled the whole contraption.

Games were also a feature of children's parties. Blow football, pinning the tail on the donkey, snakes and ladders, and quoits and blow football proved popular distractions before cake and jelly. Although Mrs Beeton does not list 'picnic', 'party' or 'children' in her index she does mention lemonade – the cloudy type of course!

By the end of the First World War education was only compulsory for children up to the age of 14 and was only raised to 15 in 1944 with the passing of the 1944 Education Act. The children of wealthier parents had the option of further education of course and a system of secondary education integrating higher grade elementary schools had been introduced in 1902. The 1917 Secondary Schools Examination Council was established to administer the new School Certificate and Higher School Certificate. Prior to the Second World War less than 2 per cent of 18-year-olds went to university, there being around 50,000 students in some 30 universities or university colleges in Britain in 1939, and the majority of these were male with women constituting less than a quarter of the university student population.

For most ordinary school children in the inner cities during wartime, about the only dramatic change in what many considered the drudgery of lessons was frequent air-raid drills and of course, on occasions, the real thing when youngsters quickly fled to the shelter in the face of enemy bombs.

It wasn't just bombs dropped from the air which threatened youngsters. In December 1914 the German high seas fleet managed to get near enough to the northeast coast of England to shell coastal towns there, spending nearly an hour raining 1,150 shells on Hartlepool alone and leaving 102 people dead including 9 soldiers, 7 sailors and 15 children. Britons were outraged when further casualties were inflicted on Scarborough and, picturing damage from German naval artillery to a civilian house, a popular British recruiting poster of the time sported the headline: 'No 2 Wykeham

Incorporating the Bulletin of the National Association of Spotters' Clubs, Aeroplane Spotter *was published on alternate Thursdays, 'For The Alert'. It promised to equip 'air-minded' schoolboys with everything they needed to keep up to date with developments in aeronautics.*

Street, Scarborough . . . four people were killed in this house including the wife . . . and two children, the youngest aged 5'.

Although the first air raid on Britain took place on 21 December 1914 when a German aeroplane dropped a few puny bombs on Dover, it was not until January 1915 when two German Imperial Navy Zeppelin airships, the L3 and L4, heading for industrial buildings on Humberside made landfall over the East Anglian coast, bombing as they went, that the full potential of aerial warfare dawned on the British.

Zeppelin L4 dropped the first bomb to fall on British soil at Sheringham, on the north Norfolk coast. Fortunately, it did not explode. However, bombs dropped at Kings Lynn did detonate and 14-year-old Percy Goate became the first British child to die as a result of enemy action in Britain.

Further Zeppelin raids struck inevitable terror throughout the war. Towards the end of the conflict the capability of German fixed wing aircraft had improved considerably and in June 1917 in the first daylight raid by Gotha bombers 162 civilians were killed in London. Among them were eighteen schoolchildren slaughtered when a bomb fell on their primary school in Poplar.

During both world wars children did their bit to support the war effort, often being roped in as emotional blackmail to encourage people to contribute to war bond drives and keep the war economy from flagging. During the Great War schoolchildren were encourage to organise 'flag days', selling patriotic paper emblems which raised money for funding the war effort. In the Second World War many schools organised 'Spitfire funds', raising money towards a target published on a kind of price list – a Spitfire or Hurricane cost £5,000, with £20,000 for a twin-engined aircraft and £40,000 for a four-engined bomber. Considering that a single torpedo allegedly cost more than £10,000 at the time, the price of a Spitfire represented a real bargain.

Newspapers published weekly running totals and printed lists of donors and their specific contributions, such as 'My week's pocket money – Fred Smith aged 7', 'My first week's old age pension – 10 shillings towards our Spitfire', etc. More than 6,000 school savings groups were started in 1940.

Toys were a treat, especially for working class kids who might only expect such delights for birthdays or at Christmas. Because many toy factories, such as Lines Brothers, their Tri-ang factory at Merton producing more than 1,000,000 Sten Guns during the Second World War, were engaged in war work there was a shortage of new toys anyway. Those parents who could afford them soon discovered that what supplies of toys, such as FROG's 'Interceptors' and 'Penguins', respectively flying and non-flying model aircraft, pre-war products of Tri-ang's factories, or Meccano sets, Hornby railways and Dinky Toys made in the late Frank Hornby's (he died in 1936) Binns Road factory in Liverpool, were available were

Famous for their maps and atlases, London's George Philip & Son also produced this rather ingenious die-cut calculator which helped plane spotters dial up the armament and performance figures of different modern war planes.

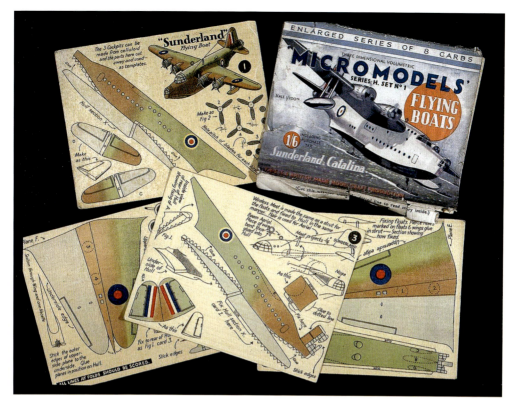

For only 1s 6d enthusiastic youngsters could purchase 'Flying Boats', one of Geoffrey Heighway's new Micromodel card kits which were introduced in 1940. This set included delightful replicas of both the Sunderland and Catalina.

soon in short supply. By 1910 about 200,000 hollow-cast lead toy soldiers were leaving William Britain's north London factory each week and his success encouraged other British firms, such as Johillco and Crescent, to participate in this burgeoning market. By 1914 it is estimated that W. Britain was manufacturing something in the order of 15,000,000 figures a year, most of which went to the home market. Britain's best customer was W.H. Gamage, proprietor of the People's Emporium in Holborn.

By 1941 Britain had converted their manufacturing tools to help the war effort. Rival Johillco's Islington factory was unable to take advantage of the opportunity to fill, or at least part fill, the void caused by Britain's absence from the market because it had been destroyed in the Blitz and didn't reopen until 1946. Interestingly, had Britain continued with the pre-war level of toy production the same quantity of military playthings, toy soldiers and the like would not have been produced that had been twenty years before. After the First World War the almost universal clamour for peace had made such items much less popular and encouraged the manufacturer to explore new avenues. Britain's famous 'Home Farm' set, agricultural accessories and zoo animals being the result of this shift in emphasis.

The lack of new toys and the relative expense of the limited supply remaining in toy shops encouraged children to swap their old toys at 'toy exchanges' or simply construct their own novelties from paper or card.

Of course a lot of the available playthings, again made of paper or card, had a wartime theme. Pop-out card models had been popular since the Boer War and as soon as aircraft, tanks and submarines took the stage during the First World War numerous publishers produced such card kits. However, in 1940 something really quite special arrived on the paper model market when Geoffrey Heighway introduced Micromodel. Miniaturising the established concept of the printed paper model, he enabled ships, great building or even a set of locomotives to be printed on an assortment of small paper sheets which all wrapped up into a compact package the size of a postcard. Enormously popular, these delightful creations were also ideal for delivery via the post. Priced at just 1s per packet, the first of Heighway's printed card Micromodel sets was 'The Romance of Sail', a collection of six miniature sailing ships. This set was followed by further wartime issues which included 'Weapons of War', 'Tanks', 'Allied Fighter Planes' and 'Flying Boats'.

Young boys devoured the *ABC of Aeroplane Spotting*, played card games with pictures of soldiers and sailors on them or perhaps threw a dart at a board with a picture of Hitler where the bullseye would normally be located!

In 1919 Harry Gibson formed H.P. Gibson & Sons Limited and traded successfully until his premises in London were completely destroyed during the Blitz. By this time, however, Gibson's company had launched a number of successful board games, each with military themes, which had proved popular with British children during both world wars.

Three games in particular, 'Aviation', 'Dover Patrol' and 'L'Attaque', which was originally designed by a French woman, Mademoiselle Hermance Edan, in 1908, plus a more complicated incorporation of all three, a game called 'Tri-Tactics', kept youngsters as engaged as PC games like 'Call of Duty' do today.

When the blackout was imposed on London and other major cities across Britain from 1 September 1939, apart from making it more difficult for enemy bombers to navigate after they had crossed the nation's coast, it also encouraged entire families to stay indoors after sunset.

It was anyway pretty dangerous to go outside. Street lights had been switched off at the mains, vehicle headlights were masked to show only a crack of light, and stations were lit by candles, an enforced darkness Britain endured until 23 April 1945. A limited blackout had been introduced in 1915, but then the lights were only dimmed rather than extinguished all together and only when a Zeppelin was known to be en route. The Germans had held their first blackout exercise in Berlin in March 1935, an event comprehensively reported in the British press. So, by 1939, the British authorities left nothing to chance. It's difficult for us to imagine today how much this transformed everyday life, but the impact of darkened streets could be overwhelming. Little wonder then, that with only partially illuminated automobiles driving along unlit roads, by the end of the first month of war there had been 1,130 road deaths attributed to the blackout.

The *The Black-out Book*, a publication that went some way to alleviating the boredom of the enforced darkness caused by wartime, featured a quotation by G.K. Chesterton, well-known author of the *Father Brown* detective books.

Of all modern notions, the worst is this: that domesticity is dull. Inside the home, they say, is dead decorum and routine; outside is adventure and variety. But the truth is that home is the only place of liberty, the only spot on earth where a man can alter arrangements suddenly, make an experiment or indulge a whim.

With over 500 games, puzzles, jokes, literary snippets and features such as 'A thought for the petrol-rationed motorist', 'What happened to the shilling?' and 'What to do when sleep won't come', *The Black-out Book* provided a useful distraction during the Blitz.

Author Sydney Box was a writer and film producer and, from 1946, the managing director of Gainsborough Pictures. Responsible for such classics as *The Seventh Veil* (1945, which won him a best screenplay Oscar), *Holiday Camp* (1947) and *Quartet* (1948), he also produced over 100 propaganda shorts for the government and the armed services during the Second World War. Most of his screenplays were written in collaboration with his wife, Muriel, and their collaborative work was published under the pseudonym 'Evelyn August'.

Comics, a perennial favourite with children since Edwardian times, were also a faithful companion for the young in wartime. Before the arrival of what we now know as comics, so-called 'Penny Dreadfuls' flourished from the 1830s onwards. Primarily horror stories, they were filled with vampires, werewolves, pirates and tales of daring highwaymen There were also more wholesome publications aimed at youngsters including the *Boys' Own Magazine*, *Every Boy's Magazine* and *Young England* and, from 1866, *Chatterbox*. In 1879, when the British Army suffered a crushing defeat at the hands of the Zulu at Isandlwana, the *Boys' Own Paper* first appeared. This was followed in 1892 by Cassell & Company's story paper *Chums*, an equally famous publication which sustained youngsters prior to the First World War.

Comic Cuts and *Illustrated Chips*, progenitors of the classic format of sequential comic strips which we take for granted today, came on to the British market just before the turn the twentieth century, but it wasn't until

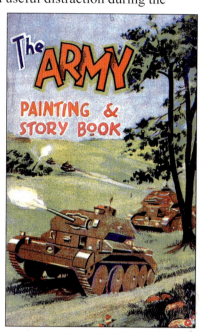

British tanks and British aircraft reign supreme in both these 'Painting and Story Books'. The reality, as the youngsters learned when they grew up after the war, was that other than machines like the Spitfire and Lancaster most British weapons were distinctly inferior to those of the enemy.

the late 1930s that perennials such as the *Dandy* (December 1937) and *Beano* (30 July 1938) established the format we take for granted today. On the other side of the Atlantic kids comics developed in a uniquely different way with the arrival of *Action Comics #1* a month before the *Beano* first appeared in Britain. Featuring the first appearance of Superman, *Action Comics #1* entered the record books in 2011 when this first edition sold at auction for a record $2 million, becoming the most valuable comic book of all time.

Young people in Britain were also served by authors who catered just for them. Young girls enjoyed Carolyn Keene's famous Nancy Drew stories, which first appeared in 1930, as well as the Judy Bolton mystery stories series, which were first published in 1932 and kept female readers enthralled until 1967.

Another hugely successful female author, but this time one who catered mainly for boys having penned *Just William*, the first of a huge series of novels about school boy William Brown in 1922, was Richmal Crompton. A suffragette, she had initially trained as a schoolmistress, teaching classics, but after been struck with polio, she took up writing full-time instead. Crompton penned thirty-eight 'William' books all together; her last, *William the Lawless*, was published posthumously in 1970.

Collectors of wartime ephemera, however, are most keen on the books she wrote at the time of the Munich Crisis, starting with *William the Dictator* in 1938, and continuing with *William and Air Raid Precautions* (1939), *William and the Evacuees* (1940), *William Does His Bit* (1941) and *William Carries On* (1942). Early editions of any of these hugely popular works (Crompton sold more than 12 million copies of her books in the United Kingdom alone) in good condition (no 'foxing' – see the Chapter 7) and complete with their illustrated dust-wraps now command increasingly high prices.

In *William and Air Raid Precautions*, one of my favourites, our eponymous hero gets caught up in the zeitgeist of the times and decides to set up his own civil defence post: 'I've thought of lots of games you could play with gas masks, but no one'll let me try. They keep mine locked up. Lot of good it'll be in a war locked up where I can't get at it. Huh!' Having decided to form an ARP Junior Branch, William and his friends Ginger, Henry and Douglas set about creating a sign for their new post which Douglas fashioned from cardboard torn from the box in which his mother kept her best hat and on which, in blacking 'borrowed' from the kitchen, was scrawled the legend:

> Air Rade Precorshun
> Junier Branch
> Entrance Fre.

Great stuff. Readers had more than 250 pages to enjoy, many of which were richly illustrated by Thomas Henry who had been drawing Crompton's William since 1919 when he first appeared in magazine serialisation. Though he worked with her for forty-three years, Henry allegedly only met Crompton once, at a book festival luncheon in Nottingham!

Boys and girls alike enjoyed Enid Blyton's Famous Five series in equal measure, the first book, *Five on a Treasure Island*, first appearing in 1942.

When they weren't reading or involved in family games, children, like their parents, spent hours listening to the radio. Princess Elizabeth, The Queen made her first public speech on 13 October 1940, a radio address to the children of the Commonwealth.

> In wishing you all 'good evening' I feel that I am speaking to friends and companions who have shared with my sister and myself many a happy Children's Hour.
>
> Thousands of you in this country have had to leave your homes and be separated from your fathers and mothers. My sister Margaret Rose and I feel so much for you as we know from experience what it means to be away from those we love most of all.

After addressing children from each country within the Commonwealth and expressing her and her sister's desire to visit such far-off lands as soon as peace would allow, she finished her speech by saying:

> Before I finish I can truthfully say to you all that we children at home are full of cheerfulness and courage. We are trying to do all we can to help our gallant sailors, soldiers and airmen, and we are trying, too, to bear our own share of the danger and sadness of war.
>
> We know, every one of us, that in the end all will be well; for God will care for us and give us victory and peace. And when peace comes, remember it will be for us, the children of today, to make the world of tomorrow a better and happier place.
>
> My sister is by my side and we are both going to say goodnight to you.
>
> Come on, Margaret.
> Goodnight, children.
> Goodnight, and good luck to you all.

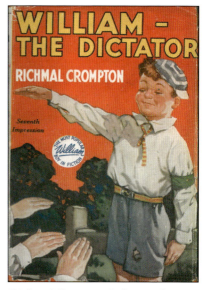

Richmal Crompton's famous Just William *series of thirty-nine books chronicle the adventures of the mischievous schoolboy William Brown. Published between 1921 and 1970, though the 11-year-old protagonist never gets any older, each William book reflects the time in which it was written. First published in 1938,* William the Dictator *contains ten stories each designed to show autocracy in a bad light. It is now one of the rarest William books.*

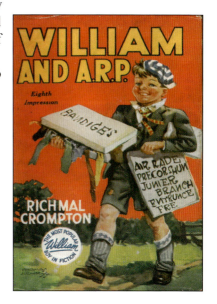

William and Air Raid Precautions *dates from 1939. Wartime provided Richmal Crompton with much inspiration and in this book and* William and the Evacuees, *which followed in 1940, it provided the mischievous schoolboy with a vivid backdrop.*

Between the 1920s and the outbreak of the Second World War, the BBC broadcast two distinct nationwide radio services: the BBC National Programme and the BBC Regional Programme. Together with a service specific to London, the Regional Programme included programming originating in six regions. However, on 1 September 1939, the BBC merged these two programmes into one national service from London. One of the reasons they said they did this was to prevent enemy aircraft from triangulating the locations of the different transmitters and using them as navigational beacons to aid targeting. This new service was named the Home Service, which was also the internal designation at the BBC for domestic radio broadcasting to keep it distinct from the fledgling Television Service and Overseas Service departments.

Since 1922 the BBC had broadcast *Children's Hour*, transmitted daily from 5p.m. to 6p.m., the time of day during the week when children could be expected to be home from school. Aimed at an audience aged about 5 to 15 years, it was imbued with the somewhat puritanical values of Lord Reith who joined the British Broadcasting Company Ltd after the First World war and by the late 1930s had risen to the lofty position of Director-General of the British Broadcasting Corporation which had been created under a Royal Charter.

Children's Hour was hugely popular, and presenters, such as Derek McCulloch, as 'Uncle Mac' of *Children's Favourites* and *Children's Hour* fame, became major celebrities. McCulloch was also the head of children's broadcasting for the BBC from 1933 until 1951. Ending with the sign-off line, 'Goodnight children, everywhere', McCulloch's children's programmes attracted a wartime audience of more than 4 million children.

As an escape from the hardships and suffering of the American depression following the Wall Street Crash of 1929 newspapers in the United States offered their readers a variety of illustrated new strips. Buck Rogers first appeared in 1929, with Dick Tracy following in 1931, Flash Gordon in 1933, Li'l Abner in 1934 and Prince Valiant in 1937. These features became so popular that commentators declared that many American citizens chose their daily newspaper based on the comic strip within it.

It wasn't long before these fictional characters developed a huge fan base and a ready market for merchandisers, ranging from cereal premiums to books and magazines dedicated entirely to a particular character.

In 1932, the Buck Rogers' radio programme, notable as the first science-fiction show on radio, relating the story of hero Buck who finds himself in the twenty-fifth century but fortunately accompanied by the beautiful and strong-willed Wilma Deering and the brilliant scientist-inventor Dr Huer, hit the airwaves. It was broadcast four times a week for fifteen years, from 1932 to 1947.

Flash Gordon, a science-fiction adventure comic strip originally drawn by Alex Raymond in 1934, soon migrated to radio where the adventures of Flash, Dale Arden and Dr Hans Zarkov (sounds familiar?) really took flight. Stories took the three of them to the planet Mongo, home of Emperor Ming, the evil ruler of the planet.

During this time American and British children, but mostly boys I guess, devoured similar science-fiction stories in a hugely popular American publication, *Amazing*

Stories, which was launched in April 1926 by Hugo Gernsback's Experimenter Publishing. It was the first magazine devoted solely to science fiction.

In 1935 Dick Tracy had moved from comic cuts to the radio, when Mutual produced the show for North America's New England region until in 1937 NBC took the show, and broadcast it across the United States until 1948.

Dick Barton Special Agent was the BBC's answer to Dick Tracy, but it arrived too late to entertain British youngsters who had to be content with *Children's Hour* instead. Broadcast on the BBC Light Programme from 1946 to 1951, Dick Barton was the BBC's first daily serial, airing at 6.45 each weekday evening. It featured ex-Commando Captain Richard Barton (Noel Johnson, later Duncan Carse and Gordon Davies), who, with his mates Jock Anderson (Alex McCrindle) and Snowy White (John Mann), solved all sorts of crimes, escaped from dangerous situations and saved the nation from disaster time and again. At its peak it had an audience of 15 million.

While British children didn't perhaps share the excitement of listening to their comic-book heroes on the wireless, they could, at least, revel in American pulp fiction on screen, enjoying Flash Gordon, who featured in three serial films starring Buster Crabbe: *Flash Gordon* (1936), *Flash Gordon's Trip to Mars* (1938), *Flash Gordon*

Despite the emergency restrictions which limited the quality and supply of printing paper soon after Allied troops had landed in France on D-Day, publishers made sure children could read about some of the technology used.

Conquers the Universe (1940) and a twelve-part Buck Rogers serial film produced in 1939 by Universal Pictures Company at their local picture palace.

In the 1940s children in Britain didn't go to the 'cinema', or to see a 'film' or a 'movie', they went 'to the pictures'. And on Saturday mornings many cinemas organised special, cut-price film shows especially for children. The programmes generally consisted of cartoons, a 'B' movie and the main feature, all interspersed with newsreels and serials designed to encourage youngsters to go again the following Saturday so as not to miss an instalment.

The usherette, or ice-cream lady as she was known by the children, would perform a variety of duties to assist in the smooth operation of the establishment and to ensure the safety of all patrons. Her duties included collecting tickets and showing people to their seats, selling ice creams and refreshments during the intermission and cleaning up after the hordes of children rushed for the exits at the end of the programme!

Regular visitors to ABC Cinemas (Associated British Cinemas), a cinema chain established in the 1930s, would inevitably join the 'ABC Minors', the first major Saturday cinema club for children. At the beginning of each Saturday morning session, the 'ABC Minors Song' would be played to Abe Holzmann's famous march, while the lyrics were presented on the screen with a bouncing red ball above the words to help all the children sing off the same hymn sheet as it were.

> We are the boys and girls well known as
> Minors of the ABC
> And every Saturday all line up
> To see the films we like, and shout aloud with glee
> We like to laugh and have a singsong
> Such a happy crowd are we.
> We're all pals together.
> We're minors of the A–B–C.

The final line 'A–B–C' was shouted at full blast by the assembled audience.

While youngsters shared their parents' enthusiasm for patriotic films such as *First of the Few*, known as *Spitfire* in the United States, the 1942 British film directed by and starring Leslie Howard as R.J. Mitchell, the designer of the Supermarine Spitfire, alongside co-star David Niven, who played RAF Squadron Leader Geoffrey Crisp, and no doubt enjoyed William Walton's stirring score, there's little doubt that the big hitters came out of Hollywood. And, despite the war, the Californian studios didn't disappoint.

Early in 1940 Walt Disney's animated film *Pinocchio* was released to acclaim. However, its undoubted artistry was eclipsed later that year with the world premiere of *Fantasia*. Released in a unique, multi-channel format, Fantasound, the film also marked the first use of the click track, a series of optical marks made on the film to indicate precise timings for musical accompaniment while recording the soundtrack, the forerunner of today's multichannel surround system.

In 1940 Bugs Bunny also made his debut, first appearing in the animated cartoon *A Wild Hare*. *Dumbo* followed in 1941 and the tear-jerker *Bambi* in 1942. These big

American animated blockbusters not only appealed to worldwide audiences, or rather the audiences of unoccupied Allied nations, they also avoided getting into trouble at home by compromising the United States' neutrality until it entered the war in December 1941.

Until then restrictions proclaimed that cinematic or radio dramas could not involve stories featuring sabotage, subversion, or spying within the United States. Heroes could not be seen to favour one side or the other and broadcasters could not openly side with any of the combatants. Certain productions managed to circumvent these proscriptions by playing the patriotism card and celebrating the American way of life.

In February 1940 radio listeners had tuned in to hear movie director Louis de Rochemont laud the Maginot Line and speak of the invincibility it gave to France against a possible German assault. Subsequently, viewers of Movietone and Pathé News newsreels saw that this invincible bulwark proved to be no obstacle against blitzkreig.

Children listening to 'Captain Midnight' (aka Charles J. Albright) in late 1941 heard their hero striking 'fear into the hearts of foes of democracy and freedom' in Japanese-occupied China. The actors on one broadcast of the *Lux Radio Theater* in 1941 donated their salaries to the China Relief Fund.

American children fought the Second World War in front of their radio sets. They joined the likes of *Don Winslow of the Navy*, the story of a naval aviator who bombed ships, attacked Nazis and hated Japanese. 'America's ace of the airways', 'Hop Harrigan', an 18-year-old freelance aviator, was every listener's 'big brother', an American warrior to the core. Harrigan did everything and always very well. He flew bombing runs, engaged in dog-fights with enemy aircraft, rescued his wounded pal while dodging German machine-gun bullets and even escaped from a concentration camp.

American heroes abounded. There was *Terry and the Pirates*, *The Sea Hound*, *Jungle Jim*, Superman, Tom Mix, The Green Hornet and *Jack Armstrong, the All-American Boy*, a creation of General Mills which presaged this famous American giant's later involvement in merchandising.

When the United States did enter the war, the federal government decided upon a course of voluntary self-censorship and as early as January 1942 (when the United States had not been at war for a month), the Office of Censorship published its Code of Wartime Practices for American Broadcasters which stated the official position on programmes that might provide information helpful to internal spies and saboteurs, or the enemy's military.

Although they were never subjected to aerial bombardment, even Americans wondered what future wars might bring as the cover of this 28 February 1939 edition of Look *suggests.*

Stations were urged to watch carefully those quiz and discussion programmes where such things as secret coded messages, telegraphed requests for specific songs or announcements of forthcoming meetings might suggest a subversive intent.

The United States government stated: 'Free speech will not suffer during this emergency period beyond the absolute precautions which are necessary to the protection of a culture which makes our radio the freest in the world.'

Free speech was not foremost in the minds of the authorities in Nazi Germany but at least in 1938 the government introduced the so-called 'people's receiver, the *Volksempfänger*, dubbed the Goebbels-Schnauze (Goebbels' snout), a radio set for every family in the Reich and all for a cost of only 35 marks. One of the reason's Goebbel's propaganda department was so enthusiastic about the distribution of this receiver was that the population would have no excuse for ignoring the Führer's speeches and now boys and girls, and their parents of course, could settle down beside the wireless and, tuning in to Großdeutscher Rundfunk, could listen to *die Stunde der Jungen Nation* (the hour of the young nation) and listen to the leader rant on in his distinctively rough Austrian accent.

On the radio, German children could also hear Walter Groß, head of the Nazi Party's Racial Policy Office, speak to them about racial purity. What follows is an excerpt from a radio talk, entitled 'Blood is Holy', aimed at youth that he gave on 7 August 1935. It outlines the fundamentals of Nazi racial thinking in a way intended for children.

> Dear German Boys and Girls!
> As we talk about blood and race this evening, we are discussing a theme that is in the centre of today's intellectual and worldview battles. You all know that those who oppose our movement for political or worldview reasons have been forced more and more over time to grant the political and economic achievements of National Socialism. They can no longer be denied even by the most hostile critic. As soon as the discussion turns to National Socialism's intellectual foundations, however, as soon as the idea itself is debated upon which everything we do is based, there are objections. And as in the past, National Socialism's racial thinking is called into question or openly opposed. We see that if we survey the world press, as well as in discussions with groups within the country who still believe that they can reject individual aspects of the National Socialist worldview.
>
> I have previously spoken about what we mean by racial thinking in the broad sense.
>
> Today we once again raise anew the flag of life against the doctrine of death, and serve the future with the faithful affirmation: The blood given to us by God is holy.

Let's hope that many German schoolchildren saw through Groß's words, though I'm sure they chimed with young boys who had joined the Hitler *Jugend* and the girls in the *Bund Deutscher Mädel* (the League of German Girls).

Generally, the young are more amenable to new ideas than older people. Recently, most of the early adopters of smart phones, apps and social media platforms proved to be teenagers or younger. Youth embraces the new and perceives the full potential of innovation. It was ever thus.

One thing all youngsters had in common during the First World War was a fascination with flight – after all, its development had been a truly international thing. From the pioneering flights of Prussian Otto Lilienthal, the 'Glider King', so-called because he was the first person to make well-documented, repeated, successful gliding flights, to the Wright brothers, pioneers of the first powered and sustained heavier-than-air human flight, in December 1903, aviation was the most exciting thing on, or rather *off*, Earth.

British boys devoured the exploits of First World War fighter ace Albert Ball VC, who scored forty-four victories before he crashed to his death in 1917 aged only 21.

German youth lauded their own air hero, Manfred Albrecht Freiherr von Richthofen, the Red Baron, who incidentally upon hearing of Ball's death remarked that he was 'by far the best English flying man'.

The British also had James Thomas Byford McCudden VC, who survived until July 1918, by which time he had downed fifty-seven enemy aircraft and with six British medals and one French one, received more medals for gallantry than any other airman of British nationality serving in the First World War.

International aces also included Germans Max Immelmann and Oswald Boelcke, René Fonck and Georges Guynemer from France and American Edward V. Rickenbacker. Heady times for youngsters who followed their heroes' every exploit.

The inter-war years proved no less of a stimulation to 'air-minded' young men. Sir Alan Cobham had been in the Royal Flying Corps in the First World War but became famous after the war as a pioneer of long-distance aviation. In 1921 he made a 5,000-mile air tour of Europe, visiting seventeen cities in three weeks. On 30 June 1926, he set off on a flight from Britain (from the River Medway) to Australia where 60,000 people swarmed across the grassy fields of Essendon Airport, Melbourne when he landed his de Havilland DH.50. He was knighted the same year.

In 1927 Cobham starred as himself in the 1927 British war film *The Flight Commander* and in 1928 he flew a Short Singapore flying boat around the continent of Africa landing only in British territory.

In 1932 he started the National Aviation Day displays – familiarly known as 'Cobham's Flying Circus', which gave many people their first experience of flying and delivered the thrill of aviation to ordinary people. In fact, air shows proved so popular in Britain that the RAF Pageants, the 'Hendon Air Days' held at the famous London aerodrome every summer from 1920 to 1937, attracted enormous crowds of spectators.

Piloting the single-seat, single-engine, purpose-built Ryan monoplane *Spirit of St Louis*, 25-year-old Charles Lindbergh made history when he flew non-stop from New York to Paris, a distance of nearly 3,600 miles (5,800km), in 1927. He entered the record books as the first person in history to be in New York one day and Paris the next and received the Medal of Honor, for his historic exploit.

Lindbergh's anti-war and isolationist stance during the build-up to the outbreak of the Second World War in 1939 might have lost him a few fans in Great Britain at the time, but after the Japanese attack on Pearl Harbor he threw himself wholeheartedly behind the American war effort and his prestige remained unabated.

Britain's equivalent was not a man but a woman. Amy Johnson would be remarkable at any time but being a pioneering female English aviator, flying solo or with her husband, Jim Mollison, she proved remarkable during the 1930s.

Johnson achieved worldwide celebrity when, in 1930, piloting her de Havilland DH.60 Gipsy Moth named *Jason*, she became the first woman pilot to fly solo from England to Australia, a flight of over 11,000 miles (18,000km). She received a CBE in recognition of her achievement. In July 1931, Johnson and her co-pilot Jack Humphreys became the first pilots to fly from London to Moscow in one day, completing the 1,760-mile (2,830km) journey in approximately 21 hours. In July 1932, Johnson set a solo record for the flight from London to Cape Town, South Africa and in 1933, with Mollison, flew nonstop from South Wales to the United States. In May 1936, Johnson made her last record-breaking flight, regaining her Britain to South Africa record in G-ADZO, a Percival Gull Six. In 1940, the recently divorced Johnson joined the newly formed Air Transport Auxiliary (ATA), rising to become its First Officer. Incidentally, the ATA was one of the rare, early champions of sexual equality. Both men and women did the same job, were treated equally and took home the same pay.

In January 1941, while flying an Airspeed Oxford for the ATA, Johnson went off course in adverse weather conditions. After running out of fuel over the Thames Estuary she bailed out and although the crew of a nearby ship witnessed her decent, she landed in a heavy swell in the intense cold and her body was never recovered. In 1942, a film of Johnson's life was made. *They Flew Alone* starred Anna Neagle as Johnson and Robert Newton as Mollison. The movie was distributed in the United States as *Wings and the Woman*.

By the beginning of the Second World War British youth was thoroughly 'Air Minded'. Young boys and many young girls (who had been encouraged both by the exploits of Britain's Amy Johnson as well as America's Amelia Earheart, the first female aviator to fly solo across the Atlantic Ocean) were genned up about every modern development in the exciting field of aviation.

Youngsters devoured books and magazines about aviation. Indeed, most of the aircraft recognition manuals that were all the rage during the Second World War, though ostensibly designed to help those in the Home Guard, ARP, Observer Corps and other civil defence organisations, were actually purchased by schoolboys. Plane spotting was de rigueur and although such boys were too young to join the RAF, they were old enough for the Air Cadets.

The product of the efforts of Air Commodore J.A. Chamier, formerly a pilot officer in the Royal Flying Corps during the First World War, who upon retirement from the then RAF in 1929 became Secretary-General of the Air League. In 1938 he established the Air Defence Cadet Corps (ADCC). This was not before time because it was obvious that war was inevitable and Britain would soon need the skills of trained young men to swell the ranks of the rapidly expanding RAF, capable of piloting the new, fast, single-engined metal monoplanes.

In return for a weekly subscription of 3*d*, cadets learnt the skills that would be needed if and when they joined the RAF or Fleet Air Arm. On 5 February 1941, the

Air Training Corps was officially established, with King George VI agreeing to be the Air-Commodore-in-Chief, and issuing a Royal Warrant setting out the Corps' aims. The dramatic growth of the ATC was spectacular and within a month it had grown to virtually twice the size of the old ADCC and by the end of its first year had over 400 squadrons. A new badge was designed for the ATC and distributed in August 1941. Air Commodore Chamier devised the organisation's motto 'Venture Adventure', and this was incorporated into the design of the badge.

While many young boys (girls couldn't join the ATC until the 1980s, before that they had to content themselves with membership of the Girls Venture Corps Air Cadets formed in 1940 as part of the National Association of Training Corps for Girls) were able to make visits to wartime airfields and occasionally enjoy a flight in one of the station's resident flying machines, the exigencies of war prevented much hands-on experience in modern warplanes. Youngsters had to content themselves with flights in gliders instead. Fortunately, as it was with the youth in Germany, gliding was a craze among air-minded youth in Britain. Gliding was first introduced around 1939, and formally became part of the official training programme soon after with around ninety Gliding Schools (GSs) in Britain by the end of the war.

If anything Nazi Germany was far ahead of Britain when it came to encouraging youngsters to engage with adventurous pursuits like gliding. This is not perhaps surprising given Hitler's pronouncement in *Mein Kampf*:

> I am beginning with the young, we older ones are used up, we are rotten to the marrow. We have no unrestrained instincts left. We are cowardly and sentimental. We are bearing the burden of a humiliating past, and have in our blood the dull recollection of serfdom and servility. But my magnificent youngsters! Are there finer ones anywhere in the world? Look at these young men and boys! What material! With them I can make a new world.

As early as 30 January 1933, when Nazis in Berlin celebrated Adolf Hitler's appointment as Chancellor of Germany with massive torchlight parades, Hitler Youth units were among those in the marching columns. The Nazi *Gleichschaltung* (forced coordination) period which followed saw all German institutions and organisations either Nazified or disbanded. Baldur von Schirach, leader of the Hitler Youth, now sought to eliminate all 400 of the other competing youth organisations, throughout Germany. Not surprisingly, the Communist and Jewish youth organisations were immediately disbanded.

The late Alfons Heck was an enthusiastic recruit to the Hitler Youth. However, when he emigrated to the United States after the war he began to reflect on his time in this organisation, writing two books, *A Child of Hitler: Germany in the Days When God Wore a Swastika* and *The Burden of Hitler's Legacy*.

At 14, all Hitler *Jungvolk* were required to join the senior Hitler Youth branch, the Hitler *Jugend*, and Heck applied to the elite Flying Hitler Youth (*Flieger Hitler Jugend*), engaging on a year-long glider course. He described this extended period of glider training from late 1942 until early 1944 as the happiest of his life. At 16 Heck became the youngest student to receive Germany's Aeronaut's Certificate in glider flying.

When Hitler first came to power Germany was forbidden to possess an air force, and the *Luftwaffe* was slowly built in great secrecy. Ironically, given the turn of events less than ten years later, German military flying principally took place within the Soviet Union. Gliding was an ideal way to train young men in all the aeronautical skills an operational pilot would need without breaching the strictures of the Armistice agreement signed at Versailles. With the active support of the Nazi party, there were 50,000 glider pilots by 1937 and at the 1936 Summer Olympics in Berlin, gliding was a demonstration sport, and scheduled to be a full Olympic sport in the 1940 Games.

Although many of the youngsters in both Britain and Germany were urged to do their bit for their homeland, at least those in the United Kingdom faced only the darkness of coal mines if they were drafted against their will as one of the 'Bevin Boys'. German boys in the Hitler Youth, on the other hand, faced the real prospect of dying in the streets of Berlin, stick grenade in hand, confronting battle-hardened Soviet soldiers who had travelled hundreds of miles through the ravaged motherland, savagely put to the torch by the fathers and uncles of the trembling boys awaiting them.

CHAPTER 5

Civilian Militias – Home Guard and *Volkssturm*

The idea of a 'Home Guard' – an armed volunteer militia ready to rush to its country's defence when it was in danger – is not a twentieth-century innovation. There are numerous examples from history where civilians have been encouraged to lend a hand in the military defence of their homeland.

In the face of what they considered a threatening British military build-up in October 1774 the rebellious Massachusetts Provincial Congress urgently called for volunteers to supplement their militia resources. They suggested the establishment of 'companies of minute-men, who should be equipped and prepared to march at the shortest notice'. These minute-men comprised a quarter of the whole militia and, led by field officers, they were divided into companies of about fifty men each.

More famous for his saucy seaside postcards, Donald McGill actually began his career as a naval draughtsman, only moving into the field with which he is most associated in 1904. During the First World War McGill drew anti-German propaganda postcards. 'The Thin Red Line' dates from 1940 and characterises the Home Guard in true Dad's Army *guise. The artist continued working until 1962.*

France, an ally of the rebellious patriots, had a hand in Britain's defeat in North America. At the turn of the eighteenth century France was again at odds with the British government and now, led by Napoleon, and had decided to invade Britain. As a result of this threat, in July 1803 the government decided to raise a guerrilla force that might resist occupying forces by operating in small bodies to harass, instil panic and wear out the French Army. In July 1803 in his amendment to the Defence of the Realm Act, Secretary at War Charles Yorke wrote:

> In these times, it is better to run the hazard even of the people making a bad use of their arms, than that they should be actually left in a state of entire ignorance of the use of them. For my own part, I can safely aver, that I cannot see any real danger which is likely to accrue to the internal peace of the Country, when I consider the present dispositions and feelings of the people.

Within a few weeks of the government's appeal for help 280,000 men had volunteered to join the new militia.

In 1812, when it was Russia's turn to be challenged with a Napoleonic invasion, Emperor Alexander I decreed the establishment of a People's Volunteer Corps. Intended to augment the over-stretched regular troops and reinforce the huge open spaces of this vast county, the people's volunteer corps saw landlords provide a percentage of their serfs aged between 17 and 45 in support of the nation's struggle during the so-called 'Patriotic War'. These units were an embodiment of national pride and a great inspiration to the Russian people.

The advent of the twentieth century saw a new warfare abroad. Though it had been seriously threatened with invasion a couple of times since 1066 – first by the Armada in 1588 and then by Napoleon during the period 1803–5, Britain's geographical location as an island with no land borders with potential enemies made it somewhat impregnable. Fast ships with powerful, accurate long-range guns and, especially, aircraft changed all this. The White Cliffs and marshy estuaries were no longer a bulwark. The island's moat could be easily eliminated.

However, although the Germans possessed a capable air force during the First World War and were pioneers of airships that were capable of carrying offensive payloads that were far heavier than even the largest biplane bombers could lift skywards, the Deutsche Luftstreitkräfte was incapable of carrying an invading army across the English Channel.

And, during the years 1914–18, parachutes were only really an apparatus of escape – and generally only allocated to the lonely occupants of tethered observation balloons – pilots went without. Germany did of course have a powerful navy which was up to the job of at least getting thousands of troops across the English Channel or the North Sea, but Britain had a far bigger one capable of smashing any such attempt.

It wasn't until the Second World War that the aeroplane both threatened to deliver invading troops to Britain by parachute and also promised to act as an aerial umbrella, protecting any enemy naval or amphibious invasion force below by dropping bombs on any vessels sailing to intercept it. And it is, of course, in the Second World War when armed volunteers such as Britain's Home Guard, 'Dad's Army', really came to the fore.

Soldier, journalist, poet and Marxist politician, Tom Wintringham was all this and much more. He served as a mechanic and motorcyclist in the Royal Flying Corps during the First World War and afterwards travelled to Moscow, returning to England in order to establish a British section of the Third International, having joined the recently formed Communist Party of Great Britain. During the Spanish Civil War he commanded the British Battalion of the International Brigades, befriending Ernest Hemingway along the way. Published in 1940, New Ways of War *was a timely handbook of guerrilla warfare based on Wintringham's experiences in the Iberian Peninsula.*

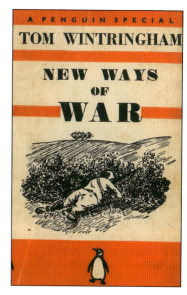

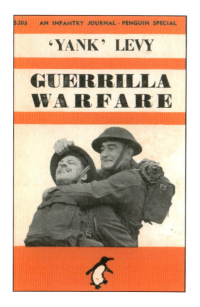

Bert 'Yank' Levy's story is as colourful as Tom Wintringham's, under whose command he served during the Spanish Civil War. A Canadian by birth, he grew up fast in the United States where his family had moved and where his father had been seriously injured when Levy was young. He said his real education was 'in the schools of hard knocks', and after enlisting in the Merchant Navy he found himself in England. By 1940, along with many of his former colleagues from Spain, Levy was teaching what he had learned at the Home Guard's Osterley Park training school. Published in 1941, Guerrilla Warfare *was a graphic record of all Yank Levy's skills.*

That's not to say that there weren't equivalents to the Home Guard in the First World War. The Territorial and Reserve Forces Act of 1907 combined the old Volunteer Force with the Yeomanry, creating the Territorial Force (TF) which was also supplemented by a Special Reserve. Containing 14 infantry divisions and 14 mounted yeomanry brigades, the TF had a strength of nearly 270,000 men. The declaration of war in August 1914 saw an immediate demand to reinforce the home forces with men who were over military age or engaged in important occupations. Initially often quite haphazardly organised and known as 'town guards', bands of eager volunteers gave up their spare time in defence of the realm, but by November 1914 an official Volunteer Training Corps was established. By 1916 this organisation had morphed into the Volunteer Force, a direct equivalent of the Home Guard of the 1940s.

On 14 May 1940, the Minister of War, Anthony Eden, made a radio broadcast asking for volunteers fit enough to march and fire a shotgun or rifle to join his new volunteer force. Desperate times required desperate measures and in the face of a rapidly deteriorating military situation on the Continent (the hasty evacuation from

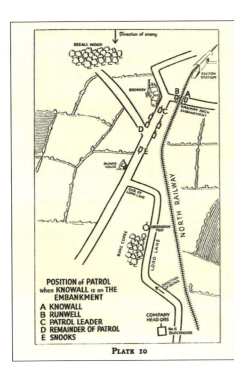

'Make each lesson as interesting as you can, and you will gain the confidence of your Command, and they will feel they are of importance to the Battalion', J.H. Levey countenanced in this spread from Home Guard Training.

For only 1s (5p) each volunteers could add one of publisher Bernards' Key to Victory *series to their pamphlets and handbooks and learn, especially, how to use imported North American weapons from manufacturers such as Springfield, Garand and Ross.*

Dunkirk would begin in twelve days' time) Eden's appeal was nothing if not earnest: 'We want large numbers of men in Great Britain who are British subjects between the ages of 17 and 65 to come forward now and offer their service in order to make assurance doubly sure. The name of the new force which is now to be raised will be the Local Defence Volunteers.'

Police stations and local government offices were besieged by volunteers eager to get their names on a rapidly growing list. Eden had expected perhaps 150,000 volunteers but the first month saw 750,000 men either serving in reserved occupations or too young or too old for military service with the regulars. By the end of June, there were over 1 million volunteers.

Churchill, who had only taken over as Prime Minister on 10 May, never liked the acronym LDV, and thought it lacked offensive spirit. Watching the disparate bunch of volunteers march up and down village streets, often armed with little more than a broomstick, wags reckoned 'LDV' stood for 'Look, Duck and Vanish'. Despite the fact that over 1 million brassards had been printed bearing the initials LDV and that despite mounting shortages many publishers had already printed handbooks for Local Defence Volunteers, some of them illustrated on these pages, on 22 July Churchill got his way and the organisation was officially renamed the Home Guard. New training manuals and 1 million replacement brassards had to be hastily produced.

Japan's entry into the war in December 1941 encouraged nations like Australia and North America, both long isolated from invasion risk by virtue of their geographical location, to consider the establishment of their own home defences. Developments in air power and the potential for high-speed amphibious assault meant that previously inviolate nations faced the risk of invasion. In the past one of the main duties of volunteer militias was to manage internal security and be on hand to put down insurrection – now their main role was as an armed supplement to regular forces and they had to be prepared to meet the invader in a combat situation.

Modelled on Britain's Home Guard, Australia's Volunteer Defence Corps (VDC) had been established in July 1940. Organised by the Returned and Services League of Australia (RSL) it was initially composed of ex-servicemen who had served in the First World War, but the government took over control of it in May 1941. Due to

Unarmed Combat. Your Answer to Invasion *by James Hipkiss (June 1941). 'Designed for the Home Guard and civilians'.*

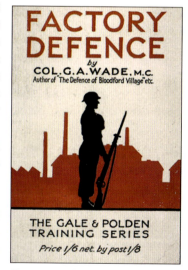

Factory Defence *by Colonel G.A. Wade MC (1941). The previous year the author wrote* The Defence of Bloodford Village *which proposed a scenario that haunted Home Guard commanders throughout the war – German parachutists landing behind the lines and linking up with Fifth Columnists.*

Japanese aggression by February 1942 membership was extended to any men aged between 18 and 60 who were working in reserved occupations. As a result, Australia's VDC reached a peak of almost 100,000 men spread right across the continent.

'He's coming south. It's fight, work or perish' read an Australian propaganda poster from 1942. It showed a Japanese soldier, rifle in hand with fixed bayonet, rushing towards across the globe towards Australia – all against a backdrop of an unfurled rising sun flag. This poster was criticised for being alarmist when it was first released – it was soon banned by the Queensland government.

But the threat was real, and elements of the Imperial Japanese forces had already drawn up plans for an attack on Australia. With the fall of Singapore in February 1942 the long-derided Japanese Army achieved a new status. Japan's was an army to be feared and one that in fact might reach Australia after all and it wasn't long before they did.

On 19 February, the bombing of Darwin took place. It was Australia's Pearl Harbor. Although the targets for the 242 Japanese aircraft involved in the attack were military, Darwin's harbour and the town's 2 airfields, bombed to prevent the Allies from using them as a staging post in their attempt to re-conquer Timor and Java, inevitably there were civilian deaths among the 240 killed. An American destroyer, the USS *Peary* was in harbour at the time and it and 22 RAAF aircraft were destroyed. It was the worst wartime loss of life on Australian soil in the country's history.

Shortly after the attack on Pearl Harbor the Japanese tasked seven of their submarines to operate close to the United States' west coast and ordered them to select targets of opportunity such as merchant men and even the American military if a suitable occasion arose.

On 23 February 1942, the Imperial Japanese Navy's submarine I-17 fired its deck canon and shells soon rained down on the oil refinery at Ellwood near Santa Barbara.

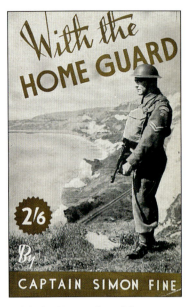

With the Home Guard *by Captain Simon Fine (1943) recounts the rapid development of Britain's volunteer defence force from humble origins when everything was improvised to a well-trained and equipped fighting force.*

Home Guard Training *by Lieutenant Colonel J.H. Levey was allegedly a bit of a rush job and published in 1940 when the Home Guard had only existed for a matter of months. It included much more drill than those guerrillas of Yank Levy (no relation) and Tom Wintringham's persuasion liked. A private in the Scots Guards in 1899, Levey went on to earn the DSO in 1917 and ended the war as Deputy Inspector General of Training to the British Armies in France and Britain.*

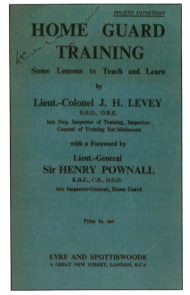

Although the shelling did only minor damages to a pier and an oil well derrick, it created 'invasion fever' all along the West Coast. The raid also influenced the decision to intern Japanese-Americans. It also marked the first shelling of the North American mainland during the conflict.

Fortunately, the United States was not without its own para-military defence force. The Militia Act of 1903 gave federal status to the militia and required the organised militia of the states to conform to Regular Army organisation and standards. It dramatically increased federal funding of the militia: between 1903 and 1916, the federal government spent $53 million on the Guard, more than the total of the previous hundred years. The act was instrumental in setting up what we now know as America's National Guard with the creation of a separate section responsible for this new organisation's affairs.

The National Defense Act of 1916 further transformed the militia from individual state forces into a Reserve Component of the US Army – and made the term 'National Guard' mandatory. It increased the number of annual training days to fifteen, increased the number of yearly drills to forty-eight and authorised pay for drills.

Because the US Army did not want to bear the financial burden of supporting troops whose only role was internal security, the Guard was disbanded following the end of the war in 1920.

However, although United States favoured isolationism and was neutral, the National Guard began mobilisation again on 16 September 1940. While the Guard originally focused on protecting local communities, it eventually grew into a force that complemented the full-time army and indeed many National Guard units would see action in both the Pacific and European theatres.

The United States Home Guard served as an option for those who wished to join the military but were unwilling or unable (due to political commitments) to deploy abroad as members of the National Guard were obliged to do. The United States Home Guard kept themselves at a high state of readiness in preparation for any threat to American soil, proving the perfect place for congressmen or other citizens who could not deploy to foreign nations, but still wanted proudly to support their country in times of need.

Although Germany was one of the main belligerents and had actually invaded numerous sovereign states early on in the Second World War, prompting the conflict to go global, as the tide of war turned against the Reich it needed its own home guard. The boot was now on the other foot.

Actually, even before Bismarck's unification, when German-speaking Central Europe comprised more than 300 political entities, many independent German states possessed armed militias.

The *Landwehr* in Prussia was first formed in 1813, and all men capable of bearing arms between the ages of 18 and 45, and not serving in the Regular Army, were eligible for call-up for the defence of the country. After Waterloo and the removal of Napoleon as a threat, the part-time *Landwehr* became an integral element in the Prussian Army, but by 1859 such troops were relegated to the second line. The Austrian *Landwehr* was officially established by order of Emperor Franz Josef on 5 December 1868. But, being insufficiently supported by the Austro-Hungarian authorities however, by the

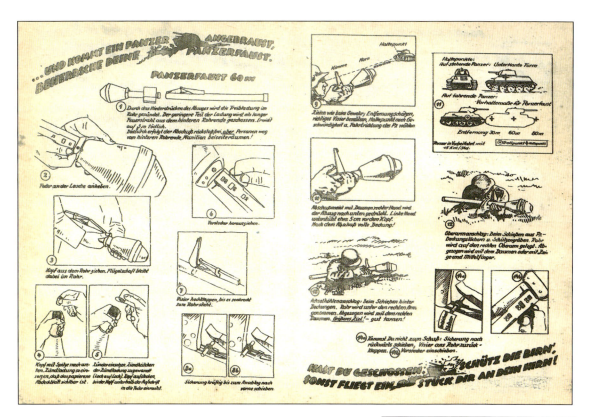

'The heaviest tank is on fire when you've the Panzer Faust at hand and even the heaviest armour isn't much when you're on target'. Development of Germany's Panzerfaust (literally 'tank fist') began in 1942 and the resulting weapon, the Panzerfaust 30, was in production by 1943. Firing a shaped charge, this weapon is the predecessor of many of the rocket-propelled grenade (RPG) platforms in use today. Most famously used by old men of the Volkssturm and boys from the Hitler Youth against Soviet tanks during the last days of the Third Reich, this powerful hand-held weapon came with a bold warning printed in large red letters on the firing tube: 'Achtung! Feuerstrahl! (*'Beware! Fire Jet!'*). After firing, the tube was discarded, making the Panzerfaust *the first disposable anti-tank weapon.*

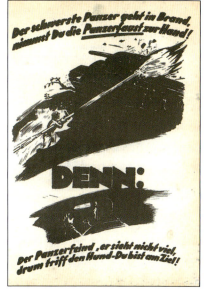

1880s the organisation had fallen into neglect and in 1887, Austrian Habsburg General Archduke Albert wrote that *Landwehr* units would not be ready to fight without two weeks' notice. The *Landwehr* system of supplementary support for the regular forces was to remain in place until 1918.

The best-known twentieth-century German self-defence force is, of course, the Second World War's stirringly named *Volkssturm*, meaning people's or national storm. This organisation became of increasing importance to Germany as the Reich began to crumble following the Soviet victory at Stalingrad in 1943 and the Allied landings in Normandy a year later.

Comprising all males aged 16–60, *Volkssturm* units fought principally on the Eastern Front, most notably in East Prussia, Breslau, along the Oder River and in Berlin. Germany's regular Nineteenth Army positioned on the Upper Rhine became so reliant on *Volkssturm* troops for infantry that it was nicknamed the 19. *Volkssturm-Armee*. This also helped engender a feeling that volunteers were joining a real, professionally armed organisation, not a rabble militia, and that if they were subsequently captured they would be treated as soldiers and not shot out of hand as guerrillas or saboteurs. Indeed, one of their principal weapons was the *Panzerfaust*, 'Tank Fist', a lethal fire and forget weapon which despatched a shaped charge that was capable of immobilising any tank on the battle field. *Volkssturm* units would be issued with shipping crates each containing four weapons. With the letters *Achtung! Feuerstrahl!* ('Attention! Fire Jet!') written in large red letters on the firing tube, warning soldiers to avoid the back blast, the Panzerfaust was the forerunner of today's Rocket Propelled Grenade (RPG). Capable of being fired by even the youngest members of the *Volkssturm* as well as boys in the Hitler Youth, this weapon was the bane of advancing Allied tank units. An example of the kind of hurriedly produced instruction leaflets issued to German fighters is shown in this book (see opposite).

I will look in more detail at the various pieces of written ephemera associated with volunteer defence forces which can still be collected by the enthusiast but, before I do, no survey of such organisations can be considered complete without mentioning Britain's super-secret Home Guard, the legendary Auxiliary Units. As we shall see, they also had reference to printed documents, and one in particular, *The Countryman's Diary 1939*, is now as rare as hen's teeth.

Popular history has planted the popular TV sitcom *Dad's Army* into the national conscience as the cultural reference point for how many in Britain think about the nation's hastily organised home defences in the wake of the collapse at Dunkirk in 1940. Then it appeared a given that the opportunist Hitler would capitalise on his successes on the Continent with an immediate invasion of Britain, the Third Reich's last remaining obstacle in Europe. Although most of the BEF had returned safely from France, it had been forced to abandon most of its modern weapons and vehicles on the battlefield and had returned armed only with rifles. An urgent supplement was required to shore up Britain's regular forces while they regrouped and reequipped. The Home Guard might, just might, provide a useful accessory. Certainly it was thought it might provide a useful, even expendable, front line in the face of a German invasion, impeding the *Wehrmacht*'s advance while regular forces could decide where and when to make a coordinated counter thrust.

Poorly armed and only barely trained, the Home Guard was, in its early days at least, the rather

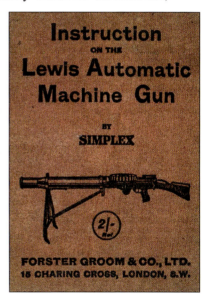

Instructions on the Lewis Automatic Machine Gun. *Though it was invented by an American, Colonel Isaac Newton Lewis, as far back as 1911, this reliable and accurate weapon remained in service until the end of the Korean War in the 1950s.*

amateurish organisation portrayed in the classic BBC comedy series. There was, however, a far more serious and potentially valuable Home Guard, the super-secret Auxiliary Units.

The story of Auxiliary Units really began when Winston Churchill appointed Colonel Colin Gubbins to establish a special force answering to GHQ Home Forces, but organised as if it was part of the existing Home Guard.

A regular soldier, Gubbins had wide experience of unconventional warfare. He had encountered the irregular tactics of the Bolsheviks during Britain's ill-judged and ill-fated intervention at Archangel during the Russian Civil war in 1919 and had confronted Michael Collin's IRA during the Anglo-Irish War of 1919–21. On both occasions he had been impressed by the capabilities of a small, well-organised unit when pitted against a much larger and better equipped foe. During the debacle of the Norwegian campaign which ultimately led to the collapse of Chamberlain's government and the ascendency of Winston Churchill, Gubbins led the Independent Companies, forerunner of the British Commandos. In November 1949 Colin Gubbins was to be chosen as the military head of the Special Operations Executive (SOE) but now his role was to provide Britain with a covert and very irregular defence force.

Gubbins had also authored a couple of important handbooks, *The Art of Guerrilla Warfare Handbook* and *The Partisan Leader's Handbook*, both of which were full of hints and tips about the various nefarious techniques irregular forces would need to employ in order to overwhelm a larger and better equipped enemy.

Gubbins was not alone in his activities but was supported by excellent and, like him, somewhat maverick subordinates. One of them, Captain Peter Fleming of the Grenadier Guards, was the brother of James Bond's creator Ian Fleming. Captain Mike Calvert of the Royal Engineers would later command the Bush Warfare School in Burma and fight in the jungles against the Japanese with Orde Wingate's Chindits.

Gubbins, Fleming and Calvert were involved in the creation of so-called Operational Patrols, which consisted of between four and eight men, often farmers or landowners who knew the land (Auxiliary Units' activities would take place under the cover of darkness) and usually recruited from men in the Home Guard who were looking for something a bit more challenging than endless drill and target practice with obsolete American P17 rifles of Great War vintage. Around 3,500 such men were distributed throughout Auxiliary Unit patrols located right across Britain. They were divided into the following battalions: 201 (Scotland), 202 (northern England) or 203 (southern England). Although they wore Home Guard uniforms, with unit flashes on their shoulders which linked them to the county in which they operated, they did not fall under Home Guard control and were not subject to the routine and discipline of those men who trained within this august organisation each week. Instead, Auxiliary Units went about familiarising themselves with every detail of their local environment and learned how to move about stealthily at night. They operated from underground hides, called Operational Bases (OBs), and should invasion actually happen were ordered to shut themselves up in their subterranean lairs and wait for a couple of weeks by when, surfacing under the cover of darkness, it was thought they would be well behind the enemy's front and able to do most damage.

The Operational Patrols were supported by Special Duties and Signals Sections

 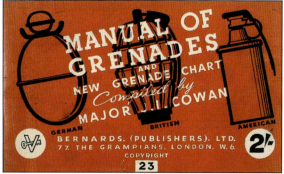

Home Guard and inquisitive schoolboy alike consumed the dozens of specialist publications like these two in publisher Bernards' Key to Victory *series:* Uniforms, Badges and Intelligence Data etc of the German Forces *and* Manual of Grenades.

comprising about 4,000 members. These were the eyes and ears of Britain's underground army, and were tasked with gathering intelligence – identify enemy units, high-ranking officers and the kinds of vehicles and heavy weapons employed by the invader.

Because Gubbins had seen how the IRA's cell system prevented British forces from penetrating and compromising the rebel's security, Auxiliary Units were established along similar lines. One Auxiliary Unit would not know about the existence, location and establishment of other units located nearby. If Auxiliers were captured they would know nothing. So secret was the organisation that volunteers didn't even tell their families about their involvement. Having signed the Official Secrets Act, their silence was mandatory and many went to their graves without even their spouses knowing about the potentially very risky work with which they had been involved.

Although secrecy and security were paramount, even the Auxiliary Units possessed printed manuals and handbooks to instruct them about the techniques of guerrilla fighting.

In 1940, the year Auxiliary Units were first established, Auxiliers were issued with a small manual cunningly entitled Calendar 1937. This was followed by *Calendar 1938*, which was published in 1942. Finally, in 1943, when the Britain was bursting with American troops as well as thousands of soldiers from the dominions and invasion was, to say the least, unlikely, *The Countryman's Diary 1939* was produced.

Emblazoned with the words 'Highworth Fertilisers do their stuff unseen, until you see results!' (Highworth in Wiltshire was the location of Coleshill House, Auxiliary Units' training HQ), this compact publication instructed readers on the use of phosphorous bombs, the application of wire garrottes against enemy sentries, the use of time pencils to detonate concealed bombs and blow up railway lines, fuel dumps and enemy stores and even how to blow the tail off a parked enemy aircraft with little more than a handful of plastic explosive.

Regular Home Guards would have been envious of the kind of equipment and written instructions with which Auxiliary Units were furnished. But even Dad's Army was provided with a range of printed advice explaining their duties and the best way to go about them.

One of the earliest handbooks was *Home Guards Training*, published by Eyre and Spottiswoode in 1940 and available for a very reasonable 1*s*. It was authored by Lieutenant Colonel J.H. Levey, with a foreword by Lieutenant General Sir Henry Pownall.

A private in the Scots Guards in 1899, Levey went on to earn the DSO at St Julien in 1917 during the First World War, ending that conflict as a Lieutenant Colonel, when he served as the Deputy Inspector of Training under Inspector General of Training General Sir Ivor Maxse. Following his appointment as Chief of Staff to the BEF in France and Belgium, in May 1940 Lieutenant General Sir Henry Pownall was given the position of Inspector General for the recently created Home Guard.

> The object of this book is to try and assist Commanders of Home Guard Units, and is in no way intended to replace official instructions or publications which have been issued or recommended. It is also hoped to assist all other ranks, many of whom have had previous military experience but may have forgotten, and have had no previous experience.

The preface began. It ended with this stirring exhortation:

> The training of Home Guards in their duties in case of invasion must be the responsibility of the local Home Guard Commanders. Meanwhile the watchword for every member should be:- 'Train yourself for your task to the utmost extent possible, in preparation for the important role you have to play in the scheme of National Defence.'

No punches were pulled on the pages of instruction within this useful pocket book.

> Home Guards are expected to be good shots and to be certain of a 'kill' if an enemy gives the slightest chance at a reasonable distance . . . What are the lessons your men require in order to reach quickly the standard of being able to shoot at, say, 200 yards so as to Kill? . . . Men should be encouraged to practice daily loading and aiming for 5 minutes in their homes, if they keep their rifles at home.

In September 1940, Mr C.H. Newton, the Chief General Manager of the London & North Eastern Railway (LNER), issued instructions to his executives concerning 'Facilities for the Home Guard'.

> I have taken an opportunity of raising the question of responsibility for the expense of providing accommodation for home guards on railway property. Up to the present we have been doing our best to meet the position by allotting disused waiting rooms, huts, spare coaches, etc., but the reports which have reached me indicate that we are coming to the end of our resources in this respect

and the question of building new structures, particularly at isolated places, will require to be considered . . . Whenever the matter is being discussed with the military authorities it should be made clear to them that the Company cannot accept this responsibility.

It seemed that the patriotic novelty of the Home Guard was not only wearing thin with the railways. After the initial rush to join the Local Defence Volunteers and subsequently the Home Guard in the summer of 1940, the RAF's victory during the Battle of Britain and the advent of shorter and colder nights, nights made more dangerous because of the Blitz, saw a slowdown in recruits to civil defence. Recruiters had to be more persuasive than before to encourage those that weren't eligible for service in the Regular Army to give up what little free time they had and join their own local defence force. 'C' Company of the 54th Kent Battalion Home Guard posted an entreaty headed 'Recruits are Wanted':

Signalling and Map-Reading for the Home Guard by H.G. Stokes, a Penguin Special published in 1941. It is now very hard to come by like many of the other Penguins from this period.

> Why? Because so many men of this Company have been called up, or have joined H.M. Regular Forces. Because more men are needed to take their places and to defend, on a properly organised basis, your homes in Chislehurst District. The chances of attempted invasion have not diminished. We are giving up a great deal of our spare time preparing to smash Germans in Chislehurst. Are you going to leave it all to us? You'll be no good if and when the time comes unless you are with us, or some other Official Defence Unit. Think it over!

Ironically, like it had with Auxiliary Units, as the likelihood of invasion diminished, the Home Guard received more and more printed advice on how to deal with it and a veritable plethora of privately produced anti-invasion leaflets and handbooks appeared, each intended to instruct those who had volunteered for home-defence duties, as well as those who were simply interested in it, how to go about resisting the invader.

London publisher Bernards was one of the most prolific supporters of civil defence. Their Key to Victory series of ultra-compact manuals were small enough to fit into the patch pockets of the new Battle Dress blouse. A particularly popular one promised full details on loading, firing, dealing with stoppages and stripping or assembling a range of weapons including automatic pistols, the 'Boys' anti-tank rifle and Northover Projector.

This guide didn't only cover conventional weapons. It also included details about the more exotic munitions with which the Home Guard was gradually being equipped. The No. 76 SIP (Self-Igniting Phosphorous) grenade, for example, in a 'Half pint clear glass bottle' was described as having a range of between 20 and 30yd when thrown by hand and 75 and 100yd if fired from the Northover Projector. Readers were told this weapon was 'immediately dangerous' and that if it was used for incendiary purposes in blitzed houses, it should have 'detonator and safety fuse attached to side of bottle to ensure breaking'. On the assumption, presumably, that an invasion had actually taken place and Home Guards might manage to wrest firearms from German soldiers, the guide also provided details about Luger and Mauser automatic pistols. About the Luger, Bernards' guide said, 'This is probably one of the most common of the German automatic pistols that may come into our hands and uses 9mm Parabellum ammunition only.' The comprehensive 'Manual of Small Arms & Special weapons' was available for a very reasonable 1*s* and could be picked up at newsagents and branches of W.H. Smith.

Although all of the privately published handbooks and guides were sincere in their intent and full of information compiled by mostly reliable sources – usually retired army officers, these unrestricted publications were not the most up-to-date resources. The most accurate contemporary data was contained in the various official Military Training Pamphlets, Army Council Instructions (ACIs) and published Army Orders (the latter often comprise multiple volumes combined in a bound pocket book), all of which were marked either 'Restricted' or 'Not to be Published', bearing the warning, 'The information given in this document is not to be communicated, either directly or indirectly, to the Press or to any person not holding an official position in His Majesty's Service.'

Any idea of just how much official information was distributed to not just the regular forces but volunteers in the Home Guard as well can be gleaned from simply looking at two ACIs, both published in 1942, which updated previous ACI information circulated in 1940.

Firstly, ACI Nos 152–4, which were revisions of orders originally published during the 'Invasion Summer' of 1940 and which had already been updated in 1941, looked at a range of issues pertinent to the growing volunteer army. The majority of this double-sided, single-sheet document was dedicated to issues concerning administrative details such as information for students attending the War Office Schools for Training Instructors in the Home Guard, but the smaller articles, 153 and 154, were far more illuminating.

Article 153 stipulated the criteria surrounding the award of Home Guard proficiency badges, adding details relating to the award of badges to volunteers who had achieved proficiency in signalling or had passed the HG's First Aid test. Article 154, on the other hand, was issued by the Quarter-Master-General and addressed the matter of 'American Small Arms and Machine Guns', which were now arriving in abundance to help fill the HG's previously depleted armouries.

> In order to assist in the identification of those American small arms and machine guns which have components common with British weapons, booklets are being produced which will give pictorial representations of weapons and parts, and the designation of both British and American components. Part numbers will be shown against the pictures and the designation . . . The booklet for 'Guns, Machine, Vickers .30-inch, U.S.A., Mark I' is now ready for distribution and units in possession of these guns (Including the Home Guard) should submit

indents on the basis of one booklet for each gun held to the C.O.O., Weedon (Commanding Officer Ordnance at Weedon, the former Napoleonic War era Military Ordnance Depot, in Northamptonshire) through to the A.D.O.S. (Assistant Director Ordnance Services), by whom they are administered for ordnance services. As and when booklets for other weapons become available, the fact will be notified in A.C.I.s.

Just how frequent these subsequent ACIs appeared can be gauged from the fact that also in 1942, the same year as numbers 152–4 were distributed, No. 780 appeared. Furthermore, this publication was four pages in extent rather than simply a single sheet.

Army Council Instruction No. 780 dealt entirely with matters medical. Perhaps Home Guard volunteers who had been injured while engaged on training exercises had been utilising emergency and medical services provided for the regular troops and tying up staff and equipment reserved for front-line soldiers because Article 1, entitled *Casualty Evacuation Scheme*, stipulated: 'In order to economise in medical and nursing personnel and equipment, Civil Defence casualty organisations will be made use of wherever possible. Only where Home Guard units are fighting near Regular Army troops will it be possible for Army Medical facilities to be available for Home Guard casualties.'

Article 3, *Medical Orderlies and Stretcher-bearers*, is equally fascinating: 'The fact that a man may receive training as a stretcher-bearer will not affect his liability to be trained in the use of weapons. If called upon to use weapons, be must not wear his 'S.B.' brassard.'

With the tide of war at last turning in the Allies' favour, Home Guard Circular No. 33, published by the War Office in August 1943, deals with issues regarding areas of complacency that had crept into an organisation which was now fully equipped but, in all honesty, unlikely ever to have to put its skills and training to use – certainly in the face of an invader.

From the following paragraph one can deduce that volunteers weren't perhaps, treating their equipment with the respect demanded of the authorities who had issued it:

> Equipment – authorised types of cleaners.
> The following details on the subject of the correct type of cleaner for use on web equipment, web anklets and respirator haversacks are published for the guidance of unit commanders.
> The only cleaner to be used will be that approved by the War Office, and is known as 'Equipment Cleaner, Khaki Green, No. 3 (W.O. specification).'
> The approved cleaner is made up of two types:
> Powder – for use on web equipment, web anklets and respirator haversacks.
> Block – for use on web equipment and web anklets only.

Item 'G' in this endless list of dos and don'ts about equipment maintenance provides some idea about the minutiae of details on which Home Guard commanders had to keep a weather eye: 'Unit Commanders will prohibit the use of cleaners obtained from other sources of supply, as well as other unauthorised practices, such as scrubbing web equipment, using bleach powder or other colouring mediums, painting with service colour paints or camouflage emulsion, etc.'

And one can't help but think of Dad's Army's elderly Private Godfrey when reading the following paragraph:

> It is the responsibility of all Home Guard Commanders to ensure that all men in their units are employed in the way most suited to their physical standard. In most cases this is being done and older men are not employed for the more strenuous tasks which the unit has to perform. There is still evidence, however, to show that men of low medical standard or advanced years are being asked to carry out duties which are beyond their powers and from a sense of duty or patriotism, or from mistaken pride, they do not disclose that they are being overstrained.

The above is not in any way intended to belittle this fine organisation of patriots who gave freely of their spare time and in the summer of 1940 faced the potential of coming face to face with a hardened enemy which by then had a succession of victorious campaigns under its belt. And, even by the spring of 1944, just weeks before D-Day and the Allied invasion of Hitler's *Festung Europa* the Home Guard was still manning the barricades with more than 100,000 men operating anti-aircraft batteries alone.

On 14 May 1944, precisely four years after the Home Guard was formed, King George, who was their Colonel-in-Chief, wrote to volunteers to thank them for their efforts.

> The burden of training and duty, dependant as it is on the needs of war, cannot fail to fall with greater weight on some than on others. To that great number of you who combine proficiency and enthusiasm in Home Guard work with responsible work of National importance in civil life, I would send a special message of thanks and encouragement.

After D-Day and the Allied advance into occupied Europe, the Home Guard was formally stood down on 3 December 1944. It was finally, officially disbanded on 31 December 1945. Male members were rewarded with a certificate, bearing a further message from the King: 'In the years when our Country was in mortal danger, [name] who served [dates] gave generously of his time and powers to make himself ready for her defence by force of arms and with his life if need be. George R.I.'

CHAPTER 6

Military Training Guides and Manuals and ARP Instructions

The new armies taking to the field at the turn of the twentieth century were very different to those who had gone to war in previous generations. For centuries soldiers had rammed iron balls down the barrels of muskets and cannons, sending them flying after igniting a charge of black powder. Indeed, so inaccurate and low powered were the firearms of the day that rival armies had to line up front of each other with not much distance between and discharge their weapons from massed ranks in the hope that a percentage of the shots expelled would inflict casualties upon their enemies. Smoke from gunpowder quickly enveloped the battlefield meaning the only way for armies to distinguish friend from foe was if they each wore uniforms of bright and contrasting colours.

Rifled barrels, percussion caps and smokeless cordite had revolutionised the battlefield. Guns were more powerful, could shoot accurately over greater distances and their discharge didn't fog the battlefield. Gone forever were high-visibility uniforms and the need for soldiers to operate in massed ranks. Camouflage and concealment was the name of the game and an understanding of the science of ballistics and the mathematics of hitting targets at long range instead of nearby over open sights became essential to military success.

The battlefield had become far more complicated. It now also occupied three dimensions as aircraft demonstrated their warlike capabilities. At sea, wood and sail had been replaced by steel and steam propulsion. Naval ships also benefitted from the improvements in ordnance enjoyed by land forces. In the Royal Navy Armstrong's rifled breech loaders were capable of hitting targets out of sight over the horizon and sailors learned about rangekeeping, the science of accurately judging a target's range and bearing. If a

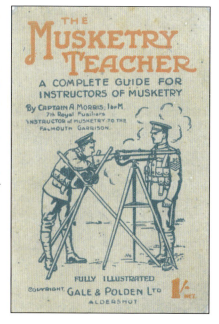

The Musketry Teacher *(Gale & Polden, 1916).*
'A complete guide for instructors of musketry by Captain A Morris, 7th Royal Fusiliers Instructor of Musketry to the Falmouth Garrison'.

Resplendent in woollen khaki serge Service Dress, complete with 1908 webbing and carrying the accurate and reliable .303 Short Magazine Lee–Enfield (SMLE), the soldiers of the British regular army who marched to the front in 1914, the 'Old Contemptibles', were a well-trained and well-equipped modern fighting force. There just weren't enough of them. Postcards like this are some of the most accessible collectables of the Great War.

Gale & Polden's Semaphore Simplified. Or how to learn it in a few hours. *Priced 6d and dating from around 1900 but used throughout the First World War, this set of illustrated cards vividly illustrates the massive developments in communications technology in the twentieth century. By late 1969 the American Advanced Research Projects Agency Network (ARPANET), the progenitor of the Internet, was ready to send messages via a nuclear-blast resilient network to US ICBM silos.*

target was visible then optical rangefinders were employed, if not, mechanical computers performed position predictions using a linear extrapolation of the target's course and speed.

While conflicts like the Boer War had already demonstrated the changing face of warfare and, in the case of the British Army, heralded the introduction of khaki uniforms and bolt-action, magazine-feed rifles, the novice conscripts who joined the armies, air forces and navies squaring up against each other from August 1914 were in desperate need of tuition in the technology of war. This requirement and the exponential rise in literacy among the working class in the late Victorian period saw a huge increase in the production and distribution of military manuals which could both be used in the field or during training before a soldier saw combat.

The principles and details of training were laid down in the Field Service Regulations and in army publications like *Infantry Training 1914* as recruits began basic training and improved their physical fitness. Basic training, as it was known, taught individual and encouraged unit discipline – team work being critical to the success of regiments, battalions and smaller units such as companies, platoons and sections. Recruits were taught how to follow commands, how to march and how to safely handle weapons. Because these former civilians were going to live 'rough' in the open, they were also taught basic field craft.

Britain did, of course, possess training bases at home, where a recruit could learn the basics of drill and the specific skills required by the arm of service (i.e., infantry, machine-gunner, artilleryman, engineer) he had joined before going abroad to be trained further and then released for active service, but, right from the start these were found to be inadequate, such was the size the Kitchener's new army had grown to. Consequently, many additional training camps were developed and traditional infantry training facilities at Aldershot and Catterick, for example, were supplemented by additional instructional barracks built at Cannock Chase in Staffordshire (known as Brocton Camp and Rugeley Camp), constructed with the permission of Lord Lichfield, on whose estate they were being built, at Clipstone in Nottinghamshire and in East Anglia and on the North Wales coast. The Infantry Battle School (INFBS) at Brecon in Wales was further extended in early 1939 and known as 'Dering Lines' after Sir Edward Dering who, in 1689, raised the 24th Regiment of Foot – the famous South Wales Borders of Zulu War fame, more recently, the Royal Regiment of Wales.

When new recruits arrived overseas their training continued and the brutal realities of what men were about to face began to sink in as they learned how to deal with the threat of gas, the wounds caused by rifle bullets, shrapnel and the nearby detonation of high explosives. Major Generals Ivor Maxse and Arthur Solly-Flood were closely involved in ensuring that soldiers learned all about the techniques of the new warfare they were about to encounter. The infamous 'Bull Ring' at Étaples, seen of the well-known mutiny by British troops subject to the notorious discipline at this camp in September 1917, is probably the most well-known of the transit camps in France and Flanders during the Great War.

Resting at Étaples on his way to the front, the poet Wilfred Owen recorded the following words about the establishment:

Because they only fly because they all follow the predictable and established aeronautical principles, aircraft all look pretty similar. This was particularly true of First World War biplanes. Knowing exactly which machine was an opponent was critical and led to the introduction of recognition manuals like this one.

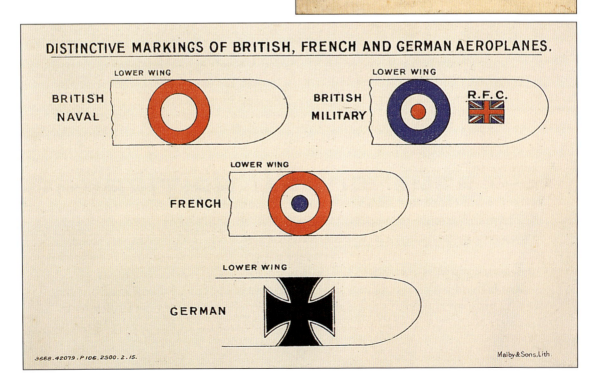

I thought of the very strange look on all the faces in that camp; an incomprehensible look, which a man will never see in England; nor can it be seen in any battle but only in Étaples. It was not despair, or terror, it was more terrible than terror, for it was a blindfold look and without expression, like a dead rabbit's.

At least British recruits enjoyed up to a year's training before they faced the enemy. German soldiers, on the other hand, often found themselves flung into the teeth of battle after only one month of the most rudimentary training. British soldiers also benefitted from a network of schools teaching specialist skills, learning how to command a platoon or company; how to be a sniper; how to use the use the primitive radio technology available; or operate machine guns like the Vickers or Lewis gun.

Alongside instruction about the weapons they might employ while on active service in France, British soldiers – most of whom had never been much farther than a visit to their nearest county town or seaside resort, and had never been abroad – were given some rudimentary tuition in the language they were to encounter. French publishers wasted no time in capitalising on a captive market keen, when not in the front line, to converse with lonely *mademoiselles* or at least order a bottle of affordable *vin rouge* from the first intact *estaminet* they could find. *Familiar French* – with phonetic pronunciation no less, was one of the many such indispensable guides available to Tommies keen to do their best when faced with the need to communicate with their Gallic allies.

'An invaluable supplement to any English-French phrase book', *Familiar French* promised to provide the idioms, colloquialisms, familiar expressions, slang expressions in common use by the French. It cost only 50 centimes. For another 1 franc 50 centimes, Boulogne-Sur-Mer-based publisher Jean Herrebrecht also offered sets of ten cards, 'artistically coloured', in the series *Sketches of Tommy's Life in France*.

> Let them know at home about your life in France by sending from time to time Mackain's post cards. This series in the artist's well known humorous style consists of four sets as follows:
> 1st Set In Training
> 2nd Set At the Base
> 3rd Set Up the Line
> 4th Set Out on Rest
> There will come a time when you may be glad to have something of this sort to remind you of the bright or funny side of the war. Take the first opportunity to secure the entire lot. These cards can be obtained at any shop which stocks 'Familiar French' – or directly from the publisher of this booklet – small notes accepted in payment.

The reader might be interested to learn that Fergus Mackain, the artist of the postcards in question which did, indeed, prove terribly popular, was a Canadian who worked his way to England at the start of the war, where he joined the British Army and served with the 23rd Royal Fusiliers. Wounded on the Somme at the Battle of

PREFACE

"FAMILIAR FRENCH" is not a common French phrase book, but it is a most useful supplement to any French phrase book you may use already.

Its aim is to give the idioms, colloquialisms, familiar expressions, slang expressions, etc., in common use by the French, but never to be found in the books.

When you are puzzled as to the meaning of a French word you can't find in the dictionary, it is probably because it is an idiom, or slang.

But if you refer to "FAMILIAR FRENCH" you'll see exactly what it means, and the sense in which it is used in colloquial conversation.

In French, as in English, there are a certain amount of slang expressions which have been introduced into the language and are widely used by everyone. It is that slang you will fin din our booklet. It is indispensable to know it if you want to understand French as it is spoken, and also if you wish to make a proper use of the Frenchman's own every day expressions.

The booklet takes practically no room in the pocket, and the phonetic pronunciation of each word is shown so clearly that you can't possibly go wrong when introducing Colloquialisms or Slang into your conversation.

However much or little you know of French, this useful booklet will provide that confident touch to your French, and supply the right word in the right place every time.

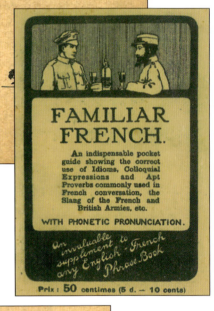

British troops who found themselves in front-line trenches in Flanders didn't only have to get to grips with incessant shelling they also needed to learn the local lingo, especially if they wanted to enjoy any free time at the rear. 'An indispensable pocket guide showing the correct use of Idioms, Colloquial Expressions and Apt Proverbs . . .', Familiar French could be their salvation.

II. — ABOUT CHARACTER PERSONAL ATTRIBUTES, etc...

A. — COLLOQUIAL EXPRESSIONS

English Equivalent or meaning.	French expression.	Phonetic Pronunciation.
A clever man.	Un homme calé.	Eun(g) omm kahlay.
A good-hearted man.	Un bon cœur.	Eun(g) bon(g) kurr.
An outspoken man.	Un homme qui a le cœur sur la main.	Eun(g) omm kee ah ler kurr sür lah man(g).
As full of tricks as a monkey.	Malin comme un singe.	Mahlan(g) komm eun(g) sanje.
He is crackbrained.	C'est une tête fêlée.	Set ünn tett fehlay.
He has bats in his belfrey.	Il a une araignée au plafond.	Ill ah ünn ahraynceay oh plahfon(g).
He is hot-headed.	C'est une tête chaude.	Seh t'ünn tett shod.
A busybody.	Un mêle-tout.	Eun(g) mell-too.
A coward.	Un poltron.	Eun(g) pohltron(g).
He speaks stuff and nonsense.	Il dit des bêtises.	Ill dee deh behteez.
He is in a brown study.	Il est de mauvaise humeur.	Ill ay der mohvayz ümurr.

ABOUT CHARACTER, PERSONAL ATTRIBUTES, etc.
(Continued)

B.—FRENCH FAMILIAR EXPRESSIONS AND SLANG

English Equivalent or meaning.	French expression.	Phonetic Pronunciation.
He is a clever chap.	C'est un type à hauteur.	Seh t'eun(g) teep ah ohturr.
A real sport.	Un chic type.	Eun(g) sheek teep.
A lucky man.	Un veinard.	Eun(g) vehnahjr.
He has good luck.	Il a de la veine.	Ill ah der lah venn.
He is dotty.	Il est maboule.	Ill ay mahbool.
He is a softy.	C'est une poire.	Seh t'ünn pwarr.
He is windy.	C'est un froussard.	Seh t'eun(g) froossahrr.
He has the wind-up.	Il a la frousse.	Ill ah lah frooss.
He has cold feet.	d°	d°
He does not feel up to work.	Il a la flemme.	Ill ah lah flehmm.
He has the gift of the gab.	Il a de la blague.	Ill ah der lah blahg.

Delville Wood in 1916, Mackain survived the war but died in North Carolina in 1924 aged only 38.

Soldiers could partake of more serious instruction by reading any of the numerous instructional guides published by Aldershot's Gale & Polden. Fully illustrated, *The Musketry Teacher, A Complete Guide for Instructors of Musketry* by Captain Morris of the 7th Royal Fusiliers, Instructor of Musketry to the Falmouth Garrison, could be purchased for 1*s*.

On the subject of ammunition supply Morris had this to say:

The ammunition carried in linen bandoliers in chargers is an idea borrowed from the Japanese, who used it with great success in Manchuria. It has the advantage of being easily portable and easily distributed. There are various means of ensuring an adequate supply of ammunition in the firing line.

Prior to an engagement issue additional rounds to each man. The issue should be as late as possible in order to avoid fatiguing the men sooner than necessary. The Germans issue as much as a man can carry without undue fatigue.

Husband ammunition during fight. Good fire control is necessary. Do not open fire at long range except when imperative or favourable target presents itself. Lack of fire discipline in the personnel of a company is responsible for a great waste of ammunition, such as opening fire without good cause. Misapplication of fire to a target i.e., the use of rapid fire where slow fire was only justified.

In the defence it should be possible to collect the ammunition of all casualties.

Reinforcements should bring up fresh supply of ammunition to firing line.

Ammunition should be sent up whenever opportunity offers during a pause in the fight. The Japanese used this method with appreciable success by sending forward all unemployed men under an officer and non-commissioned officer. The firing line was very often reinforced with the chief idea of replenishing the ammunition supply.

One non-commissioned officer and a few men should be detailed from each company as ammunition carriers. They should supply the reinforcements with ammunition.

Reinforcements may be used to replace the firing line in future advances. This method is not advisable, as it may lead to misapprehension which may entail very serious consequences.

Men should not be sent back from the firing line for ammunition, as it produces a bad moral effect. Men who take ammunition to the firing line should not withdraw until a suitable opportunity occurs.

For the purpose of arriving approximately at the number of rounds to be carried in ammunition columns, the number of rifles in units is calculated at 500 for cavalry regiments and mounted infantry battalions, and at 1,000 for infantry battalions; other units are not considered, The capacity, in rounds, of vehicles and animals allotted for small ammunition is as follows:

Each S.A.A. cart, 16,000 rounds.*

Each Limbered G.S. wagon, 16,000 rounds.**

Each G.S. wagon 40,000 rounds.

Each Pack animal, 2,000 rounds.
Each Lorry (a ton), 80,000 rounds.***
* Small Arms Ammunition (SAA) train cart.
** General Service Wagon.
*** GMC model 15 truck.

With over 150 pages packed with details which included 'Common Faults in Aiming', 'Daily Cleaning of the Rifle' and 'Judging Distance', this book was published in 1916, just in time for the Battle of the Somme when, as we now know only too well, very few British soldiers ever got the opportunity to raise their muskets offensively before they were scythed down by German machine guns.

There was a lighter side to some of the material produced for the edification of British troops in the field and possibly the most famous and successfully produced publication soldiers read with eagerness was the legendary *Wipers Times*.

While stationed in Ypres, the heavily shelled Belgian city which blocked the progress of Germany's Schlieffen Plan, their aim to sweep through the rest of Belgium and into France from the north, men of the 12th Battalion, the Sherwood Foresters (Nottinghamshire and Derbyshire Regiment), found themselves in the ruins of an old print works. Three of them, Captain Fred Roberts, Lieutenant Jack Pearson and Sergeant Harris, a Fleet Street printer in civilian life, who recognised a pedal-operated printing press for what it was, realised they had the wherewithal to produce a trench newspaper. With Captain Roberts as editor and Pearson as the sub-editor, the *Wipers Times* was born. The name was chosen because the average Tommy had difficulty with the correct pronunciation of Ypres.

A cross between a parish magazine and *Punch*, the popular British satirical magazine, the first edition of 100 copies of the *Wipers Times* was printed on Saturday, 12 February 1916. It went down a storm with the men, editions of the necessarily small print run (paper was in short supply) were read and then passed on from soldier to soldier meaning it reached a readership far in excess of the numbers produced.

The *Wipers Times* ran from February 1916 until just after the war had ended. It went through several incarnations as the Sherwood Foresters moved from location to location. In fact there were only four editions of the *Wipers Times* because in April 1916 the battalion moved to Neuve Eglise and the *New Church Times* ensued. A move to the Somme saw the short-lived *Kemmel Times* quickly followed by the *Somme Times* and then eleven editions of the *B.E.F. Times*. Two editions were printed as the war came to an end in 1918, and, fittingly, these went by the name of the *Better Times*.

It is easy to see why the *Wipers Times* and its successors proved so popular with the men in the trenches and so irksome for those in authority. Rereading a facsimile edition while I was preparing this narrative, I was struck by both how funny it was and so anarchic and contemporary in its style. I found it as subversively enjoyable as I did when I watched Monty Python in the early 1970s. It certainly hasn't dated and is a credit to the wry observations and witticisms of its authors.

There's an enormous amount of pure gold sprinkled midst the pages of Roberts' trench newspapers but I'd like to take this opportunity to present a personal selection which, I hope, reveal why they've so admirably stood the test of time.

Rightly the stuff of legend. Amid all the official communications and the dos and don'ts soldiers were subjected to while they were trapped in the few square kilometres of mud they inhabited for nearly four years during the First World War, the Wipers Times *told it like it was and was a breath of fresh air. Its sardonic, 'Pythonesque' humour is as funny now as it was 100 years ago. Editor Captain, later Lieutenant Colonel, Roberts and his sub-editor, Lieutenant Pearson, provided a real tonic for the troops.*

From the third edition of the *Wipers Times* (or *Salient News* after the 'Ypres Salient' within which the printing press was discovered in 1916) published on Monday, 6 March 1916:

Editorial

Firstly, we must apologise to our numerous subscribers for the delay in bringing out our third number. Owing to the inclemency of the weather our rollers became completely demoralised, also the jealousy of our local competitors, Messrs Hun and Co, reached an acute stage, and brought some of the wall down on our machine. But we have surmounted all these difficulties by obtaining, on the hire-purchase system, a beautiful Cropper? (I think that's the name) machine. This machine is jewelled in every hole, and has only been obtained at fabulous expense. So that we are once more able to resume our efforts towards peace, and by still telling the truth to our subscribers we hope to retain their confidence, which may have been shaken by pernicious utterings of the Yellow Press during our silence. Our great insurance scheme met with instant success, and we have already paid out three sums of 11/7 owing to an unfortunate accident on the

Zillebeke Bund, where a celebrated firm of commission agents took the knock. At the urgent request of the printing staff we have just inspected our new machine. It is certainly a ghastly looking arrangement, and we hesitate to trust our ewe lamb in its rapacious maw, but as it is either that or no ewe lamb we'll risk it. We hear that the war (to which we alluded guardedly in our first number), is proceeding satisfactorily, and we hope shortly to be able to announce that it is a going concern. So for the time being there we will leave it, and turn to graver subjects. We regret that there is still reason to deplore the inability, inefficiency, ineptitude and inertia of our City Fathers with regard to the condition of the roads (these are mostly up still), and the lighting of the town. We should like to see these matters taken in hand at once. There are many more justifiable reasons for dissatisfaction on the part of our fellow townsmen, notably the new liquor laws. We hear that the new night club, which has recently been opened near the Hotel des Ramparts prepares a beautiful 'cup' for its patrons. This is a step in the right direction, and long may it flourish. All the stars can be seen there nightly, and consequently all visitors will have reason for satisfaction. This being our grand summer number, we have doubled the price, as is usual on these occasions. Before closing we must thank our numerous subscribers for the kindness we have received, both congratulatory and financial. A Happy Xmas to you all!
THE EDITOR

There's so much more to choose from but perhaps just a couple more short excerpts. First, what about a half-page advertisement which appeared in the *Somme Times* at the height of that bloody offensive:

Are You a Victim to
OPTIMISM?
——————-

You Don't Know?
——————-

THEN ASK YOURSELF THE FOLLOWING QUESTIONS.
—————

Do you suffer from cheerfulness?
Do you wake up in the morning feeling that all is going well for the allies?
Do you sometimes think that the war will end within the next twelve months?
Do you believe good news in preference to bad?
Do you consider our leaders are competent to conduct the war to a successful issue?
If the answer is 'yes' to anyone of these questions then you are in the clutches of that dread disease.
WE CAN CURE YOU

Given the high esteem in which war poets like Owen, Sassoon, Brooke and others are rightly held today, the fact that during the conflict Roberts and his colleagues famously protested against the amount of poetry they received is another fine example of the irreverent and subversive humour exhibited by the *Wipers Times*.. OK, so it's a bit 'public school' and I'm sure it went over the heads of many of the coarser enlisted men who read it, but it is very funny nonetheless:

> We regret to announce that an insidious disease is affecting the Division, and the result is a hurricane of poetry. Subalterns have been seen with a notebook in one hand, and bombs in the other absently walking near the wire in deep communication with the muse . . . The editor would be obliged if a few of the poets would break into prose as a paper cannot live by 'poems' alone.

And finally:

> CAN YOU SKETCH?
>
> Some of you may be able to draw corks.
> Very few of you can draw any more money.
> Probably some of you can draw sketches.
> Here is a letter I have just received from a pupil at the front:
> 'The other day by mischance I was left out in No-Man's Land. I rapidly drew a picture with a piece of chalk of a tank going into action, and while the Huns were firing at this I succeeded in returning to the trenches unobserved'
> Could you have done this?
> Send a copy of the following on a cheque:– Francs 500 –
> And by return I will send you a helpful criticism and my fourteen prospectuses.
> Please sign your name in the bottom right-hand corner to prevent mistakes.

The editor, Fred Roberts, was later promoted to Lieutenant Colonel and received the Military Cross for his war service. He died in Toronto, Canada in September 1964.

Fighting on the Western Front during the First World War was characterised by long periods of boredom abruptly punctuated by moments of sheer terror when men were pushed to the edge and subjected to unimaginable horrors which would stay with them for ever, if they survived the fighting. Relief from the drudgery and monotonous routine of army life was found in entertainments such as the *Wipers Times*, love letters from home, playing cards, or in fact, reading just about anything they could get their hands on.

Perhaps because it was targeted at working class men, the heavily illustrated magazine *War Illustrated* had become one of the most popular reads among men in the trenches. In December 1915, *War Illustrated* published an article about how soldiers looked forward to and enjoyed reading books sent from Britain. The publication urged readers on the home front to send soldiers abroad as many books as they could.

Fortunately by 1914 the General Post Office (GPO) was Britain's largest economic enterprise; indeed, with over 250,000 people employed it was the largest single employer of labour in the world. It was big enough to cope with the deluge of mail to and from the front. I should point out, however, that by 1918 28,000 GPO staff had

Like Fred Roberts, Bruce Bairnsfather has entered the pantheon of the good and great who brought some normality to the troops of the western front in the First World War. Famous for 'Old Bill', the curmudgeonly but worldly-wise British soldier who adorned a thousand postcards, and who appeared in the weekly Bystander Magazine, *Bairnsfather's cartoon creation also appeared in compilations such as* Fragments from France *and* More Fragments from France, *as illustrated here. The price of original editions of these poignant reads has increased dramatically given the centenary of the First World War.*

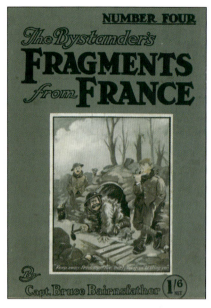

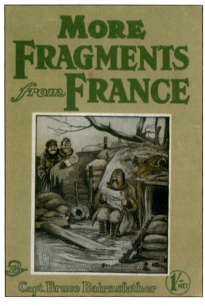

enlisted in the armed forces and that by the end of the conflict 73,000 staff had joined up. The Post Office even had its own battalion, the Post Office Rifles (POR), comprised entirely of postal staff. Sadly, like so many of the other 'pals' battalions, made up of men who knew each other in 'civvie street', the POR fought and died together, the unit suffering badly at Ypres in 1917.

All post bound for troops on the Western Front was sorted at the GPO's London Home Depot which by the end of 1914 covered 5 acres of Regent's Park. During the war the Home Depot handled 2 billion letters and 114 million parcels. The Army Postal Service (APS) was responsible for distributing mails in the theatre of war and coordinated communications with battalions, right up to the front. During the First World War up to 12 million letters a week were delivered to soldiers in all theatres of war, not just in France and Flanders but in the Dardanelles, the Middle East and Africa.

From 1915, Lord Kitchener yielded to political pressure and allowed newspaper reporters onto the Western Front. At first six war correspondents were appointed to GHQ in France and worked in a pool system for publication in the national press. They wore uniform, but were closely escorted by suspicious regular escort officers and were rarely able to report accurately on the full horror of what they saw. This was mostly, of course, because they operated some distance behind the front line! However, one journalist in particular, Philip Gibbs of the *Daily Chronicle*, achieved the respect of the politicians at home, Generals at GHQ and even the men in the trenches, when and if old copies of newspapers reached them.

Between February 1918 and June 1919, the United States Army even managed to publish its own newspaper, the *Stars and Stripes*, actually produced in France for the information, education and entertainment of the growing ranks of dough boys swelling the Allied armies.

When not in action men did, in fact, have plenty to read although it has to be said that they enjoyed lighter reading and even novels, particularly those written by H.G. Wells or Rudyard Kipling, to the latest official army bulletins about operational procedures or how to field strip a Lewis gun.

The coming of peace in 1918 brought respite to the war-weary nations of Europe. The victors, France and England, had nearly bankrupted themselves to persecute such a worldwide conflict. The Austro-Hungarian Empire had been broken up and Germany saddled with almost unimaginable reparations in accordance with the diktats of the Treaty agreed at Versailles in 1919. The United States emerged even stronger, its massive industrial capacity undamaged by war and easily able to switch to a peace-time footing and provide eager consumers with the new, benign products of the production line such as automobiles, electric cookers and vacuum cleaners. There was inevitably a surplus of military items manufactured to feed the greedy warring combatants and aeroplanes, particularly, could be purchased cheaply. The easy availability of now-obsolete but nevertheless strong and powerful aircraft led to a huge increase in barnstorming and stunt flying, particularly above the wide open spaces of North America.

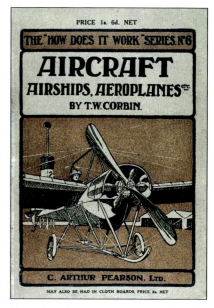

Immediately prior to the First World War there was already a thriving market for technical handbooks about new flying machines as this book, Aircraft, Airships, Aeroplanes etc, *demonstrates.*

The aeroplane didn't just promise excitement and entertainment, of course, and though peace time certainly offered the opportunity to harness modern development in aviation to explore uncharted wildernesses, flying machines were also harbingers of bad things to come.

Even by 1918 the apparently flimsy biplanes had proved themselves capable of military versatility, dropping increasingly heavy bomb loads and offering pretty stable platforms from where machine guns could be fired. As early as 1912, Bradley Fiske, an officer in the United States Navy, had taken out a patent for an aerially launched torpedo. In 1914 the Royal Naval Air Service managed the first successful aerial torpedo launch by dropping a Whitehead torpedo from a Short S.64 seaplane. The United States bought its first batch of ten torpedo bombers in 1921, and in 1931, the Japanese Navy developed the Type 91 torpedo, dropping it from a height of 330ft at a speed of 100 knots.

If these developments weren't frightening enough, the possibility that aircraft might also employ chemical weapons – poison gas, like that used to such awful effect on the Western Front, further vexed the military authorities. Despite the prophecies of the Italian General Douhet and the British author H.G. Wells, both convinced that military airpower was invincible – even the British politician Stanley Baldwin pronounced,

The Luftwaffe *flew hundreds of reconnaissance sorties over Britain and went to extraordinary lengths to ensure bombing missions were despatched to priority targets such as this industrial concern in Doncaster. Remarkably, these photographs can still be purchased and remain relatively inexpensive.*

'The bomber will always get through' in a speech to the House of Commons in 1932 – military authorities had to develop methods to counter the threat from the air.

Until the timely development of radar in the late 1930s, the only defence came in the shape of the Heath Robinson-esque, and frankly useless, Sound Locators, giant ear-trumpets supposed to be able to detect incoming aircraft before they could be visibly observed, and good old anti-aircraft (AA) guns.

In my collection I have a particularly rare 1928 edition of *Gunners' Instruction for Second and First Class Gunners* employed in US coastal artillery gun batteries. A series of useful instructions delivered in question and answer format, it makes very interesting reading:

Q. What does the propelling charge consist of?
A. Nitrocellulose powder.

Q. What does the bursting charge of a high explosive shell consist of?
A. About one-and-a-half pounds of high explosive powder.
Q What does the bursting charge of shrapnel consist of?
A. About one-fifth of a pound of shrapnel powder.
Q. What does the shrapnel filling consist of?
A. About 253 half-inch lead balls, and a smoke producing powder filled in the space between the balls.
Q. What happens when a shrapnel projectile bursts?
A. The fuse is blown off and the projectile acts as a shot gun, the lead balls being ejected through the nose at an increased velocity.

Bombing planes fly in close formations, usually with not more than 50 yards between planes. It is seldom that less than 5 or more than 18 bombing planes cross the lines in a single formation, as formations of more than 18 planes are not easily maneuvered.

During the first week of July 1937, less than ten years since this manual was distributed, the German Condor Legion launched a coordinated attack on Spanish Republican forces at the Battle of Brunete. Then, as Messerschmitt Bf-109B fighters flew high above Heinkel He-111 bombers, who were in turn co-ordinating their attack with Heinkel He-51 biplanes a further 500ft below, literally dozens of *Luftwaffe* aircraft exhibited that it was quite easy to manoeuvre massed formations of far larger size than just '18 planes'.

By 1939 it was imperative that those involved with air defence were able visually to distinguish between the warplanes of rival belligerents. Those involved in anti-aircraft and those in civil defence whose job it was to issue the warning of an incoming raid had to be capable of telling the difference between an assortment of monoplanes which by this period, because they were all designed on the same proven and published principles of aerodynamics, all looked very similar indeed.

To help gunners and observers recognise friend from foe a series of Aircraft Recognition manuals were produced. They were regularly updated as subsequent improved marks of aircraft took to the skies. For example, during the Second World War there were five basic marks of Messerschmitt Bf-109 alone, as well as numerous sub-variants of each major production run. The Spitfire actually progressed through an amazing 24 different marks during the same period when an amazing 20,300 examples of this iconic fighter were manufactured.

In April 1943 Peter Masefield, Technical Editor of the *Aeroplane* and Editor of the *Aeroplane Spotter*, wrote:

Published in reaction to the demonstrations organised by American General Billy Mitchell which revealed the vulnerability of warships and seacoast defences to air power, this copy of Gunners' Instruction *for an American coastal anti-aircraft battery dates from 1928.*

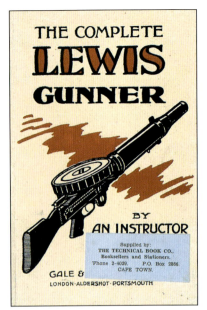

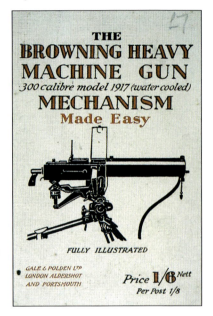

The Complete Lewis Gunner *(Gale & Polden)*. *Although invented by an American in 1911 and used throughout the First World War, as this 1941 publication shows, the Lewis gun was still in service in the Second World War and, in fact, through to the end of the Korean War in 1953.*

The Browning Heavy Machine Gun Mechanism Made Easy *(1940), another handbook from Gale & Polden's prolific lists.*

There is no short cut to aircraft recognition and the basis of all study of any particular aeroplane must begin with the silhouette. The silhouette presents the true outline and detail of the features which go to make up the machine, free from the distortion or perspective which may give a false impression in a photograph.

Recognising the different silhouettes of the myriad operational aircraft was crucial to air defence during the Second World War. OK, silhouettes weren't as crucial as radar and radio proximity fuses, but these technological developments were secret, even from those men manning AA batteries. The importance of precise knowledge about differing silhouettes was what was drummed into all those scanning the skies in search of enemy aircraft during wartime.

To aid observers and gunners they were encouraged to study not just the latest recognition manuals but to use other aide-memoires like sets of cards or posters which could be plastered on the walls of billets and examined when soldiers were involved in chores like 'bulling' their ammunition boots. Another great help was so-called recognition models, accurately scale miniatures which could be held in the hand and considered from three dimensions. A great improvement over traditional three-view recognition graphics which depicted silhouettes in plan, profile and head-on aspects and often missed distinguishing subtleties of shape and form, recognition models were

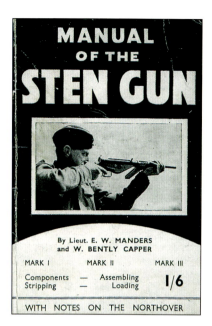 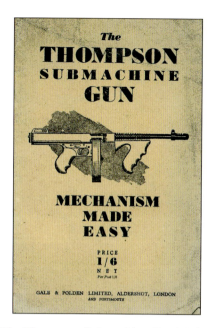

Manual of the Sten Gun. *You can see that this booklet was aimed primarily at the Home Guard because it includes notes on the Northover Projector, the very rudimentary anti-tank weapon invented by Major Robert Harry Northover, an officer in the Home Guard, who designed each one to be manufactured for under £10.*

The Thompson Submachine Gun Made Easy *(Gale & Polden, 1942).*

usually moulded in a black thermosetting polymer such as Bakelite which had taken the world by storm in the 1930s.

The War Office published *Small Arms Training Volume 1, Anti-Aircraft* in 1942. It was designed to update soldiers with the lessons learned from the various combatants who had encountered Germany's new blitzkrieg method of warfare – that is the close co-ordination and application of mechanised units moving rapidly forward beneath the umbrella of aircraft who both acted as a shield against aircraft from the opposing side and operated as highly mobile artillery softening up targets ahead which the advancing infantry could quickly envelop. Though the British Army had practised fire and movement techniques in the late 1930s and, in fact, went to war in 1939 as a highly mechanised force, it was not as adept at mobile operations as was the German Army. The PBI (poor bloody infantry) in King George's army still spent a lot of time marching to their objectives. But, as *Small Arms Training Volume 1* pointed out:

> So far as troops are concerned, probably the most vulnerable target that presents itself to aircraft is that of a column in line of march. Instructions in this pamphlet are concerned only with low flying attacks or dive bombing attacks within 2,000 feet or 600 yards (ground range). These attacks will be made at high speed and will be quickly over, allowing only three or four seconds during which effective fire is possible . . . Against undisciplined or demoralized troops air

 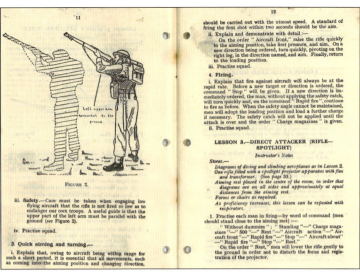

Small Arms Training Volume 1, Pamphlet No. 6 Anti-Aircraft *(1942) was a compilation of the lessons learned when British soldiers found themselves subjected to repeated air attack during the battle for France. The image of the BEF infantryman vainly trying to take out dive-bombing Stukas with a single .303 rifle shot has become iconic. 'Owing to the high speed of modern aircraft, it is essential that the fire should be delivered quickly and with reasonable accuracy.'*

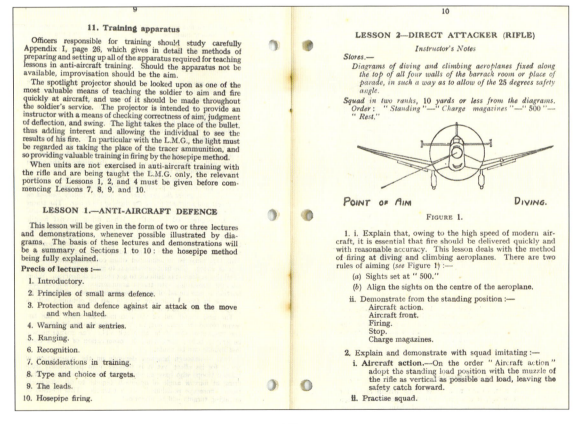

attacks may have a decisive effect. It is of the utmost importance therefore that all ranks should be trained to withstand the noise of air attack and should be imbued with the necessity of hitting back as hard as possible . . . Troops must not expect that the aircraft when hit will crash immediately. If it remains in the air for only 30 seconds it will fly two or three miles. Personnel therefore must not lose heart if the accuracy of their fire does not bring immediate results.

Soldiers were taught the importance of 'leading', which is aiming ahead of the direction of flight of an enemy aircraft, when shooting at it with rifle or machine gun. Instructors were told to educate their squads accordingly about this essential technique, one that is in fact familiar to anyone shooting game or clays with a shot gun. To help them gauge the degree of lead necessary model aircraft were fitted onto wooden stands with a rectangle of card held on a wire some distance ahead of the aircraft. Trainees then pointed an outstretched arm towards the model, using their extended fingers to judge the degree of offset between target and aiming point. *Small Arms Training Volume 1* continues: 'Explain that each man must measure for himself what part of his left hand when at arm's length will give 12 degrees from the nose of the aeroplane to the centre of the rectangle. The parts of the hand which gives the measurement at 10 yards will also give 12 degrees at any range.'

Although not involved in developments as leading edge as those taking place in aviation, soldiers also had to contend with familiarising themselves with new techniques of land warfare.

Army Form A 2022 provided soldiers with instructions to follow in the event of gas attack. They were advised that a great deal of personal decontamination could take place immediately, even on the march. Provided with pads manufactured from cotton waste, soldiers were advised to use it to remove 'free liquid' which remained on their skin and to rub the ointment with which they were also supplied 'vigorously into exposed skin for at least 30 seconds with both hands'. They were further told the following:

1. Don't put your rifle and equipment down on exposed ground.
2. Swab free liquid off web equipment – apply ointment to both sides where contaminated. You can wear it again.

All armies were equipped to deal with gas, as were air forces – the observant reader might have notice the yellow diamond patches on the wings of RAF fighters, such as the Hawker Hurricane. These were patches of a material impregnated with a chemical which would change colour if contaminated by poison gas, giving the pilot a warning sufficient to enable them to push the throttle forward and speed off towards a decontaminated airfield.

Airpower and chemical weaponry aside, armies still had to learn or relearn age-old techniques essential for them to find their way around the battlefield or move from one location to the next. Map reading and the ability for soldiers accurately to judge distance was as important as ever.

In *Military Map Reading for the New Army*, published in 1940, Captain W. Stanley

Lewis said that the ability to 'read' a map was an essential element of military education. British maps of 1in to 1 mile, 1/63,360 scale, with relief shown by orange-coloured contours and roads indicating both their surface finish and width; those suitable for speedy traffic being coloured red; poor roads shown in broken yellow and footpaths indicated by dashed lines were superior to German maps, the author argued. He continued, though very detailed, the German 1/50,000 map featured a complicated list of symbols: 'It is not a very satisfactory map, as so much has been included that its details are difficult to follow. The same criticism applies to the 1/25,000 variety; and the fact that in both types most of the material is printed in black further obscures the matter portrayed.'

Regarding night marching or marching in reduced daylight, Captain Lewis urged reference to the compass:

> Marching by night or in conditions of reduced daylight, e.g. in mist or through wooded areas, demands a special technique. To meet such emergencies the compass is graduated around the outer brass ring into 360 degrees, numbered from the lubber line, which is zero, in an anti-clockwise direction. Every 10th degree is marked and numbered thus: 10 degrees by the figure 1, 20 degrees by the figure 2, and so on. The moveable glass cover has a luminous 'director' which can be set opposite to any required number of degrees on the brass ring . . . It is possible to march by stars if they are visible. Select one at the outset, but remember that all stars move through the circle of 360° in 24 hours, i.e. 15° in one hour. Therefore a constant check, say once in every quarter of an hour, is necessary; this involves calculating a fresh bearing.

When it came to judging distance, the other topic covered in *Military Map Reading for the New Army*, the author said that although technical instruments existed to help with this task, it was often necessary to make estimates by eye. This was no easy task the reader was told, but it was suggested that judging distances based on the lengths of well-known spaces such as the 22yd of a cricket pitch or the 120yd of a football pitch was helpful.

> The various distances on a rifle range should be studied and recorded in the memory. It is always useful to remember that 110–130 walking paces cover about 100 yards. The height of the individual, his length of pace and rate of progress determine the exact relation between number of paces and distance travelled. You will always find that there is a tendency to place distant objects farther away than they actually are; only experiment can guide you upon the amount of allowance which must be made.

From the moment war was declared in 1939, the War Office bombarded, no pun intended, soldiers, regulars and new recruits with a never-ending series of A5 size Military Training Pamphlets.

Troop Training for Light Tank Troops was published in November 1939. The fact that it had 'NOT TO BE TAKEN INTO FRONT LINE TRENCHES' emblazoned on the front cover is, perhaps, an indication of what a shock blitzkrieg was about to deliver to the men of the BEF, who had more or less taken up the positions in Northern France (they weren't allowed to enter neutral Belgium) that their fathers had occupied in 1914. Another indication of the innocence and unpreparedness of British troops, even armoured ones, is given by this description of the role, application and capabilities of a light tank troop which only comprised three puny Vickers-Armstrong MkVI tanks, each with hull armour that was only 4mm thick and an offensive armament of two machine guns:

> The light tank is armed with two weapons, a heavy machine gun for use against tanks, and a medium one for use against exposed personnel. It also carries a pair of smoke projectors from which smoke candles can be fired to produce a smoke-screen to protect the tank from observation of fire. The projectors may, on occasions, be used also to throw a grapnel and line to tow away light obstacles which have been placed by the enemy to obstruct the tank's advance. The armour, mobility and fire-power of the three tanks of a troop, put in the hands of the troop leader comprise a unit with great powers of reconnaissance and considerable fighting value.

It should be remembered that the nonsense above was written during the period of the 'phoney war' when Anglo-French armies dug in along the Belgium border or behind the vaunted Maginot Line, a period when nothing happened save the dropping of propaganda leaflets over opposing lines with each side either arguing their cause or trying to demoralise troops shivering in slit trenches as they endured one of the coldest winters on record.

When the fighting did start in earnest in May 1940 British armour was found to be wanting. The tiny size of Britain's armoured component was so insignificant that it was almost entirely placed under French command. What tanks survived their encounters with the much better deployed German panzers and the pinpoint accuracy of Stuka dive-bombers were left in France after the BEF escaped from Dunkirk and the other French beaches. No wonder Montgomery later said of this period that the entire British Army was not prepared for a full-scale exercise, let alone a war, in 1939.

The Universal or Bren Carrier was one of the rare success stories, as far as British armoured vehicles deployed early on in the war was concerned. It was another machine built by Vickers-Armstrong at Newcastle upon Tyne. Published in 1940, *Military Training Pamphlet No. 13* reveals some interesting details about the little tracked vehicle which found ubiquity in almost every theatre British or Commonwealth troops fought. These are the stores the fully equipped Bren Carrier went into action with: 'Bren gun, 22 magazines, spare parts bag, spare barrel and tripod. Anti-tank rifle and 8 magazines. Flags – red and blue.' 'Flags! In mechanised warfare?' I hear you ask. *Pamphlet No. 13* provides the answer:

> If the carriers are on the move, the noise will prevent verbal commands being heard. In such circumstances the section commander will hold the red flag horizontally and dip it two or three times towards the ground. Whilst the carriers are coming to a halt, the duties detailed above will be carried out by the crew.

Albeit slowly, the British Army was learning new methods and adapting to the revolutionary concepts of coordinated armour, mechanised infantry and close air support which the *Wehrmacht* so ably demonstrated. Britain certainly wasn't idle after the failure in France. War production was up and new machines were going from the drawing board and into production faster than ever before. In fact, by the end of 1940, Britain's aircraft output exceeded that of Nazi Germany. If the rules were changing, Britain was determined to master them. *Military Training Pamphlet No. 42, Tank Hunting and Destruction* caught the new mood at the War office:

> Tanks well served and boldly directed have established a superiority on the battlefield which is out of all proportion to their true value; the problem is now to reduce the menace to its true perspective even when elaborate equipment is not available. It has been proved that tanks, for all their hard skin, mobility and armament achieve their more spectacular results from their moral effect on half-hearted or ill-led troops. Consequently, troops which attempt to withstand tanks by adopting a purely passive role will fail in their task, or at the best only half complete it. Tank hunting must be regarded as a sport – big game hunting at its best. A thrilling, albeit dangerous sport, which if skilfully played is about as hazardous as shooting tiger on foot, and in which the same principles of stalk and ambush are followed.

This was all very well of course, but the army wasn't engaged with large cats in the jungle and it was no longer mainly led by men of aristocratic bearing who had the time and resources for big game safaris. Britain's new army leaders comprised a hard core of regulars with experience gained in the First World War, although many more still were simply grammar school boys whose vocational path had been interrupted by the war. The reality was, that in 1940 at least, the British Army simply didn't have weapons of the calibre required to knock out the latest panzers. This can be evinced when one considers the list of weapons available to soldiers who did indeed manage to spring a German tank from its lair. Among a list of armaments available, which included Molotov cocktails, Phosphorous grenades, the Sticky (ST) grenade, the Harvey flame thrower (a 22-gallon capacity tank of flammable liquid mounted on a wheeled trolley!), the Northover (bottle) mortar (designed for Home Guard use to enable them to launch the AW (Allbright and Wilson) bomb, a potentially lethal milk bottle), the only proper weapon available was the Boys Anti-Tank Rifle. *Military Training Pamphlet No. 42* continues: 'The anti-tank rifle penetrates the armour of the light tank, and that of some heavier models when fired at short range. It is effective against the tracks of the heaviest tanks yet encountered.' The Boys rifle was almost useless, as the pamphlet so casually explained; unless it was fired at short range. And, it may have penetrated the armour of light tanks, British light tanks, but is was ineffective against the latest German tanks. Furthermore, as one Home Guard veteran told me, it had a fearful kick that was enough to dissuade soldiers from ever reaching for it!

There was one rifle the British soldier could depend on: The trusty Lee–Enfield .303 SMLE, the same weapon troops used in the trenches used during the First World War. Although the No. 4 version of this excellent weapon would replace the trusty

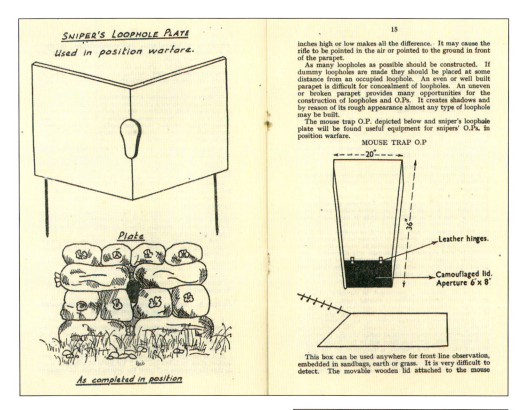

Notes on the Training of Snipers, Military Training Pamphlet No. 44 *was published in 1940. The sentence: 'An even or well built parapet is difficult for concealment of loopholes' reveals that instead of the rapid movement inherent in blitzkrieg, Britain's high-command still foresaw the likelihood of trench warfare.*

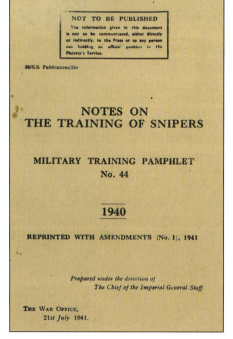

Mk III rifle which had served the army so well since 1907, it was, to all intents and purposes, the same weapon.

Snipers in the British Army even employed a variant of this classic firearm using the Rifle, .303 Pattern 1914 which was only declared obsolete in 1947.

Military Training Pamphlet No. 44, Notes on the Training of Snipers pulled no punches when it said:

> The primary object of a sniper is to kill. Sniping is an old art which came into much prominence during stationery warfare, and its importance was increased by the introduction of the telescopic sight rifle. During the short period of open warfare which occurred during the Great war in 1918 (and also in the recent

fighting both in Norway and in France), snipers proved to be indispensable, and by their use of ground, endurance, and expert shooting, were able to put large numbers of enemy weapons out of action by operating on the flanks of the attacking troops. They also succeeded, on several occasions, in putting enemy gun batteries out of action by shooting down the gun crews.

Notes on the Training of Snipers praised the qualities of the British Army service sniper rifle:

The combination of Sniper Rifle (Patt '14) and telescopic sight is an extremely accurate weapon. The sniper should be capable of taking full advantage of its accuracy. It is capable of producing a one-and-a-half inch group at 100 yards. Although groups at 100 yards as large as four and five inches are acceptable, the soldier should realize that he is not of much value as a sniper unless he can make groups of three inches or less at that range.

Every branch of the armed services had pages of instruction to rely upon. Though a lot would have been very similar to the old salts who served in the Royal Navy at the time of Jutland, sailors in the Royal Navy during the Second World War had lots of new stuff to learn. Naval weapons like the Hedgehog (also known as an Anti-Submarine Projector) was an anti-submarine weapon developed by the Royal Navy to counter the U-boat stranglehold which threatened to starve Britain of food and resources. Based on the British Army's Blacker Bombard 29mm Spigot Mortar, the Hedgehog fired a number of small spigot mortar bombs from spiked fittings. These exploded on contact and achieved a greater success rate than traditional depth charges.

Collectors of Royal Navy wartime ephemera should also keep an eye out for any leaflets or training manuals associated with ASDIC (an acronym usually wrongly claimed to stand for Anti-submarine Detection Investigation Committee, but actually a conjunction of words to disguise some of the device's top-secret components such as quartz piezoelectric crystals), the RN's revolutionary anti-submarine detection system, a prototype of which was ready for testing by mid-1917, only used on HMS *Antrim* in 1920. ASDIC started production in 1922. Beginning work a bit later than the Admiralty but following a parallel course, the United Stated Navy developed Sonar (SOund Navigation And Ranging), their technique for detecting and attacking submerged enemy submarines. Anything whatsoever to do with either ASDIC or SONAR should be snapped up without delay.

Those in the RAF could refer to *The Kings Regulations and Air Council Instructions for the Royal Air Force*, a weighty tome of almost 4,000 pages which covered almost every detail imaginable concerning the operation and administration of Britain's military air arm. In December 1940 a reprint of the 1928 edition, with appendices and index, was published. The Air Ministry preface included the following forthright words: 'Air and other officers commanding, and commanding officers, will be held responsible that these regulations are observed by officers and airmen under their command, and that any local instructions or orders that may be issued are not inconsistent with the regulations here laid down.'

This copy of Infantry Training Volume 1 Infantry Platoon Weapons *dates from 1955 and was the possession of a Lance Corporal in the Buffs. The British soldier's uniform and equipment had further evolved towards the end of the Second World War and by D-Day many troops wore the new Mk III 'turtle' helmet. The outbreak of the Korean War in 1950 was a further spur for change and a new battledress – the 1950 Pattern, made of heavy duty cotton sateen material and based upon the US M1943 uniform which included zips and vents to aid ventilation and was, quite obviously, more comfortable and practical than the old woollen serge battle dress, soon equipped British troops.*

There's quite an assortment of official wartime or interwar RAF material still available on the collectors' market – though RFC material is naturally much scarcer and consequently more expensive. If you do happen to find anything to do with British military flying which predates 1 April 1918, the date when the Royal Flying Corps and the Royal Naval Air Service (RNAS) merged to form the Royal Air Force, you've struck gold.

But it's more likely you will unearth RAF combat reports (RAF Form 1151 or 'Form F'), which detail the time, date, height and outcome of individual combats or perhaps, even better, individual pilot log books (RAF Form 414), the blue book-cloth covered square record pads charting the operational activities of pilots. At the time of writing examples of vintage log books in good condition were available from around £50, but costing more if they belonged to fighter pilots on operational duties during wartime and even more expensive if they detailed dogfights and, the cherry on the cake, combat kills.

It wasn't all commands and serious book learning of course. Each of the three services also published their own, less officious material. *TEE EMM*, the RAF's Training Memorandum, was published on a monthly basis from April 1941. It enabled Bill Hooper's legendary Pilot Officer Prune, who did everything wrong, to show the potential error of not doing things right. The inside back cover of *TEE EMM* Vol. 5. No. 3, June 1945, featured a stark cartoon showing simply a wooden cross bearing the letters 'RIP'. Below the mound of grass into which the memorial was planted read the words: 'His pilot couldn't be bothered to strap himself in'.

On a lighter note a small classified ad at the bottom of the last column of text in the publication simply said:

STOP PRESS
Latest War Results.
2.21 a.m. Allies beat Germany

'Bored – Stiff!' A very interesting leaflet distributed among offices and factories and intended to reinforce the notion that training and preparation was crucial and that there was no excuse for idleness. Inattention and inefficiency was destined only to lead to disaster.

Each of the armed services published an assortment of information to keep those in uniform up to date with operational activities to do either with the arm of service they worked for or, on a more general basis, the political developments that might soon see the war come to a conclusion and them 'de-mobbed' back into 'civvie street'.

Alongside *TEE EMM* the RAF also published an official fortnightly magazine called, appropriately, *Royal Air Force*. There was also *Evidence in Camera*, a regular RAF publication exhibiting some of the results of RAF Medmenham, the home of the RAF's photographic reconnaissance unit operations (PRU) in the European and Mediterranean theatres.

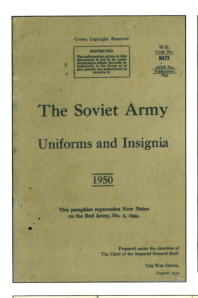

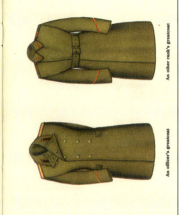

The Soviet Army Uniforms and Insignia 1950 *superseded* New Notes on the Red Army, *published in 1944. A lot had changed in the relationship between the former Allies since then. As the Soviet Union consolidated its controlling grip over the states of the Eastern Bloc in March 1946 Churchill famously said: 'From Stettin in the Baltic to Trieste in the Adriatic, an iron curtain has descended across the Continent.' This was followed by the Berlin blockade over the winter of 1948/49, the formation of NATO and North Korea's invasion of South Korea in June 1950. Although Russia and the West didn't come to direct blows (discounting Soviet 'advisors' piloting MiG 15s against the USAF Sabres over Korea that is) the cold war and the opposing doctrines prepared for the worst. At this time the United States still enjoyed a lead in the possession of nuclear weapons but this advantage was to be shortlived.*

Many other similar publications can be picked up relatively cheaply and all make fascinating reading as well as good investments for the future. *Union Jack*, the British Army's own newspaper, initially covering operations in North Africa and the Middle East, where it amalgamated with *Eighth Army News* and later extended its coverage to cover operations in Italy and Greece, and *Soldier*, first produced by the War Office for Montgomery's 21st Army Group in 1945, are but three publications associated with the army which can still be readily found. *Soldier* is still going strong nearly seventy years later! There's *Neptune*, for Merchant Seamen, those unsung heroes of the Merchant Navy, and *Flight Deck* for the Fleet Air Arm and *Navy News*, reporting on all that happens in the Senior Service since 1954. The choice is virtually endless.

Armies, of course, train for war whether or not conflict is imminent. Like Boy Scouts, they have to be

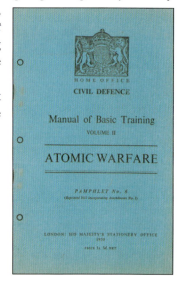

The year 1950 also saw the publication of a series of Manuals of Basic Training in Atomic Warfare *published for the Civil Defence Service (CD). This is pamphlet No. 6. Disbanded in May 1945, the Civil Defence Corps was revived in 1949, and set about retraining members, some of whom had been members of the ARP during the Blitz, in the new techniques required to deal with casualties should nuclear Armageddon become a reality.*

Photo No. 7. HIROSHIMA. Reinforced concrete building about 300 yds. from the centre of damage, which is to the left of the photograph. There was no serious structural damage, although a roof panel was depressed and some internal party walls were deflected. Designed for earthquake resistance, this building has a composite reinforced concrete and steel frame.

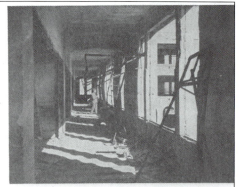

Photo No. 9. HIROSHIMA. Reinforced concrete school 500 yds. from the centre of damage, which is to the right. The frame of this building was of special design (portal) and resisted the lateral forces. The outside walls were of continuous reinforced concrete, and although they were deflected, as seen, they did not fail.

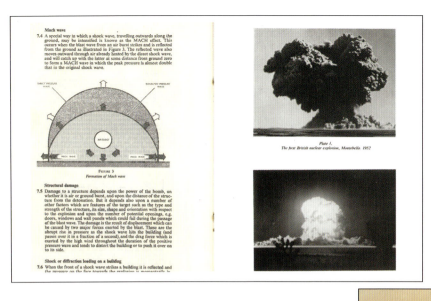

This manual, Nuclear Weapons, *was used by those engaged in civil defence activities in Devon. Illustrated within is an individual dosimeter in transparent plastic sheath and a portable contamination meter. The Geiger-Müller counter 'Meter, Contamination, set No. 1' was the first such outfit widely distributed to those in civil defence. Using two 150-volt batteries, many such units remained in service until the 1980s. On 3 October 1952 'Operation Hurricane', the test of the first British atomic bomb, was detonated off the Montebello Islands near Western Australia. Because British scientists had been involved with the American Manhattan Project the weapon was not dissimilar to Fat Man, one of the weapons dropped on Japan in 1945.*

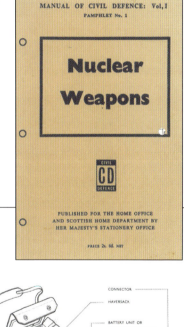

Plate 7.
Individual dosimeter in transparent plastic sheath

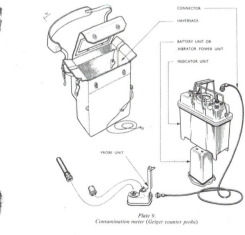

Plate 9.
Contamination meter (Geiger counter probe)

prepared. Consequently, the War Office carried on producing military training pamphlets instructing soldiers on how to use the weapons with which they were issued and what the likely equipment and composition of their likely enemies amounted to. Similarly, airmen and sailors learned the latest tricks of their trade by genning up on the latest published information. But, as fighting men got to grips with new uniforms and helmets, ironically based on those worn by their most recent adversary, the German Army, and pilots climbed into the cockpits of warplanes that, now devoid of propellers, were thrust skywards by powerful jet engines, they found themselves embroiled in a new war, the cold war. The West's fighting men faced a daunting new enemy: the Warsaw Pact – the combined armed forces of the Soviet Union and its acolytes.

But there was another threat which everyone faced – a weapon of virtually infinite destructive power – the atom bomb. Of necessity, military training pamphlets got bigger and comprised numerous supplements and appendices as soldiers studied page after page of advice about how to deal with nuclear, biological and chemical threats. They learned that should nuclear weapons be used, they would go into battle after donning protective NBC outer garments, what the British troops called 'Noddy Suits' because of their pointed hoods that were reminiscent of the hat worn by Enid Blyton's famous children's character!

It became important to study the uniforms, weapons and tactics of the Soviet Army. I have an early post-war British Army training guide which details the uniforms and equipment of Soviet forces in my collection and this very rare, 1950 vintage publication is shown in this book. As it adapted to the new conditions of a nuclear stand-off, the RAF also had its work cut out. From 1956, Britain's first operational nuclear weapon, the Blue Danube free-fall bomb, was carried by the V-bombers (Valiant, Victor and Vulcan) of the RAF's strategic bomber force. Soon it was the Royal Navy's turn when the Polaris submarine-launched ballistic missile system entered service in 1968 (the V-bombers were withdrawn from the nuclear role in 1969). From 1994 onwards, British submarines switched to the far more powerful, and no less controversial, Trident nuclear missile system. Fortunately for the compliers of military training pamphlets, there was suddenly a lot of new information for soldiers, sailors and airmen to get to grips with.

As with all militaria, collectors of printed ephemera should always try to purchase items that are in the best condition. Check that all the pages are intact and that bindings are sound. Avoid anything that has been scribbled on in biro – unless it is the authentic scrawl of the soldier, sailor or airman who was reading the publication in an operational context. As with all collectable books or magazines, first or early editions of military publications will command a premium price but offer far better rewards as far as investment opportunities are concerned. And, as is the case with all collectable items, especially delicate vintage printed ephemera, once purchased, such items should be conserved with care. And protecting your prized finds is the subject of the next and final chapter.

CHAPTER 7

Looking After Your Collectables

*R*ust Never Sleeps is the 1979 album by one of my favourite musicians, Canadian singer-songwriter Neil Young and his band Crazy Horse. Young used the same title for his tour, signalling his determination to avoid artistic complacency and fatigue, even though, like all of us, he was getting that bit older and weather worn.

Using this, I have to admit, rather contrived link to the topic of this chapter – how preserve things in the best condition – I aim to show collectors some of the techniques they might employ to impede the inexorable degenerative process of decay. We won't encounter 'rust' perhaps, although in the case of printed ephemera, 'foxing', which old documents sometimes suffer from, is a similar kind of oxidation, but the following advice will help enthusiasts keep their collectables in the best possible condition.

Entropy, that lack of order or predictability, leading to a gradual decline into disorder is, I'm afraid, the natural state of this expanding universe. We only ever see wine glasses smash. We never see them reassemble. Fortunately, some of this inevitable decline and fall can be slowed down at least. There follows some easy ways to start the redemption process and hold on to your vintage bits and pieces.

One of the best ways to prevent damage to printed ephemera is to make sure delicate paper items are stored correctly. Certainly, you should avoid displaying your paper memorabilia, books or pictures in direct sun or even

Ideally, postcards like these First World War examples – the German example: 'A Five Minute Burner', and the French: 'Journée du Poilu' ('The poilu's holiday', about a poilu's Christmas leave from the front), should be kept in special albums. After all, they've survived 100 years and it is the collector's duty to see that they last even longer.

If you are lucky enough to possess an original lithograph of one of Dutch artist Louis Raemaekers' xenophobic but none the less beautiful drawings such as this one, Aren't I a loveable fellow?*, care must be taken not only to store it in an acid-free archival folder, but that if it is displayed it is not exposed to direct sunlight.*

artificial light. Whenever possible, also keep papers and books in containers. They are best kept in the dark.

Light is one hazard, damp is another – humidity will encourage mould to grow. And don't keep your collection in an excessively warm place either, such as above a radiator, for example. It's generally best to avoid fluctuating temperatures and aim if possible for a constant of 66 °F/19 °C.

Putting papers or books in places where they will come into contact with polluted or impure air, for example, near an opening window or in a room with a coal fire is also to be avoided. If you live with any heavy smokers, wait until they are out, out of cigarettes or asleep before removing your treasures from their display sleeves. We are all familiar with the qualification 'from a smoke free home' on eBay listings. Believe me, nicotine, tar, smoke and the components of the dangerous cocktail of about

4,000 chemicals in cigarettes all contribute to taking the edge off a pristine collectable. As they do with a smoker's lung!

Booklice, members of the order *Psocoptera*, which contains about 3,200 species worldwide, can often be found hidden in the pages, often near the spine stitching and glue residue, of vintage books. Adult booklice can live for six months. Besides damaging books, they also sometimes infest food storage areas, where they feed on dry, starchy materials. They are scavengers and do not bite humans. Booklice prefer the dark, and they like temperatures of 75 to 85 °F. Because they need a high humidity in order to survive, storing books in cooler but perfectly dry places will prevent them from thriving.

Named because of the fox-like reddish-brown colour of the stains left by this affliction, 'foxing' is the term for the age-related spots and browning seen on vintage paper documents and books. It is thought that the rust chemical, ferric oxide, caused by the effect on certain papers of the oxidation of iron, copper, or other substances in the pulp or rag from which the paper was made, is the main contributor to this problem. As with the issue of booklice, high humidity also encourages foxing.

However, paper is not only prone to attack from external factors. The very integral constituents of the product itself, the ingredients in its manufacture, can contribute to paper's decay. Until the mid-nineteenth century, recycled rags were used as part of the paper manufacturing process. Later, increased demand led to the substitution of wood pulp for papermaking. But, unless it is chemically treated, wood pulp contains lignin, and over time this substance causes the paper to become acidic and subsequently discoloured and brittle, eventually disintegrating. We all know old newspapers are yellow in hue.

In the late 1930s paperbacks often came with removable dust jackets such as this volume about Hermann Göring, the last commander of Manfred von Richtofen's famous 'Flying Circus' (Jagdgeschwader 1) and at the time of publication, in 1933, president of the Reichstag. At the time, the author, Martin Sommerfeldt, was the Minister of the Interior's press officer. Collectors should search for examples complete with their original dust jackets.

Even if your collection contains items high in lignified material, newspaper cuttings, for example, you can help prolong their life by storing them in lignin-free, or 'acid-free', containers and display boxes. Not all modern papers and card are lignin-free, and where possible these should be stored in acid-free archival quality storage wrappers and boxes.

Even if you can't get hold of, or afford, acid-free archival storage materials, avoid wrapping items in newspaper, between sheets of cardboard or in brown envelopes. Good quality white paper and envelopes contain fewer impurities and should be used instead.

Vintage photographs shouldn't be kept in the kind of commercially available albums used to exhibit family holiday snaps because these are likely to contain a high degree of impure substances. Colour photographs are the most sensitive items in your collection and prone to very rapid fading if not stored correctly. That is out of the light. They are best kept in chemically stable polyester, polythene or polypropylene enclosures but not in PVC, which will break down over time and emit hydrochloric acid as it goes brittle. Photographically safe paper, of low sulphur content, such as Glassine papers are best used as interleaving papers between fine photographs, art prints and in bookbinding. Such coverings, sleeves, are especially useful in protecting vintage ephemera from damage from the acids resulting from handling.

Never use adhesive tape (Sellotape, etc.) or sticky labels on items you wish to keep. In time the adhesive will migrate into the paper, staining it and leaving a sticky residue behind.

I'm often asked why sunlight or more properly ultraviolet light (UV) causes colour to fade. Well the technical term for such bleaching is photo degradation. The light-absorbing colour particles called chromophores, the part of a molecule responsible for its colour, are present in all inks and dyes and the colour we perceive is a result of the amount of light that is absorbed by these components in a particular wavelength. Ultraviolet rays can break down the chemical bonds of chromophores and thus fade the colour reflected from an object. Some things are more prone to fading, such as dyed textiles, certain inks and paint pigments, particularly reds. Objects that reflect the light more, repelling dangerous ultra violet, are naturally less prone to fading.

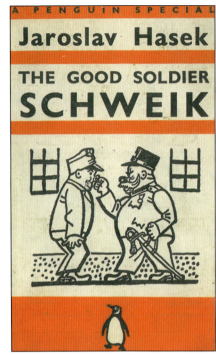

Penguin Specials are becoming more and more collectable. To ensure their preservation they should be kept in stable environments – so not in the loft or garage from which when removed they will generally be exposed to dramatically increased temperatures. The Good Soldier Schweik recounts the adventures of a malingering Czech soldier caught up in world events since the assassination of Archduke Franz Ferdinand of Austria.

A measure known as the Blue Wool Scale calculates and calibrates the permanence of dyes. Traditionally, this test was developed for the textiles industry but it has now been adopted by the printing industry as measure of light fastness of lithographic and digital inks.

The process involves taking two identical samples and placing one, the 'control', in the dark. The other sample is placed in the equivalent of sunlight for a three-month period. A standard blue wool textile fading test card is also placed in the same light conditions as the sample under test. The amount of fading of the sample is then assessed by comparison to the original colour. A rating between 0 and 8 is awarded by identifying which one of the eight strips on the blue wool standard card has faded to the same extent as the sample under test.

'Permanence' or 'fastness' refers to the chemical stability of the pigment in relation to 'any' chemical or environmental factor, not only light but including heat, water, acids, alkalis or attack by mould.

Often overlooked, the myriad War Emergency leaflets which dropped through letter boxes during and immediately after the Munich Crisis in 1938, and which continued throughout the war, are hugely important historic records. They are also very fragile and in need of careful conservation.

Founded in 1846, the Smithsonian Institution, located in Washington, DC, is the world's largest museum and research complex, consisting of nineteen museums and galleries, a National Zoological Park, and nine research facilities. Its Museum Conservation Institute (MCI) is considered one of the world's leading authorities on conservation and combines state-of-the-art instrumentation and scientific techniques with a unique knowledge of materials. The Smithsonian publishes a set of guidelines to everything from archival document preservation to fabric conservation and I can't recommend this institution highly enough.

All this talk of 'chromophores' and 'photo degradation' might sound a bit highfalutin and to some might suggest a degree in bio-chemistry is required in order

Period photographs are an important part of the historic record and should not be discounted. They can also be purchased relatively inexpensively. Fortunately, being printed on black and white bromide paper, photos like the two seen here, of a wardens' post and beaming fireguard, will survive without fading for generations to come.

to keep collectables in good order. But to be honest, day to day conservation, the maintenance of the average collection, is not rocket science. Here are my top ten tips:

1. Store everything neatly in a clean dry atmosphere and avoid moving things from warm to cold places – this will encourage mould growth.
2. Keep things clean – wear linen gloves when handling very old or delicate documents.
3. Keep printed items and photographs, especially colour ones, away from direct sunlight.
4. If you want to frame and display vintage items, don't hang them on walls, or place them on shelves, directly opposite windows.
5. Ideally keep things flat not rolled.
6. Don't wrap things in newsprint or brown paper – if you don't have access to archival, acid-free paper, use good quality white paper or card.
7. Don't store photographs or old documents behind plastic sheets in self-adhesive picture albums – use 'A-sized' folio display sheets as used by graphic designers.
8. Keep old books upright or interleaf them with bubble wrap to avoid their spines cracking.
9. If packaging lots of items for storage, try to stack together items of the same size. For example 'foolscap' documents, common in Britain and the Commonwealth before the adoption of the international standard A4 paper in 1975, are 8.5 by 13.5in (215.9 by 342.9mm) and if stacked on top of A4 is 8.3 by 11.7in (210 by 297mm) will suffer from creasing damage.
10. Make sure you have an accurate inventory of what you have, its provenance and where it is stored!

Many original period illustrations are executed in a kind of opaque water colour known as gouache. British firm Winsor & Newton has been making such paints since founders Henry Newton and William Winsor established the firm back in 1832. When asked how 'fugitive' some designer gouache colours are they explain thus:

> The fading of a colour is due to the pigment and the methods which are used in painting. The permanence of a colour is described by Winsor & Newton using the system of AA, A, B and C. AA being Extremely Permanent and C being Fugitive. Fugitive means 'transient', some fugitive colours may fade within months. For permanent paintings it is recommended that only AA and A colours are used as these are not expected to fade. Light Purple has a B rating and Parma Violet a C rating, fading over a 10 year period would not be unexpected with these colours.

As far as lithographic inks are concerned, the inks used for posters, magazines and the colour plates in books, magenta and yellow tend to fade faster than black and cyan. This is why we often notice that advertisements and posters left in shop windows exposed to natural sunlight soon adopt a distinctly blue hue.

In the last thirty or so years, the major photographic manufacturers have developed

Form C.E.O.2A

Issued by the Ministry of Home Security and the Scottish Home Department

CIVIL DEFENCE DUTIES (Compulsory Enrolment) ORDER, 1942
PARTICULARS OF EXEMPTIONS

A. GROUNDS WHICH EXEMPT A PERSON FROM ENROLMENT.

1. Special Exemptions for Women.

(a) Having care of a child.

If you have the care of a child (whether your own or not) under the age of 14 who lives and sleeps where you live and sleep.
Give particulars on the application for registration. If any change takes place subsequently, inform the local authority.

(b) Pregnancy.
To claim exemption produce a medical certificate to the local authority.

2. Fire Guard Duties at Business Premises and Government Premises.

If you are performing, outside your working hours, fire prevention duties under arrangements in force for the premises.
Ask your employer for the appropriate certificate and send or take it to the local authority, or ask him to send the appropriate joint certificate to the local authority. (*Note*: Men may in certain cases be required to perform reduced periods of duty with the local authority.)

3. Forestalling Duties at Business Premises and Government Premises.

If you are performing, outside your working hours, duties undertaken to forestall or mitigate hostile attack for periods amounting to not less than forty-eight hours in each period of four weeks.
Ask your employer for the appropriate certificate and send or take it to the local authority, or ask him to send the appropriate joint certificate to the local authority.

4. Vital work at Industrial Premises for exceptionally long hours (men).

If the premises where you work are industrial premises used for vital work and you are employed at those premises for exceptionally long hours and if you obtain a certificate (on Form D.2 or D.3) signed by or on behalf of the appropriate authority.
Ask your employer for the appropriate certificate (on Form D.2) and send or take it to the local authority, or ask him to send the appropriate joint certificate (on Form D.3) to the local authority.

5. Work at Business Premises for exceptionally long hours (women).

If you are employed at your place of work for exceptionally long hours.
Ask your employer for the appropriate certificate and send or take it to the local authority, or ask him to send the appropriate joint certificate to the local authority.

6. Night Work.

If you are employed in night work on a weekly shift system for not less than one week in four or are ordinarily employed in night work on not less than five nights in twenty-eight.
Ask your employer for the appropriate certificate and send or take it to the local authority, or ask him to send the appropriate joint certificate to the local authority. (*Note*: You may in certain cases be required to perform reduced periods of duty with the local authority.)

7. Membership of the Civil Defence Services of the local authority with whom you register.

If you are performing civil defence duties, other than fire prevention duties, in the area in which you live, for not less than forty-eight hours in each period of four weeks, in pursuance of an undertaking given on or before the date of the registration notice.
Give particulars of the undertaking you have given on the application for registration.

8. Membership of the Civil Defence Services of some other local authority or county council.

If you are performing civil defence duties, other than fire prevention duties, in the area of some other local authority or county council for not less than forty-eight hours in each period of four weeks, pursuant to an undertaking given on or before the date of the registration notice.
Obtain the appropriate certificate from the local authority or county council of whose Civil Defence Services you are a member and submit it to the local authority with whom you register.

9. Directions to perform Civil Defence Services.

(a) If you are employed with a local or harbour authority, in compliance with directions given by the Minister of Labour and National Service, at a Control or Report Centre, as an Air Raid Warden, or as a member of a First Aid, Ambulance, Rescue, Decontamination or Civil Defence Messenger Service, or of any service carrying out functions relating to the extinction of fires exercisable by a local authority.
(b) If you are employed part-time with a local or harbour authority in any capacity mentioned in paragraph (a) above, taken up in pursuance of a requirement in that behalf, subsequently to your release from whole-time services with the same authority in any such capacity.
Satisfy the local authority that you are so employed.

10. The Civil Defence Reserve.

If you are a member of the Civil Defence Reserve or (as a result of being called up under Section 2 of the National Service Act, 1941) are serving with the Civil Defence Reserve.
Obtain a certificate from the office of the Regional Commissioner in whose area you are stationed and send or take it to the local authority. (*Note*: If you are only a *temporary* member of the Civil Defence Reserve, having been transferred to it for a limited period under the Civil Defence (Employment and Offences) orders, 1942, you should claim exemption under paragraph 7, 8 or 9 above as a member of a local authority Civil Defence Service.)

11. The National Fire Service.

If you are performing duties in a rank in the National Fire Service for not less than forty-eight hours in each period of four weeks.
Ask your Divisional Officer for the appropriate certificate and send or take it to the local authority.

12. Stretcher-bearers.

If you are enrolled by a Government Department, a local authority, a county council or any body or person having the management of a hospital for the purpose of giving assistance without remuneration in connection with the admission or transference of patients, in pursuance of arrangements made by the Minister of Health or

[P.T.O.

Some documents, such as this one detailing the compulsory enrolment for Civil Defence Duties and the ways those on the home front either unfit for military service or in reserved occupations were eligible for exemption, were printed on cheap newsprint and are very delicate. Newsprint is made using untreated, ground wood fibres with impurities remaining after processing that include resins, tannins and lignins, which promote acidic reactions when exposed to heat, light, high humidity or atmospheric pollutants. This causes the paper to become brittle and deteriorate, often rather quickly. Careful storage in archival display sheets is recommended.

more stable dyes for colour photographs and the good news is that these modern photographic prints will only fade a little in as long as 100 years, if kept in average home conditions – but, again, not in direct sunlight or bright tungsten light.

Though manufacture and processing of this excellent material ceased in 2010, Kodachrome was introduced by Eastman Kodak in 1935. Transparencies ('slides') exposed on this non-substantive, colour reversal film were a staple of still photographers for decades and for many years it was mandatory to use Kodachrome for images intended for publication in print media. Fortunately, this film always featured very stable dyes, meaning Kodachrome images will last decades with very little fading – especially if mounted slides are not used in a slide projector too regularly. Even sixty-year-old Kodachrome slides look nearly new.

Similarly, because it uses thirteen layers of azo dyes sealed in a polyester base, Cibachrome prints will not fade, discolour or deteriorate for an extended time. Like many other collectors, I got into the habit of making Cibachrome copies of transparencies and printed items and these have proved perfect for display purposes. Sadly, in 2012, in response to declining market demand attributed to the expanding popularity of digital photography, manufacturer Ilford announced the final production run of Cibachrome (now called Ilfochrome Classic).

But there it is, aside from monochrome (black and white) bromide prints, which possess almost limitless qualities of permanence, Kodachrome and Cibachrome, two of the best colour photographic materials, are now lost to us. Only time will tell just how stable some of the modern inkjet prints will be but they should keep their colours and vibrancy much longer than colour photo prints. Many have been 'lightfastness' rated for more than 100 years. Be warned, though, prints made on some papers can take several days to finally stabilise – a phenomenon known as 'short-term colour drift'. It occurs mainly with cheaper dye inks and can lead to uncertainty about what the final print colour balance will be. Regardless of which type of ink your printer uses,

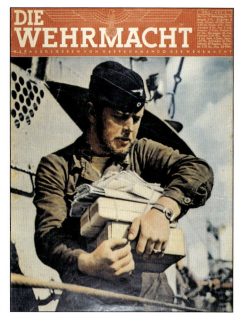

The Third Reich led the way in the production of colour magazines. Now, over seventy years since they were printed, these publications are not as robust as they once were. Ideally, they should be stored in archival sleeves or envelopes and supported by acid-free stiffeners.

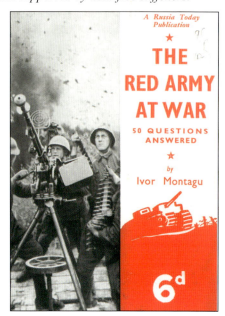

Try to avoid writing on the surfaces of vintage documents and if you do use pencil which can be erased.

Original newspapers provide really interesting collectables and they are fast becoming an investment. Truly ephemeral and never meant to be kept, they were printed cheaply on paper rich in lignin, which might make wood stiff and trees stand upright but also makes newsprint brittle. Consequently, many of those that were saved have long since turned to dust. 'Pilotless Plane Raids: Official', the Star, *Friday, 16 June 1944 – barely ten days after D-Day and Britons discovered that Germany still had secrets up her sleeve and the V1 was just the first of them.*

high-quality, acid-free papers are more stable than standard papers, which is why they are used for all archiving and fine-art applications. Pigment inks are slightly more stable than most dye-based inks, although the differences have been reduced with the introduction of highly stable dye ink sets in recent years. To obtain the maximum stability from your inkjet prints, give each print a minute or two to dry then cover it with a sheet of plain paper. Leave the covered print for at least 24 hours before framing it or storing it in an album. Inkjet prints last longest when framed behind glass or encapsulated in plastic ('laminated') to protect them against airborne pollutants. This is also a good way to protect traditional photos against light, dust and moisture – as well as airborne fungal spores.

Airborne fungal spores might sound a bit alien, even frightening, but we are all familiar with dust. Not to be confused with atmospheric dust which is the product of geological 'saltation', tiny eroded particles transported by the wind, which end up in the troposphere and are eventually deposited back on Earth, domestic dust, dust in homes, offices and other human environments contains small amounts of just about everything. Plant pollen, human and animal hairs, textile and paper fibres, human skin cells . . . you name it, all contribute to the domestic dust problem. And if you've got an open coal fire – don't get me started.

'Snappy Snaps May Help The Japs Watch the Backgrounds'. Although colour leaflets were generally printed on better quality material than newsprint and consequently less prone to acid attack, lithographic inks are still 'fugitive', that is subject to colour fade if exposed to natural light.

So, my last bit of advice is simply this, keep everything covered. Either in drawers, display cases, transparent portfolio sheets or even simple cardboard boxes, but keep things covered!

And talking of keeping things covered, there's no point in taking the time to maintain your valuable collection in tip-top condition if, by no fault of your own, it suffers damage or theft. It's easy to purchase collectables insurance and most of the established insurance companies and independent brokers will offer comprehensive cover of one kind or another to suit your needs.

First off you naturally need to estimate the value of your collection and determine the amount of insurance you might need. Don't forget, you need to insure your collection for 'replacement value' – what it would cost if you had to search for similar items in good condition and buy them all over again on today's market. If your collection is even more than a few years old it will have almost certainly appreciated in value since you first began acquiring items. Recently in Britain, home front, especially Home Guard and Air Raid Precautions (ARP) items have greatly increased in value. You need to compile and maintain an inventory of your collection and if you have receipts for certain expensive items retain them to provide proof and expedite claims in the event of a loss. Keep a copy of your inventory in a secure, secondary location from where your collection is housed (such as a safe deposit box). A good method to further accomplish this is to email the inventory to yourself and then you can access it from any computer. If you have suffered loss you must contact your insurer's claims department as soon as possible, stating the type and location of loss, the date of the loss and the claim amount. You will need to have your records on hand when contacted by the claims adjuster, and any photographic or video evidence of your collection and any police reports which will provide a crime number and greatly help to substantiate your claim will be of enormous help. When taking photos or video of your collection, be sure to concentrate on any and all markings or details that will help authenticate particular items.

APPENDIX 1

Inside the Third Reich

In *Mein Kampf* Hitler said that propaganda must always address itself to the broad masses of the people and that it should be presented in a popular form so as not to go over the head of the average man in the street. He wrote:

> The art of propaganda consists precisely in being able to awaken the imagination of the public through an appeal to their feelings. Finding the appropriate psychological form that will arrest the attention and appeal to the hearts of the national masses. The broad masses of the people are not made up of diplomats or professors of public jurisprudence nor simply of persons who are able to form reasoned judgment in given cases, but a vacillating crowd of human children who are constantly wavering between one idea and another. Propaganda must not investigate the truth objectively and, in so far as it is favourable to the other side, present it according to the theoretical rules of justice; yet it must present only that aspect of the truth which is favourable to its own side.

Hitler put his idea about crude messages appealing to lowest common denominator in society into practice when he re-established the *Völkischer Beobachter*, the Nazi Party's daily newspaper in 1925. In 1926 *Der Angriff* also made it on to the 'must read' list of the party faithful and from 1933 its editor, Joseph Goebbels, was installed as Germany's permanent Reich Minister of Propaganda, holding that office until Nazi Germany was defeated in 1945.

During Goebbel's tenure as propaganda maestro the Third Reich produced some of the most striking, albeit racially offensive and crude, official communications ever issued by an elected body.

Goebbel's proudly exclaimed that, 'It would not have been possible for us to take power or to use it in the ways we have without the radio.' Funkstunde (Radio Hour) *was the Third Reich equivalent of the* Radio Times *and regularly featured the Führer on its cover.*

Introduced in July 1938, the Kennkarte *was the basic Third Reich identity document and every German citizen was issued one and expected to produce it when confronted by officials.*

This particular Kennkarte *was issued in 1943 and rather optimistically states that it is valid until July 1948.*

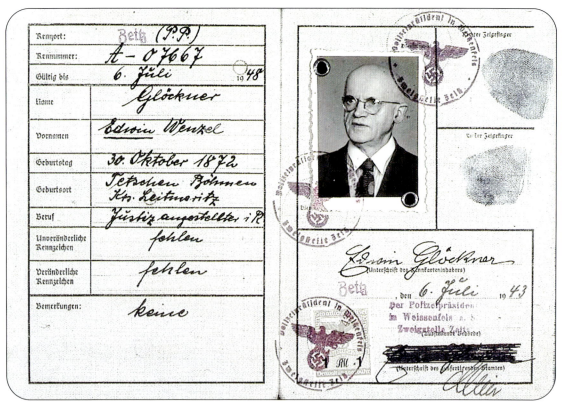

Shortly after he was elected chancellor in 1933 Hitler made Nuremberg the city of the Reichsparteitag *(Reich Party Congresses)*. This souvenir postcard celebrates the Reichsarbeitsdienst *(translated as Reich Labour Service and abbreviated RAD)*, which both militarised the workforce, indoctrinating it with ideology. However, the RAD make a major contribution to reducing unemployment during the depression and economic turmoil that spawned the Nazis.

This picture wallet celebrates the Luftwaffe's achievements in the skies above Warsaw, Paris and London.

Once the capital of Thuringia and a focal point of German enlightenment, for writers like Goethe and Schiller, composers like Franz Liszt, artists like Klee and Walter Gropius, founder of the Bauhaus movement, Weimar also gave its name to the short-lived democracy of the Weimar Republic period. It was also one of the cities that got mythologised by the National Socialist propaganda as this ten-year anniversary of the Nuremberg Rally testifies.

The cult of the Führer was everything in Nazi Germany, which Britain's propagandists well understood as this series of pages from a small photo booklet so admirably illustrate. In Berlin in 1937 the Nazi leadership opened a major exhibition, Gebt mir vier Jahre Zeit ('Give Me Four Years Time'), about the accomplishments of the Hitler regime in the four years since they came to power, reversing the humiliation of Versailles and promising good times ahead. Dropped from RAF aircraft, this booklet shows the German people actually what they got – broken promises, death on the frozen wastes of Russia and Italy, an erstwhile ally and inspiration for Hitler, turning its back on the Reich and pulling out of the war.

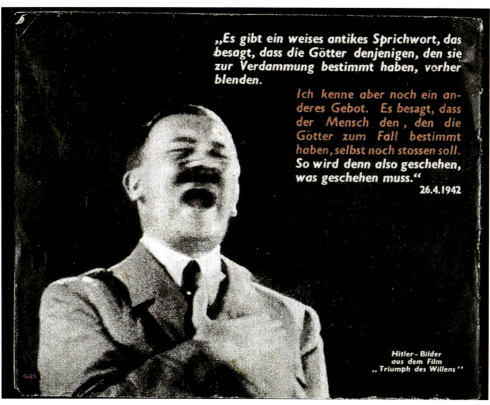

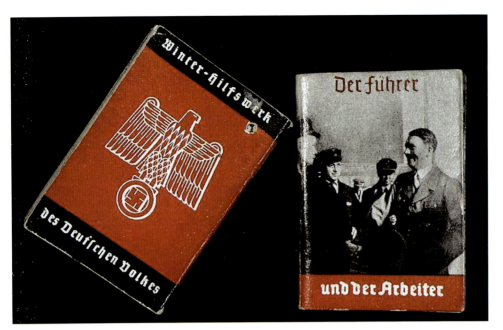

Dozens of miniature books like this one, The Führer and the Workers, *full of photographs of Hitler embracing the masses and revealing little of the reality of this demonic character, were snapped up in their millions by the faithful.*

As might be expected of the head of state, Hitler was even beatified on postage stamps.

This fundraising Gedenkblatt *(commemorative sheet) for the German Red Cross dates from 20 June 1941. On 22 June the Third Reich invaded Soviet Russia and from then on such events would become more and more commonplace.*

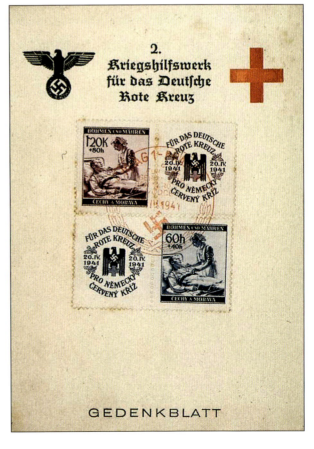

Dropped in bundles over the Reich by Allied aircraft, this bookmark is self explanatory. On one side the expression on the face of *Reichsmarschall* Hermann Göring, the leader of the *Luftwaffe*, turns from pleasure to pain as German cities experience terror bombing of the kind he happily inflicted on French and Polish cities. The reverse asks a series of questions most Germans wanted the answers to: 'How many have to fall in Russia? Why hasn't the Luftwaffe got enough aircraft? Why is England not starved? When will our rations be further reduced? Why is the Führer never seen in bombed cities? How many people are executed each day in Germany? Why does the government suppress all the Allied declarations about their policy to Germany after Hitler's fall? Who said not a single enemy bomber would attack the Ruhr?'

Consisting of the Heer *(army), the* Kriegsmarine *(navy) and the* Luftwaffe *(air force), at its inception in 1935 the* Wehrmacht *appeared invincible.* Die Wehrmacht *magazine, which was published from 1936 to 1944, was designed to promote the activities of the combined service. This edition shows an ill-clad soldier on the Eastern Front.*

For twenty-five years the Völkischer Beobachter *(People's Observer) served as the mouthpiece of the Nazi Party. It first appeared as a weekly newspaper in 1920 but from 1923 fed the party line to the German public on a daily basis. These two photos show the front and back of a British reprint of the paper which was dropped over Germany by RAF bombers. It contrasts Hitler's confident announcement that the destruction of Bolshevism would soon be decided*

(entschieden) after the Wehrmacht invaded the Soviet Union in 1941 with the reality of the situation in 1942 as the German 6th Army was overrun at Stalingrad, the turning point of the European war and the Führer was accused of lies (lügen) and is going to lie again. 'The writing is on the wall', it says 'it's going wrong.'

APPENDIX 2

Auxiliary Units

The Home Guard is characterised by the image of cadres of patriotic but hopelessly amateurish volunteers prepared to defend Britain in the event of a Nazi invasion with any means that came to hand, broomsticks if necessary. The BBC's wonderful *Dad's Army* has, of course, fixed this impression in most people's minds. There was, however, an alternative Home Guard in Britain in 1940 and a super-secret and potentially deadly one at that – GHQ Auxiliary Units. These units were made up of specially trained volunteers who would go underground, literally, waiting in their subterranean Operational Bases (OBs) until the enemy passed overhead whereupon, after dark, they would emerge and be ready to cause mayhem. Established by Colonel Colin Gubbins (who later became the military chief of the Special Operations Executive, better known as SOE), as cover 'Auxunits' were given Home

Wartime photo of Raydon Patrol Group No. 5 (Suffolk) Auxiliary Unit. Part of 202 Battalion, this picture was taken in October 1944 long after the Allies had breached Hitler's Fortress Europa and only one month before the entire organisation was officially stood down. (via Chris Pratt BRO Museum, Parham)

Guard battalion designations: 201 (Scotland), 202 (northern England) and 203 (southern England). Approximately 3,500 men involved in the so-called 'Operational Patrols' were trained on weekend courses at Coleshill House near Highworth, Wiltshire and a further 4,000, largely civilians, were engaged with the Special Duties Sections and trained to identify vehicles, high-ranking officers and other targets, using dead-letter drops or one of the 200 or so secret transmitters to pass information back to headquarters.

The Countryman's Diary 1939, *the Auxiliary Units' handbook of mayhem, is possibly one of the rarest pieces of British wartime ephemera. It was, in fact, one of the three main training manuals which the Auxiliers used. The* Calendar 1937 *was the first, given to volunteers in 1940, and the* Calendar 1938 *was distributed in 1942 – the 1939 edition was available from 1943 onward when the likelihood of Nazi invasion had passed. Humour is evident in its production. The inscription 'Highworth's Fertilisers Do There Stuff Unseen Until You See Results!' was a reference to Coleshill House in Highworth, the Auxiliary Units' national training base.*

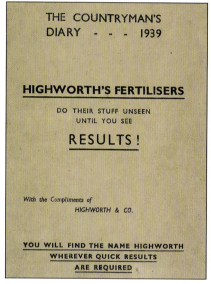

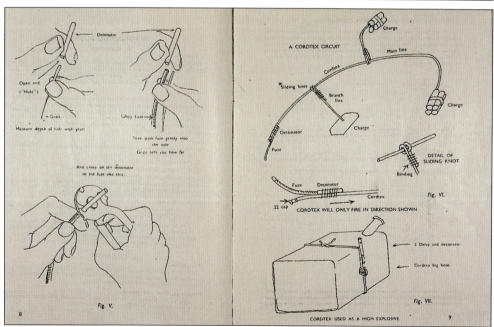

This spread and the ones with it were copied from my friend, the late Auxilier Geoffrey Bradford's copy of The Countryman's Diary *and shows how to detonate plastic explosives with the application of lengths of Cordtex fuse and percussion switches. Covert demolition of enemy vehicles and fuel dumps was one of the Auxiliary Units' primary objectives.*

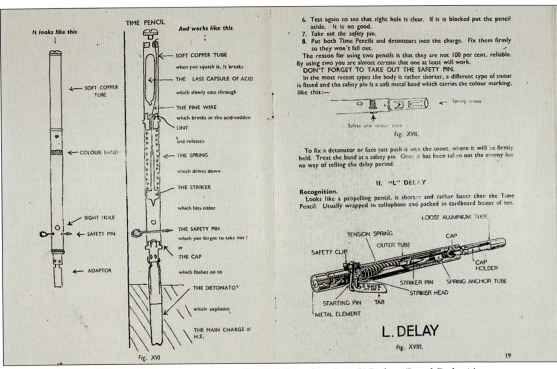

The Auxunit's time pencil, proper name 'Switch Number 9 or L Delay (Lead Delay)', was one of a series of reliable but simple time-delay switches which either operated by the action of acid degrading a retaining wire or, like this one, using the principle that lead wire will stretch and break in a time which could be measured. The breaking of the wire inside caused a spring to release a striker which ultimately set off a percussion cap and detonated the explosives it was connected to.

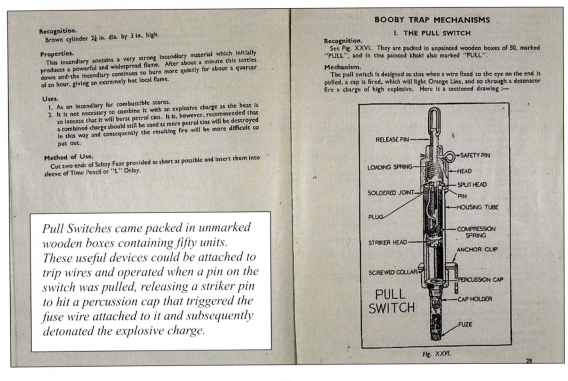

Pull Switches came packed in unmarked wooden boxes containing fifty units. These useful devices could be attached to trip wires and operated when a pin on the switch was pulled, releasing a striker pin to hit a percussion cap that triggered the fuse wire attached to it and subsequently detonated the explosive charge.

TARGETS

I. SHELL AND BOMB DUMPS

In the initial stages shell dumps will probably be fairly common, but bomb dumps will be left in France. In the later stages (if any) bomb dumps may be established in these islands. Dumps will always be spread out in the same way as petrol dumps.

Small shells are usually packed in wood, wicker or metal cases. If possible, open one of these and lay a charge of 1 lb. Plastic or 1½ lb. primed Gelignite in direct contact with the side of the shell. Time Pencils can be used to fire the charges.

Large shells and bombs are less likely to be cased, and a charge of 2 lb. Plastic or 3 lb. primed Gelignite should be laid on the side. If the bombs are unfuzed, fill the fuze pocket with explosive instead. (Fig. XXIX.) If bombs are fuzed, charge should be placed on side of bomb opposite the fuze pocket.

If shells or bombs are found in a lorry, attack them—not the lorry.

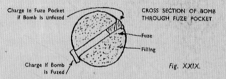

Fig. XXIX.

II. PETROL DUMPS

Petrol dumps usually consist of a large number of stacks of petrol tins spread out over a wide area. Each stack will be of 1,000 or more tins and they may be as much as 500 yards apart. They will probably be covered with camouflage material so it should be easy to conceal your charge. The charge should consist of a series of Cordtex or Primacord big knots, as shown in Fig. XIV on page 15. After pulling the knot tight, a length of about 9 inches should be cut off with the knot and a double loop formed on the free end (as in the unit charge), so that a series of knots can be connected up on a ring main. The main should be detonated by time pencils as in the unit charge. Knots should be pushed in between pairs of cans at intervals through the dump. Knots should *not* be more than 3 jerry cans apart. In large dumps concentrate on the up-wind end of the dump. The heat and wind will help to spread the fire.

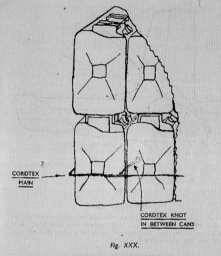

Fig. XXX.

III. AEROPLANES

The tail is the best part to attack. The following are two good methods:—

(a) Place a unit charge *inside* the fuselage at the top of the tail wheel. (There is usually an opening so that the tail wheel can be drawn up during flight.)

(b) Place a unit charge between the flat end of the elevator and the corresponding flat surface on the fuselage shown as XX in Fig. XXXI, or between the bottom of the rudder and the corresponding flat surface on the top of the fuselage shown as YY in Fig. XXXI.

Everything the committed guerrilla needed to know about the best way to destroy things like fuel dumps, stocks of ammunition and aeroplanes. Auxiliers were taught that it required a surprisingly small amount of plastic explosives (PE) to immobilise an aircraft for good. All that was needed was a fistful of the 'plastic' applied to the rear of the fuselage and, Voilà!, *there goes the tail plane.*

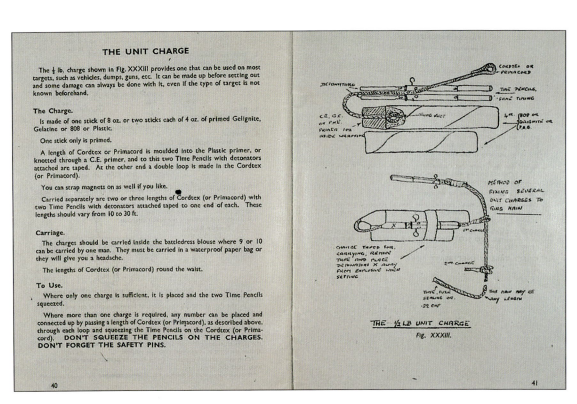

The standard Auxiliary Unit half-pound 'Unit Charge' was a universal explosive charge which, as The Countryman's Diary *explained, could be used on most targets such as vehicles, dumps and enemy weapons. As it could be prepared in advance and carried to the target where it would require little additional preparation before it could be used, it was extremely versatile.*

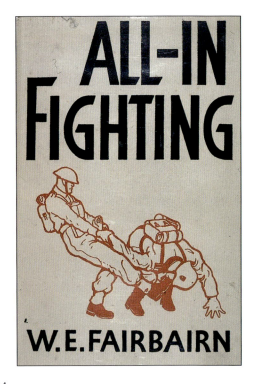

This has been reprinted many times and paperback facsimiles can be found on the collectors' market today, but this is an original, first edition hard-back copy, and consequently very rare, of William Ewart Fairbairn's famous guide to hand-to-hand or close combat. Fairbairn originally served with the Royal Marine Light Infantry and then joined the Shanghai Municipal Police (SMP) in 1907, learning many of his unarmed combat techniques in Shanghai's red light district. He is equally famous for the stiletto-shaped FS Fighting Knife he designed in partnership with Eric Anthony Sykes and which was made famous by British Commandos but also distributed to Auxiliers, it being the ideal weapon for silent killing.

APPENDIX 3

Penguin Specials

Publishing was in the blood of Penguin founder Sir Allen Lane. In 1919 he joined the family firm, Bodley Head, working as an apprentice to his uncle and founder of the company, John Lane. By 1925 Allen had risen to become managing editor but, following a dispute with some of Bodley Head's other directors about the wisdom of publishing James Joyce's controversial book *Ulysses*, Lane and his brothers Richard and John decided to establish the quite separate Penguin Books division in 1935. It became a separate company the following year. Lane's innovation was the introduction of quality paperbacks, good reads for everyone but cheap enough to be sold from vending machines. Penguin paperbacks were a run-away success and Lane went on to start the Pelican and Puffin brands in 1937 and 1940 respectively. Penguin became world famous when it published an unexpurgated edition of D.H. Lawrence's *Lady Chatterley's Lover* as a means of testing the Obscene Publications Act 1959.

Penguins are famous for their simple yet coordinated jacket designs; three horizontal bands, the upper and lower areas colour-coded according to which series they belonged to and, in the central white panel, the author and title printed clearly in Gill Sans type. A 21-year-old office junior, Edward Young, created the iconic Penguin logo.

During the war years Penguin published many bestselling manuals such as *Keeping Poultry and Rabbits on Scraps* and *Aircraft Recognition*. It also supplied its popular books to the services and POWs. When rationing was introduced in March 1940 a paper quota was allocated by the Ministry of Supply to each publisher as a percentage of the amount used by that firm between August 1938 and August 1939 – fortunately this had been an enormously profligate period for Penguin, whose books where everywhere. So, Penguin's paper supplies weren't as restricted as other publishers' quotas.

> Blackmail or War *by Geneviève Tabouis (1938). French historian and journalist Geneviève Tabouis repeatedly warned about Hitler's rise and Nazi re-armament. Writing in dismay about the reality of German unification with Hitler's homeland of Austria, the author said: 'Chancellor Schuschnigg did not yield to force but the threat of force and there is no knowing what the ultimate effects of the Anschluss may be.'*

The Air Defence of Britain *by G.T. Garratt, R. Fletcher, L.E.O. Charlton (1938)*. 'Three well-informed authoritative writers discuss urgent problems of Air Defence'. One of them, Air Commodore Lionel Evelyn Oswald Charlton, was already a well-known writer on the subject. While serving as a British infantry officer he fought in the Second Boer War. During the First World War, Charlton rose to high rank within the Royal Flying Corps and then joined the Royal Air Force on its creation. In 1928 Charlton resigned his position as the RAF's Chief Staff Officer in Iraq because he objected to the bombing of Iraqi villages.

What Hitler Wants *by E.O. Lorimer (1939)*. 'Dedicated in sorrow and mourning to the memory of the Democratic Republic of Czechoslovakia whose heroism, steadfastness and self-restraint, during the dark days of September 1938 have won her people a fame as imperishable as the infamy of her foes and the humiliation of her friends.'

Why Britain is at War *by Harold Nicolson (1939)*. English diplomat, author, diarist and politician, Sir Harold George Nicolson was also the husband of writer Vita Sackville-West. 'This book describes in simple terms the stages by which the French and British governments became convinced that Herr Hitler was determined to adopt methods of force in place of the appeasement which they continually offered him.'

Stalin and Hitler *by Louis Fischer (1940). 'The reasons for and the results of the Nazi-Bolshevik pact'.* The son of Orthodox Jews who had fled the pogroms of Alexander III, Louis Fischer was an early supporter of Stalin. He also supported the International Brigades under the control of Joseph Stalin during the Spanish Civil War. In 1938 Fischer returned to the United States where he published Stalin and Hitler, *which attempted to rationalise the startling reasons for the non-aggression pact between such polar opposites.*

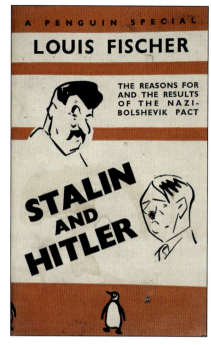

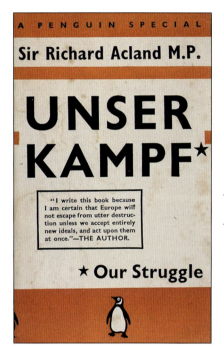

Unser Kampf (Our Struggle) *by Sir Richard Acland MP (1940). 'The trouble about this war is that it is the second such war to make the world safe for democracy and fit for heroes to live in. Because nothing was done to stop aggression in Manchuria, Abyssinia, Spain, Austria, Czechoslovakia, Lithuania or Albania this war must be fought with a clear policy for a new post-war order.'* Acland was one of the original founders of the Campaign for Nuclear Disarmament (CND).

Must the War Spread? *by D.N. Pritt KC, MP (1940).* Barrister and Labour Party politician Denis Nowell Pritt visited the Soviet Union in 1932, as part of the New Fabian Research Bureau's 'expert commission of enquiry'. A supporter of Stalin, George Orwell said he was 'perhaps the most effective pro-Soviet publicist in this country'. In 1940 Pritt was expelled from the Labour Party for defending the Soviet invasion of Finland. Must the War Spread? *was ultra-sympathetic to the Soviets and led him to be greatly disliked by many of his colleagues.*

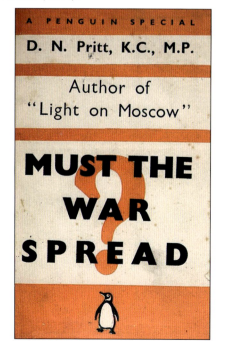

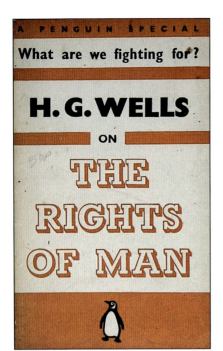

The Rights of Man *by H.G. Wells (1940).* Many observers contend that in putting before an international public the idea that international consensus about the 'Rights of Man' had to be part of any attempt at building a better international society post-war, the famous author of *The Time Machine* and *The War of the Worlds* laid the foundations for the 1948 Universal Declaration of Human Rights. However, Wells, who died in 1946, would never live to see his ideas become reality.

Science in War *(1940).* 'The full use of our scientific resources is essential if we are to win the war. Today they are being half used. Written by twenty-five scientists, all of whom speak with authority in their own fields.'

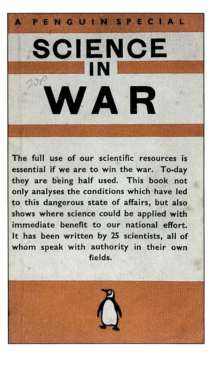

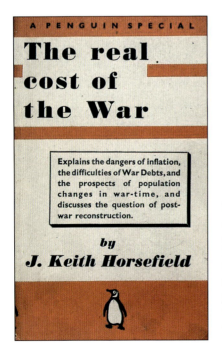

The Real Cost of the War *by J. Keith Horsefield (1940).* Economist Horsefield (author of *The International Monetry Fund 1945–65*) 'explains the dangers of inflation, the difficulties of War Debt, and the prospects of population changes in war-time, and discusses the question of post-war reconstruction'.

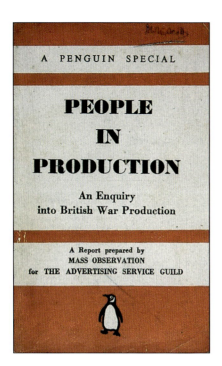

People in Production. An enquiry into British war production. A report prepared by Mass Observation for The Advertising Service Guild *(1942). At a time when there was some concern about possible inefficiencies in British industry Mass Observation surveyed some eighty firms, speaking to management, foreman, shop-floor workers and trade unionists. This popular paperback was a sequel to* Britain by Mass-Observation – The Science of Ourselves *(1939), in which the work of Tom Harrison and Charles Madge's team of well-meaning eavesdroppers threw new light on to many aspects of British society.*

Wartime 'Good Housekeeping' Cookery Book, *compiled by the Good Housekeeping Institute (1942). Now one of the rarest and most collectable Penguin Specials, this collection of recipes from the famous magazine founded in Massachusetts in 1885 and its august 'research institute', which can be traced back as far as 1900 with the establishment of its pioneering 'Experiment Station', proved a real winner with cooks trying to make ends meet with the meagre products of rationing.*

Bibliography

Briggs, Asa. *Go To It!*, Mitchell Beazley, 2000
Doyle, Peter. *British Postcards of the First World War*, Shire Publications, 2012
Evans, Harold. *Pictures on a Page*, Pimlico, 1978
Gloag, John. *Modern Publicity in War*, The Studio Publications, 1941
Hardie, Martin and Sabin, Arthur K. (eds and selectors). *War Posters. Issued by Belligerent and Neutral Nations 1914–1919*, A & C Black Ltd, 1920
Lewis, John. *Collecting Printed Ephemera*, Studio Vista, 1976
Low, David. *Years of Wrath: A Cartoon History: 1932–1945*, Victor Gollancz, 1949
Make Do and Mend, Ministry of Information, 1943, IWM facsimile, 2007
Nelson, Derek. *The Posters That Won The War*, Motorbooks International, 1991
Nelson, Derek. *The Ads That Won The War*, Motorbooks International, 1992
Overy, Richard. *The Road to War*, 2nd edn, Penguin, 1999
Railway Posters and the War, Railway Gazette, 1939
Souter, Nick and Tessa. *Illustrator's Source Book*, Macdonald Orbis, 1990
The Protection of Your Home Against Air Raids, HMSO, 1938, Old House Books facsimile, 2012
The Wipers Times, Introduction by Christopher Westhorp, Conway, 2013
Thomas, Vicki (ed.). *Mabel Keeps Calm and Carries On – The Wartime Postcards of Mabel Lucie Attwell*, The History Press, 2013
Walker, Susannah. *Home Front Posters of the Second World War*, Shire Publications, 2012

Index

'ABC Minors', 116
Abyssinia (Ethiopia), invasion of, 34
Aeroplane, the, 39
Aeroplane Spotting, 107–10
'Agreements of the People', Levellers, 1647, 15
Air Defence Cadet Corps (ADCC), 120
Air Raid Precautions (ARP), 9, 57, 58, 59, 75
Air Training Corps (ATC), 121
Airey Houses, 86
All Quiet on the Western Front, 33
Amazing Stories, 103, 114
Anschluss, 34
Antiques Roadshow, 41
Asquith, Herbert Henry, 55
Atholl, Duchess of, 45
Attwell, Mabel Lucie, 66, 76
Auxiliary Units, 132, 133, 135, 190–4

'Baedeker Blitz', 77
Bairnsfather, Bruce, 54, 150
Baldwin, Stanley, 57
Barter Books, 41
Beaverbrook (Lord), 10, 21,
Beggarstaff Brothers, 50
Bevin Boys, 68
Bevin, Ernest, 66–8
Bíró, Mihaly, 29
Black, A&C, 30
blackout, 110
Blackshirts, the, 45
Blue Wool Standard, 172
Boer War, 18
Boydell, Phillip, 71
Bracken, Brendan, 42, 44
Brangwyn, Sir Frank William, RA, 24
Brighter Blackout Book, 91, 99

British Council Against European Commitments, 45
British Movietone News, 81
British People's Party (BPP), 45
British Union of Fascists (BUF), 45
Brown, Gregory, 24
Buchan, John, 21, 22
Buck Rogers, 114
Bund Deutscher Mädel (BDM), 118
Butler, Rab, 106

Capon, Georges Émile, 25
Children's Hour, 114
Churchill, Winston, 22, 42, 46
Cibachrome, 177
cigarette cards (collecting), 78
Clark, Kenneth, 42, 76
Cobham, Alan (Sir), 119
cold war, 87–9
Committee of Imperial Defence, 42
Committee on Land Utilisation in Rural Areas, 84
conservation, 169–80
'Controlled Commodity' (CC41), 72
Cooper, 'Duff', Alfred, 1st Viscount Norwich, 42, 44, 46
County of London Plan, 85
Crazy Gang, the, 96–7
Crimean War, the, 18,
Crown Film Unit, 80
Cruikshank, George, 17
Cry Havoc, 33
Cundall, Charles Ernest, 76

Dad's Army, 131, 138
Daily Courant, 16
Dalton, Hugh, 73
Death of a Hero, 33

Defence of the Realm Act (DORA), 22, 55
Defence (General) Regulations 1939, Regulation 18B, 43, 44
Devonshire Regiment, 7
Diablo, 106
Dick Barton, 115
Die Wehrmacht (magazine), 187
Disney, Walt, 116

Edwardian Welsh Guards (poster), 6
Emergency Factory Made (EFM), housing, 86
Engelhard, F.K., 28
Entente Cordiale, the, 18
Entertainments National Service Association (ENSA), 97–9
ephemera (definition of), 7
evacuation of Children (Operation Pied Piper), 104–5
Examiner, the, 17
Expert Committee on Compensation and Betterment, 84

Faivre, Jules-Abel, 25
Familiar French, 143, 144
Field Service Regulations, 141–68
Flagg, James Montgomery, 26
Flash Gordon, 114
Flight, 39
Forster, Harold, 43, 67
Fougasse (Cyril Bird), 43
Fouqueray, Charles, 25
Fragments From France, 150
Franklin, Benjamin, 17
Fraser, Peter, 67

Gale & Polden, 38
Games, Abram, 43, 61, 81
gas (attack), 61, 63, 64
General Production Division (GPD), 42
Gillray, James, 17
Girls Venture Corps Air Cadets, 121
Gloag, John, 46, 47
Goebbels, Paul Joseph, 49

Goebbels-Schnauze (Goebbels' snout), 118
Göring, Hermann, 187
GPO film unit, 79, 80
Großdeutscher Rundfunk, 118

Haldane, J.B.S., 58
Hardy, Bert, 82
Harrisson, Tom, 43, 68
Henrion, F.H.K., 43
Him, George, 43
Hitler, Adolf, 33, 36, 182–6
Hitler Youth, 121
HMSO, 37
Hoare, Samuel, 58
Hogarth, William, 17
Hohlwein, Ludwig, 22, 49
Home Guard, 124–8, 138
Home Intelligence Division (HID), 42
Home Publicity Division (HPD), 42
Hopkinson, Tom, 82

ITMA, 100

Jackson, Ernest, 24, 25
Jobson, Ron, 67
Johnson, Amy, 120
Joyce, William ('Lord Haw-Haw'), 45
Just William, 112–13

Kaiser Wilhelm II, 15, 16
Kealey, E.V., 25
Kealy, Pat, 67
'Keep Calm and Carry On,' 10, 12, 40, 41, 42
Kennington, Eric, 24
Kennkarte, 182
Kitchener, Horatio Herbert, Field Marshal, 1st Earl Kitchener, 25, 54, 102
Kodachrome, 177
Korda, (Sir) Alexander, 9, 33
Krafter, Roland, 28, 29
Kürthy, George, 29

Lane, (Sir) Allen, 195
'Last Appeal To Reason' (Adolf Hitler), 36
League of Nations, 32, 33
Leete, Alfred, 23, 25
Lehmann, Otto, 28
Leroux, Jules Marie Auguste, 26
Levy, 'Yank', 37
Lewis, (Dr) Bex, 41
lightfastness, 177
lignin, 178
Lindbergh, Charles, 119
Lloyd George, David, 54
London Gazette, 16
Low, David, 46
Lymington, Viscount, 45

McGill, Donald, 123
Maher, George, 101
Make Do and Mend, 72
Manchester Guardian, the, 19
Mass Observation, 43, 68–71
Masterman, Charles, 20, 22
Mein Kampf, 33, 50, 121
Miller, J. Howard, 49
Ministry of Information (MOI), 10, 40, 42
Mosley, (Sir) Oswald, 45
Mount, Reginald, 43
Munich Crisis, 35, 104
music hall, 91–6

Nachshen, Donia, 72
Nash, Paul, 24, 25
National Guard (US), mobilisation of, 129
National Registration, 53, 62
National Socialist League (NSL), 45
Nelson, Derek, 48
New Towns Committee, 86
No More War Movement, 32
Nuclear Warfare, 165–8

Observer Corps, 42
Office of Censorship (US), 117

Olivier, (Sir) Laurence, 99
Orpen, (Sir) William, 24
Orwell, George, 44
Oxford Gazette, 16

Panzerfaust, 130
Partridge, Bernard, 24
Pathé, Charles, 80
Peace Pledge Union (PPU), 32
Penguin Specials, 195–9
permanence (fading, protection against), 173–9
Picture Post, 82
Plain Truth (leaflet), 17
Plontke, Paul, 28
Polte, Oswald, 28
Ponsonby, Arthur, 29
postcards (history of), 74, 75
prefabs, 86
Preissig, Vojtěch, 27
Prondzynski, Lieutenant von, 52
Protect and Survive, 89
Puchinger, Erwin, 28

Raemaekers, Louis, 9, 20, 21, 28, 170
Raleigh, Henry, 28
rationing, 59, 65, 66
Reith, Lord John Charles, 42, 86
Remarque, Erich, 33
Report on Alleged German Outrages, 20
Review, the, 17
Roll, Auguste, 25
Rothermere (Lord), 10
Royal Commission on the Distribution of the Industrial Population, 82–3
Russell, Bertrand, 46
Russell, William Howard, 17

Sheridan, Professor Dorothy, MBE, 70
Shipp, Reginald, 73
Soviet Army (uniforms), 165
'Squander Bug', 71
Swift, Jonathan, 17

Things to Come, 9, 33

Times, The, 17
Tomlinson, Herbert, 43
toys, 108–10

U-boat, 54
Union of Democratic Control, 29
UV light, 172

Vietnam War, the 18
Vogenauer, Ernst Rudolf, 49
Völkischer Beobachter, 188, 189
Volkssturm, 130–1

War Artists Advisory Committee (WAAC), 76
War Damage Act (1941), 87
War Damage Commission, 87
War Posters. Issued by Belligerent and Neutral Nations 1914–1919, 30
War Propaganda Bureau, 8, 20

War Resisters' International, 32
Wellington House, 21,
Wells, H.G., 33
Willette, Adolphe, 26
Wintringham, Tom, 37
Wipers Times, 146–9
Witt, Jan le, 43
Woods, Charles, 67
Woolton pie, 66
Women's International League for Peace and Freedom, 32
Women's Land Army (WLA), 69
Women's Social and Political Union (WSPU), 55

Young, Ellsworth, 27

Zec, Philip, 43
Zeppelin, 56, 108